I0485793

From Startup to Maturity: A Case Study of Employee Creativity Antecedents in High Tech Companies

Copyright © 2010, 2015 Yoram Solomon
All rights reserved.
ISBN: 1519112203
ISBN-13: 978-1519112200

Printed by CreateSpace, An Amazon Company

ALL RIGHTS RESERVED. No Part of this book publication may be reproduced, stored in a retrieval system, or transmitted in any form or by any means—electronic, mechanical, photo-copy, recording, or any other—except brief quotation in reviews with attribution to the author, without the prior permission of the author.

From Startup to Maturity: A Case Study of Employee Creativity Antecedents in High Tech Companies

Yoram Solomon

CORTLANDT CAMMANN, Ph.D., Faculty Mentor and Chair
SHELLEY R. ROBBINS, Ph.D., Committee Member
JOSEPH C. PICKEN, Ph.D., Committee Member

Raja K. Iyer, Ph.D., Dean, School of Business & Technology

A Dissertation Presented in Partial Fulfillment
Of the Requirements for the Degree
Doctor of Philosophy

Capella University
February 5, 2010

Abstract

Companies start their lives as startups, privately funded, small, focused, and not profitable. As they mature, they often become publicly traded, profitable, much bigger, and involved in multiple projects. Christensen (1997) found that startup companies are more innovative than mature companies. Amabile (1988), Ekvall (1996), and others developed a list of organizational factors affecting the creativity of individuals in organizations. The purpose of this study is to explore the differences in the organizational climate and personal context for creativity between mature companies and startup companies, and the resulting differences in the level of experienced individual creativity between those companies. This exploratory, interview based case study used a sample of 20 participants who worked for both startup and mature companies, and explored the differences in the participants' experiences of creativity and the factors contributing to, or inhibiting creativity. This study found that individuals experienced higher degree of creativity in startup companies than in mature ones, that the organizational factors conducive to creativity were perceived as higher in the startup companies, while the organizational factors inhibiting creativity were perceived as higher in the mature companies, explaining the experienced higher degree of individual creativity in startup companies, and potentially explaining why startup companies are more innovative than mature ones. The study did not find significant differences in personal context factors between the two types of companies.

In memory of Dr. Cortlandt (Corty) Cammann, my instructor, my mentor, my sounding board, and my friend, who has unexpectedly graduated from this life leaving a legacy of learning and teaching as his gift to this world. He will be sorely missed.

Acknowledgments

First and foremost, I would like to thank Dr. Cortlandt (Corty) Cammann, my mentor and dissertation committee chair. Corty helped me refine the dissertation topic almost a year before I embarked on the dissertation journey and before I asked him to be my mentor, simply because he was interested in the topic and wanted to help me. Corty passed away the week I completed this dissertation.

I would also like to thank Dr. Shelley Robbins and Dr. Joseph Picken who served on my dissertation committee and provided me with valuable feedback, and assured I kept my own voice, and finally, Dr. John Whitlock who guided me with my research approach, and stepped in as my mentor at the final stage of the dissertation process.

I would like to acknowledge the people who supported my study: Paul Werp and Dr. Bill Krenik, my supervisors in the first part of my doctoral studies, and Greg Kalush who supported me during the dissertation phase. I would like to thank Deborah Shute, an innovation evangelist who used the research I conducted while it was still ongoing, to improve the creativity and innovation levels in the company we share and call "home."

I would especially like to thank twenty main study and two pilot study participants, whose names are kept confidential. Many of them told me during the interviews: "maybe I am not your typical participant". To them I would like to say: You are *all* unique, and each of you in your own way and experiences helped me understand this topic and make sense of this study. I hope that in return this study would help you with your career, be it in a startup company or a mature one.

Finally, I would like to thank my wife, partner, and friend, Anat, and my two lovely daughters, Maya and Shira, who supported and accepted me through this journey.

Table of Contents

List of Tables

List of Figures

Introduction to the Problem

"Those who live by the sword are *shot* by those who don't" (Hamel, 1998). Innovation, and particularly radical innovation has the power to change industries and the competitive positioning of companies within those industries (Schumpeter, 1934, 1942). Entrepreneurial startup companies consistently disrupted markets and caused mature companies to fail (Christensen, 1997). Why are startup companies more radically innovative than mature companies?

Innovation is defined as the implementation of creative ideas (Freeman & Engel, 2007; Galbraith, 1982; Zhou, 2003). Innovation is an *organizational* process, while creativity is an *individual* process driven by a delicate combination of personal characteristics, personal context, and organizational climate for creativity (Amabile, 1988). This study attempted to understand how individuals experienced the transition from a startup to a mature company (or vice versa), through changes in their individual creativity, the differences in the organizational climate for creativity, and the differences in their personal context as those affected creativity. It was an exploratory case study of employees who moved between the two types of organizations, startup companies and mature companies, and could therefore compare those differences.

Background of the Study

Innovation is important for organizations' survival, achieving competitive advantage and superior financial performance, as an appropriate response to environmental and technological changes, and in some cases as a source of quality of life improvement to society as a whole. A 2008 Boston Consulting Group survey showed that the majority of executives considered innovation to be one of the top three strategic priorities for their companies (Andrew, Haanaes, Michael, Sirkin, & Taylor, 2008).

However, there is also a general agreement that small entrepreneurial companies are more innovative than mature, established ones (Abernathy & Utterback, 1978; Acs & Audretsch, 1988; Christensen, 1997; Leifer et al., 2000). Amabile (1998) claimed that in large organizations "creativity gets killed much more often than it gets supported" (p. 77), while Christensen (1997) claimed that management was doing its job while, in the process, missed market disruption events and drove their companies to obsolescence through lack of disruptive innovation.

By the simplest definition, innovation is the implementation of a creative idea (Amabile, Conti, Coon, Lazenby, & Herron , 1996; Galbraith, 1982; Roberts, 2006). Large organizations do not suffer a disadvantage in the implementation process, as the mature companies have advantages in terms of access to risk project financing (Ahuja, Lampert, & Tandon, 2008), access to employees, legitimacy, brand, alliances, structures, and processes (Freeman & Engel, 2007), their management quality (Khan & Manopichetwattana, 1989), and their ability to customize the work environment (Haner, 2005). The question is then raised whether large companies suffer from a significant disadvantage in the creativity of their employees (Amabile, 1998), and if so—why?

Employee creativity research can be found in the intersection between management science and psychology. Workplace creativity research historically started with qualitative studies of critical incidents, contrasting cases of high creativity with cases of low creativity, and extracting factors that affected creativity (Amabile & Gryskiewicz, 1987; Haner, 2005; Isaksen & Lauer, 2002). Those factors could be categorized into three groups: personal characteristics and creative capabilities (before entering the workplace), personal context (outside the workplace), and organizational climate. The organizational climate was the most researched of the three, and defined by Ekval (1996) as an "attribute of the organization, a conglomerate of attitudes, feelings, and behaviors which characterizes life in the organization, and exists independently of the perceptions and understandings of the members of the organization" (p. 105). Previous research started by identifying factors from interview narrative analysis, followed by creating creativity climate assessment instruments, which were then used to measure how certain organizations provide employees with a climate conducive to creativity. However, those instruments were not used to compare different types of organizations, with the exception of Ekvall (1997) who conducted a comparative study using the Creative Climate Questionnaire (CCQ) to compare the climate of several divisions from several companies to rank them on the "radically innovative" to "stagnant" spectrum, confirming the 10 factors in CCQ.

The current study built mainly upon prior research done by Amabile and Gryskiewicz (1987), Amabile (1988), Amabile et al. (1996), Amabile, Barsade, Mueller, and Staw (2005), and Ekvall (1996). The current study added a dimension of the *type* of organization (startup vs. mature), and how it interacted with the other dimensions addressed by prior research.

Statement of the Problem

Prior research identified differences in the level of innovation between startup and mature companies (Freeman & Engel, 2007). However, most studies and theories focused on the strategic actions that *companies* must take, in positioning them in the intersection of markets and technologies (Christensen, 1997). The topic of individual creativity was addressed by different studies, suggesting different factors affecting creativity, whether personal or institutional. Amabile et al. (1996) defined a model of organizational and group factors affecting individual innovation, based on which the KEYS survey instrument was developed. However, the instrument was not developed as a *comparative* tool to address the differences in individual level of creativity or the differences in the climate and factors affecting this creativity between multiple organizations. KEYS (as well as CCQ, SOQ and other instruments that are reviewed in Chapter 2) was developed as a quantitative tool to assess the organizational behavior through a survey, rather than a rich personal interpretation by the employees, as could only be understood through qualitative interviews. Prior research has only addressed the relationships between organizational factors and creativity, but did not compare the levels of those factors in different organizations and thus left a gap in the understanding of the differences in employee creativity, organizational climate, and personal context that may lead to the differences in individual creativity between the two types of companies—startup and mature. Understanding these differences as seen through the employee perspective may provide an explanation of why startup companies are more innovative than mature companies.

Purpose of the Study

The purpose of this study was to explore the perceived changes in creativity of individuals who moved between mature companies and startup companies (in both directions), and how they perceived the differences in the organizational climate and in their personal context that may have affected those changes in their creativity. The practical implications are in understanding the transition that a startup company goes through as it matures, as experienced by its employees, and as it affects their creativity.

Rationale

Christensen (1997) and others stated the startup companies are more innovative than mature companies. An organization has three main "controls" over the successful delivery of innovation to the market: hiring creative employees, establishing a climate conducive for creativity, and once the creative idea was generated—implementing it and delivering innovation. Creativity is the basic building block for innovation (Amabile et al., 1996; Zhou, 2003), affected by individual creativity characteristics, organizational climate, and personal context. Understanding the differences in the climates for creativity and personal context between the two types of companies, as perceived by employees who were exposed to both types of companies, may allow understanding of the reason mature companies are less innovative than startups.

Research Questions

Three research questions were the focus of this study, and considered from the employees' perspective, comparing the environment of the two types of organization:

1. *How do employees who worked in both startup and mature companies experience the differences in their own creativity between the two types of organizations?*
2. *How do employees who worked in both startup and mature companies experience the differences in the organizational climate for creativity between the two types of organizations?*
3. *How do employees who worked in both startup and mature companies experience the differences in their personal context between the two types of organizations?*

Significance of the Study

There is a significant body of knowledge in the area of different factors constituting the organizational climate for creativity. The focus of the existing body of knowledge was in identifying the different factors, and the level and direction of the direct impact or moderation that they provide to individual creativity. However, no research was done to explain the differences in innovation between entrepreneurial startup companies and mature companies in terms of (1) differences that employees experience in their own level of creativity between the two types of organizations, (2) differences that employees experience in the climate for creativity between the two types of organizations that could affect their level of creativity, and (3) differences that employees experience in their personal context in the two types of organizations that could affect their level of creativity. This study added those three comparisons, as perceived by employees who moved between the two types of organizations, and were therefore in a position to compare the two.

Definition of Terms

Creativity. The definition of creativity chosen for this study is Amabile's (1988): "the production of novel and useful ideas by an individual or small group of individuals working together" (p. 126).

Electronic Product Industry. For the purpose of this study, electronics industry means companies that build electronic hardware, software, semiconductors, electronic content (data), and electronic development tools.

Innovation. Innovation is an organizational process that begins with a creative idea that is implemented to deliver a new product, service, process, or business model to the market place. West and Farr (1990a) defined innovation as "the intentional introduction and application within a role, group or organization of ideas, processes, products or procedures, new to the relevant unit of adoption" (p. 9).

Mature Company. A mature company is in a late stage in its life cycle, is generating significant revenue, and is self sustained (funds its operations through revenue generated by selling products or services). At this phase, the company has a larger number of employees, and in many cases is publicly traded at a stock exchange, allowing the public to trade its stock. The mature company typically has more than a single product line. For the purpose of this study, a mature company was defined as a company that does not meet the definition of a startup company.

Organizational Climate. A climate is an "attribute of the organization, a conglomerate of attitudes, feelings, and behaviors which characterizes life in the organization, and exists independently of the perceptions and understandings of the members of the organization" (Ekvall, 1996, p. 105). Isaksen, Lauer, Ekvall, and Britz (2000) defined climate as "the recurring patterns of behavior, attitudes, and feelings that characterize life in the organization" (p. 172). It can also be defined as the shared perceptions of "how things are like around here" (Anderson & West, 1998). For the purpose of this study, organizational climate means the aggregation of factors that will specifically affect creativity of individuals within this organization.

Radical Innovation. Radical innovation is known by different names: disruptive technology (Christensen, 1997), creative destruction (Schumpeter, 1934), and also as "a product, process, or service with either *unprecedented* performance features or familiar features that offer potential for *significant improvements* [italics added] in performance or cost" (Leifer et al., 2000, p. 5). The further away that a new product, service, of business model is from the mainstream, the more radical it is.

Startup Company. The typical life cycle of a company begins at the startup phase, in which the company generates little or no revenue. This cycle may last several years. Funding is achieved through investments by the owners-founders, by "angel investors"—wealthy individuals willing to assume the high risk associated with this early stage company, by venture capitalists (VC), and by other institutional, private investors. During this phase, the company is typically held privately by its owners and investors. The company is small, and is focused on delivering the *first* (and only) product or service to the marketplace. There is a continuum between startup companies and mature companies, through the growth cycle of the company, and this study focused on the two ends of this continuum to maximize the contrast.

Assumptions and Limitations

Assumptions

One assumption was made at the outset this study. As the literature review and conceptual framework (Figure 3) show—there are three antecedents of employee creativity in the workplace: individual characteristics, organizational climate for creativity, and personal context. To explore the differences individuals experience in their personal context and organizational climate as they affect the individuals' creativity through studying individuals who moved between the two types of organizations—it is assumed that the individual characteristics of those individuals have not changed during the transition. Although it is expected that a few acquired characteristics (such as skill and experience) will always improve over time, it was assumed that other characteristics (such as risk taking, confidence, cognitive style and others) remain relatively constant.

Limitations

The study is limited first by confining it to the electronic product industry, and specifically to electronic hardware, software, content, semiconductor, and development tool companies. Different studies showed aspects where different industries behaved differently, and therefore it was not clear that the findings of this study could be generalized to other industries (Baldridge & Burnham, 1975; Stevens & Burley, 1997), and therefore this study was limited to the electronic product industry.

Another limitation was the researcher's lack of research interview experience. Interviewer error can be a major source of bias through "failure to record answers accurately and completely... failure to consistently execute interview procedures... failure to establish appropriate interview environment... inappropriate influencing [researcher] behavior" (Cooper & Schindler, 2003, pp. 246-249). A field test was conducted to assure that the interview schedule itself was appropriate, and a pilot test was conducted to assure interview schedule appropriateness, as well as allow the interviewer to practice the interview process. However, the researcher's lack of prior experience should be considered as one of the study's limitations.

Nature of the Study

This study was an exploratory, interview based case study, aiming at understanding how individuals experience the differences in their creativity, the organizational climate, and personal circumstances between two types of organizations: startup companies and mature companies. The study used open ended interviews, exploring the experiences that individuals who worked for both environments, as told in their own words. Meaning was then extracted from the narrative generated by those interviews to understand the transition that those individuals experienced, the differences they experienced in their level of creativity, and the differences they experienced in the organizational and personal contexts as they went through that transition. The selection of qualitative interviews was made as a result of a subjectivist-interpretivist preference of the researcher, the desire for "the richness and complexity that make research realistic" (Rubin & Rubin, 2005, p. 2), and since "qualitative research allows researchers to get at the inner experience of participants, to determine now meanings are formed through and in culture, and to discover rather than test variables" (Corbin & Strauss, 2008, p. 12). The study used open ended interviews, using comparative questions, and deploying the critical incident technique. The results were also coded and quantitative analysis was used to confirm the conclusions from the qualitative narrative data analysis.

Organization of the Remainder of the Study

The following chapters are organized as follows: Chapter 2 contains a review of the literature on innovation and creativity, and explains the conceptual framework leading to the research that will be conducted. It addresses the differences and relationship between the terms innovation and creativity, and reviews prior research of antecedents of employee creativity (individual characteristics, personal context, and organizational climate). It also reviews methodologies used in prior workplace creativity research. Chapter 3 describes the research methodology and design that were used in this study. Chapter 4 includes the results from the study and within case data analysis, as well as cross case data analysis. Finally, Chapter 5 includes a discussion of the findings, the implications of those findings to research and practice, limitations of the current study, and recommendations for future research.

2. Literature Review

Introduction

The management problem addressed by this study was that startup companies are more innovative than mature companies, and often disrupt the markets for mature companies as those fall into obsolescence. With employee creativity being a basic and critical building block for organizational innovation, the focus of this study was to explore the differences between the environments of startup companies and mature companies leading to differences in the level of creativity of employees of the two, affecting the level of innovation generated by the two. Creativity (an individual function) by itself is not the organizational goal—innovation is, and therefore this literature review begins with a discussion of the importance of innovation to the organization, review of definitions of innovation, types of innovation (beyond new products), the distinction between radical innovation and incremental innovation, and the importance of the two. The terms innovation and creativity are often used interchangeably in literature, and therefore the literature review continues with the distinction between innovation (an organizational function) and creativity (an individual function), and the relationship between the two. The topic of individual creativity in the workplace is then explored in detail through a review of definitions of creativity, summary of the creative process stages, and an overview of antecedents of employee creativity. Those were categorized into personal characteristics, personal context, and organizational climate. Intrinsic motivation has the strongest influence over employee creativity (Amabile, 1988), and therefore is reviewed in greater detail. Intrinsic motivation includes autonomy, support for creativity, challenge, recognition, availability of resources, and team dynamics. All antecedents of employees creativity are listed in Table 1 along with the domain they are in, the effect they have on employee creativity, and the organizational control (or lack thereof) over them. Finally, this review of the literature concludes with a review of research methodologies used in prior employee creativity research, and the suitability of different methodologies for different research objectives. The focus of this study is in exploring the differences in factors affecting individual creativity in startup and mature companies. The reader who wishes to focus on individual creativity is advised to skip directly to the "Individual Creativity" section that begins on page 37.

Innovation and the Organization

Importance and Implications of Innovation

There are four important outcomes and implications of innovation to the organization: (1) organizational survival (Abbey & Dickson, 1983; Amabile, 1988; Ancona & Caldwell, 1987; Brown & Eisenhardt, 1995; Cutler, 2000; George, Works, & Watson-Hemphill, 2005; Gryskiewicz & Taylor, 2003; Mone, McKinley, & Barker III, 1998); (2) competitive advantage and financial performance (Abbey & Dickson, 1983; Bassett-Jones, 2005; Bharadwaj & Menon, 2000; Damanpour, 1990; Devanna & Tichy, 1990; Engle, Mah, & Sadri, 1997; Miller, Fern, & Cardinal, 2007; Moore, 2004; Oldham & Cummings, 1996; Tellis & Golder, 1996; Turnipseed, 1994); (3) appropriate response to environmental and technological changes (Ancona & Caldwell, 1987; Basadur & Hausdorf, 1996; Brown & Eisenhardt, 1995; Burnside, 1990; Christensen, 1997; Dougherty & Hardy, 1996; Drucker, 1985a; Kanter, 1989; Khan & Manopichetwattana, 1989; Lant & Mezias, 1990; Lynn, Morone, & Paulson, 1996; Mauzy & Harriman, 2003; Peters & Waterman, 1982; Prahalad & Hamel, 1990; Schumpeter, 1942; Szymanski, Kroff, & Troy, 2007; Tushman & Anderson, 1986; Zahra, 1993); and (4) economical and quality of life improvements to society in whole (Leifer et al., 2000; Skarzynski & Gibson, 2008; Stevens & Burley, 1997; Tellis, Prabhu, & Chandy, 2009; West & Farr, 1990).

An annual survey conducted by the Boston Consulting Group showed that 66% of the 3,000 executive respondents considered innovation to be one of the top three strategic priorities for their companies (Andrew et al., 2008). Szymanski et al. (2007) claimed that innovation is the Holy Grail of the corporate world, while Brown and Eisenhardt (1995) stated that "[innovation] is among the essential processes for success, survival, and renewal of organizations, particularly for firms in either fast-paced or competitive markets" (p. 344). The term "competitive advantage" was best defined by Barney (1991) as the implementation of value creating strategy not implemented by a current or potential competitor. Bharadwaj and Menon (2000) used the percentage of revenue from new products in total revenue as playing an important role for companies facing top line (revenue) growth challenges, suggesting that innovation is required. Peter Drucker (1954) claimed that there are only two essential functions for the business: marketing and innovation. Kanter (1989) and Brown and Eisenhardt (1995) focused on the fast and increasing rate of change as an important factor in the need for innovation. George et al. (2005) concluded that company longevity dropped from 65 years in 1925 to 10 years in 1998, due to inability to sustain growth through innovation.

While one of the reasons for the importance of innovation is the response to market dynamics, there are cases where such response led to reduced innovation. Leifer et al. (2000) claimed that the imitation of the Japanese

1980's success in incremental process innovation led to American companies responding by *reducing* the level of innovation, and focusing on quality and manufacturing efficiency.

Schumpeter (1942) defined the market changes as "new consumer's goods, the new methods of production... the new markets, the new forms of industrial organization..." (p. 83). Skarzynski and Gibson (2008) claimed that innovation fundamentally changes customer expectations. Stevens and Burley (1997) emphasized the role of innovation in increasing the standard of living in society. However, they stated that in the high-tech industry, only 15% of innovations turn into significant financial successes. Tellis et al. (2009) conducted research linking innovation, firms, and nations. They claimed that innovation is crucial not only to the growth of firms, but also national economies. Tellis and Golder (1996), breaking the myth of the importance of being first to market in favor of being the market leader, identified innovation as one of the five critical factor of becoming a market leader (along with vision, persistence, commitment, and asset leverage).

In summary, for many reasons ranging from company survival to overall contribution to society—innovation is very important, if not critical to organizations.

Definition of Innovation

There is more than a single definition of innovation in the literature. In a book summarizing innovation definitions and research review, West and Farr (1990a) coined one of the most comprehensive definitions of workplace innovation: "the intentional introduction and application within a role, group or organization of ideas, processes, products or procedures, new to the relevant unit of adoption, designed to significantly benefit the individual, the group, organization or wider society" (p. 9). Review of this and other definitions of organizational innovation showed three categories of definitions: (1) definitions focused on innovation generated in the organization and impacting the world outside (Basadur & Hausdorf, 1996; Drucker, 1985a; Engle et al., 1997; Mone et al., 1998); (2) definitions focused on the adoption of external innovation by the organizations (Damanpour, 1990; Downs Jr. & Mohr, 1976; Scott & Bruce, 1994; Thompson, 1965); and (3) definitions focused on the process of innovation (Amabile et al., 1996; Drucker, 1985b; Freeman & Engel, 2007; Galbraith, 1982; Mone et al., 1998; Peters, 2004; Roberts, 2006; Scott & Bruce, 1994; van de Ven, 1986).

The first group of definitions is focused on innovation generated by the organization. Basadur and Hausdorf (1996) defined innovation as "deliberately changing procedures to make new, superior levels of quantity, quality, cost, and customer satisfaction possible" (p. 21). Drucker (1985a) defined it as "the specific tool of entrepreneurs, the means by which they exploit change as an opportunity for a different business or a different service." (p. 19). "Newness" is a major core element in this category of innovation definition, as Szymanski et al. (2007) discovered in their meta-analysis. The "newness" aspect of the definition of innovation was challenged by King (1990), stating that innovation does not have to have something new. Szymanski et al. (2007) also emphasized the *meaningfulness* (to the customer) component of innovation, rather than newness.

The second group of innovation definitions is concerned with *adoption* of innovation conceived outside of the organization. Damanpour (1990) defined innovation as "adoption of an idea or behavior that is new to the adopting organization" (p. 126). Thompson (1965) defined innovation as "the generation, acceptance, and implementation of new ideas, processes, products or services" (p. 2). Pierce and Delbecq (1977) added "... for the first time within an organization setting" (p. 28).

Finally, the third group of definitions focused on the *process* of innovation. Amabile et al. (1996) defined innovation as "the successful implementation of creative ideas within an organization" (p. 1155). Freeman and Engel (2007) suggested: "innovation refers to a process that begins with a novel idea and concludes with market introduction" (p. 94). Galbraith (1982) stated that "[i]nnovation is the process of applying a new idea to create a new process or product" (p. 6). Peters (2004) claimed that innovation is unpredictable, and the result of "uncontrolled skunkworks". "Skunkworks" was considered the source of radical innovations such as Intel's microprocessor and 3M's "Post it Notes". Roberts (2006) explained that "[i]nnovation is the translation of a new idea from its initial state to its actualization in practice as a full-blown innovation" (p. 597), and van de Ven (1986) specified: "development and implementation of new ideas by people who over time engage in transactions with others within an institutional context" (p. 604).

Additional definitions beyond the three categories included one from Mone et al. (1998), who offered a broad definition covering both process and outcome categories: "any action that either puts the organization into new strategic domains or significantly alters the way the organization attempts to serve existing customers or constituents" (p. 117). West and Farr's (1990b) definition, quoted in the beginning of this section, seemed to be the only one incorporating all three elements of the definition: creation of something new, adoption of new technology, and innovation process. Downs Jr. and Mohr (1976) conducted a meta-analysis of innovation research, and operationalized the innovation variable as: time of first adoption of the new innovation (most common definition), whether it was adopted or not (binary), and the extent to which the organization has implemented the innovation.

Types of Innovation

Innovation was intuitively associated with new *products* (Abernathy & Utterback, 1978), but literature discussed additional types of innovations, with respect to the output they generated: (1) new products, (2) new policies, (3) new methods and processes, (4) new services, (5) ancillary (beyond the traditional functions of the organization), (6) new sources of raw material, (7) new organization or structure of an industry, (8) new businesses, (9) new strategies, (10) application innovation (new uses for existing technologies), (11) experiential innovation (improve customer experience), (12) marketing innovation (new customer-touching processes), (13) business model innovation, (14) new technologies, (15) new information systems, (16) administrative (Acs & Audretsch, 1988; Damanpour, 1990; Engle et al., 1997; Hamel, 1998; King, 1990; Lynn et al., 1996; Mone et al., 1998; Moore, 2004; Sandberg, 1992; Taylor, 1990; van de Ven, 1986). The different types of innovation also imply different levels of impact on the industry. For example, a new technology might have higher impact than a new product, or a new use of an existing product (Andrew et al., 2008; Solomon, 2007). In fact, even when considering only products, Andrew et al. (2008) defined five levels of innovation: new-to-the-world products, new products targeting new customers, new products for existing customers, minor changes to existing products, and cost reduction of existing products while maintaining the same value to the customer.

There is a continuum between incremental innovation and radical innovation (Christensen, 1997; Damanpour, 1991; Ekvall, 1997; Khan & Manopichetwattana, 1989; King, 1990; Leifer et al., 2000; Taylor, 1990; Tellis et al., 2009; Treacy, 2004; West & Farr, 1990b). In their research of innovation across nations, Tellis et al. (2009) defined radical innovation as resulting in products that are radically different than existing products in the industry, or products based on radically new technologies. Radical innovation is also known as disruptive technology (Christensen, 1997), non-routine innovation (Galbraith, 1982), discontinuous innovation (Lynn et al., 1996), or creative destruction (Schumpeter, 1942). Acs and Audretsch (1988) described the products in this continuum as varying from new product categories (radical), first product in a new category, significant improvement of existing technology, and modest improvement (incremental innovation). Andrew et al. (2008) defined the continuum as ranging from new-to-the-world products (radical innovation), new products allowing penetration to new customer groups, new products for existing customers, minor changes to existing products, and cost reduction for existing products (incremental innovation). Lant and Mezias (1990) defined the range of innovation strategy from adaptive (radical innovation) strategy as new-to-population, imitative (less radical) strategy as new-to-the-company, and fixed strategy as not innovative at all. March (1991) defined the continuum between exploration (radical innovation) and exploitation (incremental innovation) by the activities that take place in each one. Exploration is characterized by search, variation, risk taking, experimentation, play, flexibility, discovery, innovation, while exploitation is characterized by refinement, choice, production, efficiency, selection, implementation, execution. Miller et al. (2007) added that exploitation uses existing knowledge, whereas exploration generates new knowledge. King (1990) did not define points along the continuum, but used the combination of novelty and riskiness as measures of radicalness of innovation. Leifer et al. (2000) defined radical innovation" as a product, process, or service with either unprecedented performance features or familiar features that offer potential for significant improvements in performance or cost" (p. 5), and described radical innovation as exploration (fundamentally new products, processes, or combination) and incremental innovation as exploitation (expanding existing products or processes).

Radical innovation has positive implications for the companies delivering it, but negative consequences to the companies who pursue incremental innovation in face of a radical innovator entering their market. Schumpeter (1934) was a pioneer in observing radical innovation, identifying economic discontinuities that occur as a result of new goods, new production methods, new markets, new supplies of materials, new organizations (such as the creation or destruction of monopolies), or "new combinations of means of production" (p. 74). He further coined the term "creative destruction", which occurs within an industry as a result of such discontinuous innovation, destroying an old economy, and creating a new one. He did not suggest this is a negative development to the industry, stating that "[t]his process of Creative Destruction is the essential fact about capitalism" (Schumpeter, 1942, p. 83), and that it causes "a complete reorganization of the industry... increase in production... supersession of obsolete businesses" (Schumpeter, 1934, p. 131). Leifer et al. (2000) attributed radical innovation with transforming the marketplace. Disruptive innovation can create and sustain above-average growth in shareholder returns (George et al., 2005), and is the only type of innovation that can lead to long term growth. New-to-market innovation has stronger impact on performance than new-to-company innovation ("me too" in the market) (Szymanski et al., 2007). Radical innovation is much more important than incremental innovation to keep a company innovative. The company has to obsolete itself and its products all the time (Taylor, 1990). Tellis et al. (2009) further claimed that radical innovation is crucial to the growth of nations, and not only companies. "It is important to include an opposing position, emphasizing the consistent growth provided by incremental innovation, where exotic innovation strategies usually get beaten by the slow and steady approach of incremental innovation" (Treacy, 2004, p. 29).

However, the competition created by creative destruction "commands a decisive cost or quality advantage and... strikes not at the margins of the profits and the outputs of the existing firms but at their foundations and their very lives" (Schumpeter, 1942, p. 84). Khan and Manopichetwattana (1989) suggested that the specific type of innovation follows the market cycle. Small, entrepreneurial companies introduce new technologies (radical innovation) when the market emerges. As the market matures, the surviving companies are large, the products commoditize, and innovation becomes cost reducing process innovation (incremental). Burgelman (1984) emphasized the importance of radical innovations to companies who exploited their incremental opportunities.

It is important to note that radical innovation may be in the eyes of the beholder. Abernathy and Utterback (1978) noted that what might be a radical innovation for a small company, could be an incremental process innovation for a large company that uses the product of the smaller company in its process. Gans, Hsu, and Stern (2002) identified industries where startup companies see themselves as suppliers of technology to large established companies and not as competitors in that market at all. Radical innovation allows industry outsiders to overcome entry barriers, and cause the incumbent players to lose their dominance (Basset-Jones, 2005). Freeman and Engel (2007) noted that "[t]he more radical or fundamental the innovation, the more difficult it is to plan the process of commercialization" (p. 96).

In summary, innovation is very important, if not critical to organizational survival, competitive advantage, financial performance, as well as improvements to society as a whole. The most comprehensive definition of innovation includes the creation of something new, the adoption of new technology, and the process in which those are achieved. Innovation comes in many different forms, including new products, services, business processes, and even administrative. There is a continuum between incremental and radical innovation. Radical innovation has a much bigger impact on the company, the market, and society as a whole.

Innovation in Startup and Mature Companies

The general agreement in the literature was that young, small companies are significantly more innovative than older, mature companies (Abernathy & Utterback, 1978; Acs & Audretsch, 1988; Christensen, 1997; Leifer et al., 2000). Abernathy and Utterback (1978) associated this phenomenon with the life cycle of the product, claiming that during the product and market introduction phase—small companies have advantage. When the product and market matures and only incremental innovation is possible—large companies have the upper hand. Most studies avoided the clear demarcation between small and large companies. Few defined small companies as companies with less than 500 employees (Acs & Audretsch, 1988; Khan & Manopichetwattana, 1989) and large companies therefore as having more than 500 employees, being in existence for more than eight years (Zahra, 1993), or being on the S&P 500 list (Bharadwaj & Menon, 2000). Freeman and Engel (2007) claimed that mature companies are challenged with disruptive innovations, as they have difficulties with high risk and long development time, and that people involved in innovation are risking their careers, with limited payoff potential. They also claimed that mature companies have problems with disruptive or discontinuous innovation because of the "creative destruction" they cause, not only to the industry, but to the company structures too. They further claimed that large corporations actually have advantages over startups in the form of capital, employees, legitimacy, brand, alliances, structures, and processes—and advantage that does not materialize in the form of innovation due to that fear of "creative destruction". Gans et al. (2002) observed that (in the electronics industry) startup companies intentionally engage in creative destruction, competing with established firms, as the main way of entering the market. Taylor (1990) generally stated that "[company] size is the enemy of innovation" (p. 105). Christensen (1997) stated that the failure of mature companies in face of the introduction of radical innovation was exactly because the companies listened to their customers and practiced continuous innovation, and missed discontinuous market changes. Christensen's "dilemma" is in the established companies' inability to break away from serving their best customers' current demands to understand how the current market is facing a disruption, and responding to it. Startup companies, with no customers, therefore do not face this dilemma, as they have no current customer to lose. Amabile (1998) claimed that (referring to large organizations):

> ...creativity gets killed much more often than it gets supported. For the most part, this isn't because managers have a vendetta against creativity. On the contrary, most believe in the value of new and useful ideas. However, creativity is undermined unintentionally every day in work environments that were established-for entirely good reasons-to maximize business imperatives such as coordination, productivity, and control (p. 77).

Rosenfeld and Scrvo (1990) found that innovation is harder in larger organization because "as size increases, there is a tendency towards greater depersonalization coupled with a decrease in lateral and vertical communication." (p. 251). The large organization is more rigid, and its culture is more uniform. Abbey and Dickson (1983) claimed that research showed that size had an effect on innovation, although not in a consistent way. Acs and Audretsch (1988) conducted a review of close to 5,000 innovations reported by trade journals, and concluded that in some industries large companies were more innovative than smaller ones, while in other industries—the opposite was true. They also claimed that small companies offer more *product* innovation, whereas large companies offer more *process, service,* and *management* innovations. Ahuja et al. (2008) conducted research that was inconclusive in the relationship between size and level of innovation. In the educational field, Baldridge and Burnham (1975) conducted research in and reached an opposite conclusion—that organization size had a positive impact on the adoption of innovation, but did not generalize it to other industries. This is an indication that the relationship between size and the effect it has on innovation may be industry related. Capozzi and Chakravorti (2006) concluded that large companies require scale of innovation to have an impact, because they cannot bet on a single breakthrough innovation, like startup companies. This was supported by Christensen (1997), who observed that small markets do not solve the growth needs of large companies—another reason for large companies not to engage in radical innovation. Dougherty and Hardy (1996) added that new ventures can be successful focusing on a single product, whereas successful mature companies have to manage the complexity of multiple products, and the fact that the introduction of new products might make their existing products obsolete.

Engle et al. (1997) posited that established corporations contribute poorly to innovations by not challenging the existing bureaucracy and many job changes resulting from promotions, and that R&D people in established corporations are isolated from business proceedings and therefore cannot offer innovative ideas. Khan and Manopichetwattana (1989) claimed that young innovative companies are less focused on the environment, and show stronger product focus than mature innovative companies. They found that both types of companies can be innovative: young companies who are highly proactive, research oriented, and risk taking; while mature companies are characterized by high management quality. Leifer et al. (2000) showed through their research that mature companies cannot radically innovate because they are caught in restructuring and operational quality improvement, allowing startup companies to become the source of most radical innovations, displacing the mature companies.

Not all large, mature companies are non-innovative. Peters and Waterman (1982) researched 62 companies considered innovative and excellent by informed observers in a McKinsey study, and Andrew et al. (2008) in a Boston Consulting Group study identified the most innovative companies as Apple, Google, Toyota, General Electric, Microsoft and more, all mature large companies, although the design of their survey would not have allowed small, startup companies to reach that list. Zien and Buckler (1997), too, studied how mature companies such as 3M, Apple, HP, Polaroid, Sony, Toshiba, and others keep innovation alive. However, the overall consensus in research is that in the process of transitioning from startup to maturity, technology companies become less innovative, and the current study intended to investigate a possible reason. Dougherty and Hardy (1996) conducted a study of 134 innovators in 15 large, mature companies (averaging 96 years of age, 54,000 employees, and $9.4 billion in revenue) and found that the problem of large organizations in sustaining innovation is due to problems in innovation-to-organization links, specifically in resources, processes, and meaning. Innovation depended mostly on the individuals, and not the organization. Such reliance on individual power is not sustainable for large companies.

In conclusion—startup companies use radical innovation to displace mature companies successfully due to many factors, but mainly due to the inertia that the established company has in its market, serving the current needs of its loyal customers, and ignoring possible disruptions to their own markets or new small markets that do not offer the mature company the desired revenue in its initial stage. As a result, new startups, which have "nothing to lose" (no established customers and market share), attack the market with radical innovation and displace the established players. This conclusion, however, is industry related, and not true for all industries. Most research supportive of this conclusion was conducted in the electronic product sector, which will therefore be the focus of this study.

The Innovation Process

Understanding the process of innovation allows understanding of the role of individual creativity in the innovation process, and is the purpose of this section. Leifer et al. (2000) claimed that there is no *intentional* process of innovation, and that radical innovation occurred in most companies in an ad hoc manner, and therefore unpredictably and infrequently, although mature companies attempt to drive radical innovation through systematic processes. Peters (2004) observed that innovation is unpredictable and the result of uncontrolled skunkworks. Rosenfeld and Servo (1990) claimed that innovation is a complex process, and can be dropped within the organization in many places. However, as opposed to these few dissenting views, the general consensus, as shown in the following, is that innovation is an orderly process, made of multiple steps. Different authors proposed different innovation process models varying in their level of detail, emphasizing different elements in the innovative process. They all included *individual creativity*, by different names, as a key component. For the purpose of the following process description, the individual creativity component will be called "generation of a creative idea".

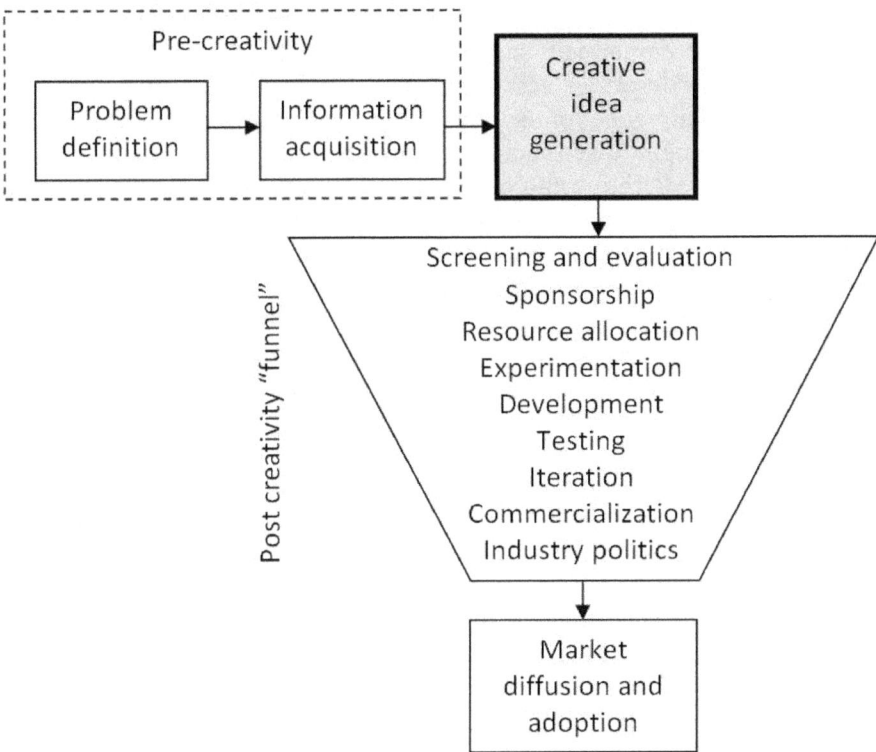

Figure 1 – The process of innovation.

Figure 1 shows the following synthesized list of steps in the innovation process: (1) initiation, problem definition; (2) acquisition of information, trend sensing; (3) generation of a creative idea; (4) screening and evaluation; (5) sponsorship; (6) resource allocation; (7) experimentation; (8) development; (9) testing; (10) iteration; (11) commercialization; (12) industry politics; and (13) market diffusion and adoption (Ancona & Caldwell, 1987; Baldrisge & Burnham, 1975; Basadur & Gelade, 2006; Damanpour, 1991; Freeman & Engel, 2007; Galbraith, 1982; Haner, 2005; Khan & Manopichetwattana, 1989; King, 1990; Lynn et al., 1996; Peters, 2004; Pierce & Delbecq, 1977; Roberts, 2006; Rosenfeld & Servo, 1990; Scott & Bruce, 1994; Solomon, 2007; Staw, 1990; Stevens & Burley, 1997; Taylor, 1990; Thomke, 2001; Thompson, 1965; van de Ven, 1986). These can be grouped into three groups: pre-creativity steps (1 and 2), the creative idea step (3); and post-creativity steps (4 through 13).

The innovation process following the generation of the creative idea is a funnel like process, in which the creative idea is screened, through a selection process, until only the commercially viable ideas are launched at the market. Stevens and Burley (1997) conducted a study based on project literature, patent literature, and venture capitalist experience, and concluded that "across most industries, it appears to require 3,000 raw ideas to produce one substantially new commercially successful industrial product" (p. 16). The funnel process they described acts as follows: 3,000 raw ideas turn into 300 ideas for which minimal action is taken (such as simple experiments, patent filing, or management discussion); 125 of the 300 ideas become small projects; 9 out of the 125 become significant projects (significant development effort); 4 out of 9 become major development efforts; 1.7 out of 4 is commercially launched; and 1 out of 1.7 (59%) is commercially successful (this last success rate varied from 40% to 67%, depending on the source of information, industry, and geography). They also claimed that the conversion rate of product line extensions (incremental innovation, as opposed to radical innovation and introduction of new products or services) was much higher.

However, care must be taken when considering this a perfect Darwinian process in which only the truly viable ideas are launched. Rosenfeld and Servo (1990) claimed that in large organizations good ideas can be dropped in the organization in many places, and they emphasized the role of champions (advocators, ligitimizers) and sponsors (with high status and track record) in driving creative ideas through the innovation funnel and not letting them drop for illegitimate reasons. Pinchot (1987) made the distinction between promoters and intrapreneurs. Promoters will promote their idea, but will not follow through to execute it, whereas the intrapreneurs (the equivalent of the champions described above) will see it through to execution, not letting it fail along the way. King (1990), Peters and Waterman (1982), Staw (1990), and Tellis et al. (2009), too, noted the importance of idea champions and change agents to the success of organizational level innovation. Leifer, O'Connor, and Rice (2001) added the concept of the radical innovation hub, an entity within the organization that can manage radical innovation throughout its life cycle. The focus is on the role of the hub to capture ideas, network, lobby, and be the link to the rest of the organization.

Innovation and Creativity

The terms *innovation* and *creativity* have often been confused and used interchangeably (Pierce & Delbecq, 1977; Thompson, 1965; Turnipseed, 1994). The two most consistent distinctions between innovation and creativity are: (1) innovation is an *organizational* function, whereas creativity is an *individual* component (Amabile, 1988; Ekvall, 1997; Farr, 1990; Oldham & Cummings, 1996); and (2) creativity is a necessary, but not sufficient *component* of innovation (Amabile, 1988; Basadur & Gelade, 2006; Basset-Jones, 2005; Cutler, 2000; Mauzy & Harriman, 2003; Rosenfeld & Servo, 1990; Zhou, 2003). Amabile (1988) stated that "individual creativity and organizational innovation are closely interlocked systems. Individual creativity is the most crucial element of organizational innovation, but it is not, by itself, sufficient" (p. 125). Bharadwaj and Menon (2000) stated that "innovation is a function of individual efforts and institutional systems to facilitate creativity" (p. 425). Basadur and Hausdorf (1996) stated that "Both improved and new methods and goods and services result from creativity" (p. 21). Basset-Jones (2005) stated that "Creativity is a necessary precondition for successful innovation" (p. 171). Mauzy and Harriman (2003) suggested the simple relationship between creativity and innovation: *creativity generates ideas, and innovation implements them*, and Zhou (2003) offered the relationship as a simple formula: Organizational Innovation = Individual Creativity + Implementation. This simple framework is described in Figure 2. The "creative idea" block is shaded, indicating the focus of this study. The importance of innovation to the organization was established in previous sections of this literature review, and the link between creativity and innovation as illustrated here justifies the focus of this study on creativity.

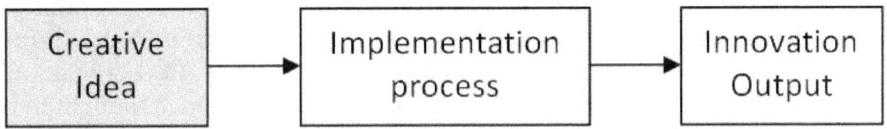

Figure 2 – Innovation and creativity.

Rosenfeld and Servo (1990) added a financial aspect to the relationship, stating that "[c]reativity refers to the generation of novel ideas—innovation to making money with them" (p. 252). West and Farr (1990), though, suggested that innovation *may* involve creativity, but that not all innovations are creative. Oldham and Cummings (1996) linked innovation to organizations and creativity to individuals, stating that "creative performance refers to products, ideas, and so forth produced at the individual level, whereas innovation refers to the successful implementation of these products at the organizational level" (p. 608).

In summary, the relationship between innovation and creativity can be summarized through (1) innovation is an organizational function while creativity is an individual one, and (2) innovation is made of the generation of a creative idea, and the implementation of it.

Individual Creativity

Definition of Creativity

In contrast with innovation, which is considered an organizational function or capability—creativity "can only be found in the head of individuals" (Anderson, 1992, p. 40). Haner (2005) added that "individual persons initiate, contribute to and evaluate all parts of creativity and innovation processes. Their individual efforts and achievements are the basis for creativity and innovation" (p. 290). As reviewed in the previous section, individual creativity is a *component* of organizational creativity, often referred to as "invention" (Galbraith, 1982). Montuori and Purser (1995), however, criticized the individualistic focus on creativity. They did not diminish the role of the individual , but put it in context: "a contextual approach to creativity will almost by necessity be interdisciplinary, historical, ecological, systemic, and aware of cultural and gender differences, while at the same time continuing to address personality issues" (p. 106). Analysis of their criticism shows that they do, in fact, agree that the creation of the creative idea is an individual function, although they wanted to emphasize the role that the organization (and other elements) play in the ability of that individual to generate the creative idea, although they did not claim that the idea generation occurs at many people at the same time, or at the organization as an entity.

Abedi (2002) claimed that the lack of a universally acceptable operational definition of creativity led to the development of multiple instruments to assess creativity, varying in what they measure. Smith (2005) summarized 100 definitions of creativity over the years. Herbert Simon's (2001, as cited by Smith, 2005) defined it as follows: "We judge thought to be creative when it produces something that is both novel and interesting and valuable" (p. 208). Shalley (1995) defined individual creative behavior as "developing solutions to job-related problems that are judged as both novel and appropriate for the situation" (p. 484).

Creativity was measured (and thus defined) as: (1) a product, (2) a cognitive process, (3) a behavior, (4) a personality trait, and (5) a creative environment or situation (Amabile, 1988; 1996; 1998; Basadur & Hausdorf, 1996; Bassett-Jones, 2005; Brown, 1989; Davis, 2009; Isaksen et al., 2000; King, 1990; Oldham & Cummings, 1996; Smith, 2005). Amabile (1988) preferred the *product* definition which, she claimed, was easier to observe and assess, and thus defined creativity as "the production of novel and useful ideas by an individual or small group of individuals working together" (p. 126). Later, she provided the conceptual definition of creativity that became the most acceptable definition today: "A product or response will be judged as creative to the extent that (a) it is both a novel and appropriate, useful, correct or valuable response to the task at hand, and (b) the task is heuristic rather than algorithmic" (Amabile, 1996, p. 35). This definition is based on subjective assessment of a *product*, and not a person or a process. She further defined the creative product as being original, appropriate and useful, and actionable (Amabile, 1998). Anderson (1992) noted that creativity is not the *knowledge* itself, but rather how knowledge it used. Barron and Harrington (1981) proposed two creativity definition categories: "creativity as socially recognized achievement in which there are novel products to which one can point as evidence, such as inventions, theories, buildings, published writings, paintings and sculptures and films; laws; institutions; medical and surgical treatments, and so on; and creativity as an ability manifested by performance in critical trials, such as tests, contests, etc, in which one individual can be compared with another on a precisely defined scale." (p. 442). Basset-Jones (2005) claimed that in defining creativity, it is difficult to separate creative product from the process that created it, since products may be intangible, and processes may result in products. Dormen and Edidin (1989) added a non- scientific definition of creativity: "the search for the elusive... moment of insight when one sees the world, or a problem, or an idea, in a new way" (p. 46), as well as the ability to adapt to change. The adaptability aspect of creativity was supported by Ripple (1989). While Runco (1993) claimed that creative performance is unpredictable, Farr and Ford (1990) stated that individual creativity is intentional and not accidental, defining it as "the intentional introduction within one's work role of new and useful ideas, processes, products, or procedures." (p. 63). Bharadwaj and Menon (2000) claimed that creativity is a thought process that can be acquired and improved through training and practice. Feldhusen and Goh (1995) were unique in defining creativity as an interactive process: "an interaction among a domain, a person, and a field" (p. 233).

It appears that the definition and measurement of creativity in terms of the *creative product* (idea) output is the most acceptable today. The characteristics of the creative idea are: (1) it is *new and different* than anything that existed before, and (2) it is *useful and appropriate* to the task it intends to serve (Amabile, 1988; 1996; Bharadwaj& Menon, 2000; Scott & Bruce, 1994; Zhou, 2003). Brown (1989) added that to define a product as creative, it has to be more than novel—it should also be *unusual*, and also include "'Transformation of constraint'—combining elements in a way that breaks through tradition and leads to a new perspective of way of viewing reality" (p. 12). Scott (1965) also emphasized that a creative idea is a result of an unusual and rare behavior. Ekvall (1997) added the dimension of elegance, supported by Smith (2005). However, one must remember that some of the creativity research was done outside the industrial setting, in the world or art, where elegance plays a more significant role than it does in the industrial world. Gryskiewicz and Taylor (2003) emphasized that the novelty or newness of the creative idea has to be significantly different than the existing ideas, thus eliminating "minor variations" from the definition of creativity. West and Farr (1990b), focused on creativity as part of radical innovation, wanted the definition of creativity to address the "absolute novelty". Oldham and Cummings (1996) measured the *usefulness* of the creative ideas by the willingness of the organization to further develop them. Shalley (1995) further extended the *usefulness* of the creative product concept to include that it should be a better way to accomplish some purpose.

Anderson (1992) and Engle et al. (1997) defined three types of creativity: *creation* (of something out of nothing), *synthesis* (of previously unrelated phenomena), and *modification* (of something that already exists so that it can perform the existing function better, perform a new function, perform same function in a new setting, or be used by someone new), and added that the three types are hard to separate in reality, and stated that the creation (radical innovation) might be mystical and possessed by few individuals, while synthesis and modification (incremental innovation) are much more widely acceptable.

The Creative Process

Different authors were relatively consistent when defining the *innovation* process, varying only at the level of detail, and sometime offering unique steps as part of the overall process. However, different authors varied significantly with respect to the definition of the *creativity* process. In some cases, the borders between creativity steps and innovation steps were blurred, and in other cases authors claimed that there is no recipe for systemic creativity (Mauzy & Harriman, 2003), or that stated that creative performance is unpredictable and there is no creative process at all (Runco, 1993). The simplest description of the process of creativity includes a single step: the creation of a new idea (Anderson, de Drew, & Nijstad, 2004; Galbraith, 1982). There were three main models used to describe the creativity process: (1) problem solving approaches, (2) breaking old paradigms and connections and making new ones, and (3) divergent and convergent idea generation.

Problem solving approaches

Three of the earlier models of the creative problem solving processes were: invention (observed need or difficulty, analysis and definition, information survey, possible solutions, critical evaluation of the solution, ongoing incubation, formulation of the new "inventions", evaluation, refinement, and acceptance of final solution) (Rossman, 1931 as cited in Brown, 1989); creative production (preparation, incubation, illumination, and verification) (Wallas, 1926, as cited in Brown, 1989); and problem solving (felt difficulty, problem formulation, possible solutions, implications of solutions, and experimental corroboration) (Dewey, 1910, as cited in Brown, 1989). The modern problem solving model of creativity is made of three stages: problem finding, problem solving, and solution implementation. At each stage—there is a two step process of ideation (divergent, uncritical generation of ideas) and evaluation (convergent, applying judgment to select best ideas) (Basadur, Graen, & Green, 1982; Basadur & Hausdorf, 1996). Davis (2009) suggested a three step model of problem solving based creative thinking: problem finding (identifying, defining, and working towards a solution); ideation (divergent thinking, categorization, and remote association); and evaluation (important to the usefulness of the creative idea). Staw's (1990) evolutionary model of creativity included only the presentation of the problem, followed by idea generation. However, he emphasized the importance of increasing variation in the organization so that new combinations can be generated. Kirton

(1976) associated creativity with problem solving behavior when developing the Kirton Adaption-Innovation measurement instrument. Farr (1990) claimed that divergent thinking may lead mostly to incremental innovation rather than radical.

Breaking and making paradigms and connections

Basadur and Gelade (2006) suggested that creativity is a two step process: *innovating* ("inventing")—breaking old connections ("old paradigms") and moving from the familiar to the strange; and *learning*—making new connections ("new paradigms") and moving from the strange to the familiar, completing a cycle. This model was supported by George and Jing (2007): "Workplace creativity often necessitates a rejection of preexisting schemas and a more bottom-up search for better ways of doing things and new ideas" (p. 607). Schumpeter (1934) defined the core of creative destruction as the creation of new combinations. Elkington and Hartigan (2008) defined "unreasonable people" as highly creative, and defined "being unreasonable" as jettisoning old, outdated forms of reasoning in favor of conceiving new ones.

Divergent and convergent ideation

Amabile et al. (2005) stated that "the probability of novelty varies with the *number* [italics added] of cognitive elements available for association and with the *breadth* [italics added] of those elements that are treated as relevant to the problem" (p. 368/ASQ). Mednick (1962) defined creative thinking process as "the forming of associative elements into new combinations which either meet specified requirements or are in some way useful. The more mutually remote the elements of the new combination, the more creative the process or solution." (p. 221). Runco (1993) emphasized the importance of the incubation stage, which provides time necessary for cognitive processes to result in associations. Haner (2005) empirically discovered that the creativity process includes both convergent and divergent activities.

Other models

Amabile (1988) defined the following creativity process: task presentation (using internal and external sources), preparation (gathering information and resources), idea generation (produce ideas or products), idea validation (Against task criteria), and outcome assessment (success, failure, or progress). She further claimed that the idea generation stage represents the entire individual or small group creativity model. Rogers' (1983, as cited in King, 1990) innovation-decision creativity process included knowledge, persuasion, decision, implementation, and confirmation. Bassett-Jones (2005) did not define a complete process of creativity, but emphasized the importance of the cross pollination of ideas to increase creativity. Haner's (2005) creativity process model was made of preparation, incubation, insight, and elaboration and evaluation. Mauzy and Harriman's (2003) process of creativity included motivation, curiosity and fear, forming new ideas through breaking and making of connections, and evaluation. They are the only authors who moved motivation from context into the process. They further defined a seven stage process of purposeful creativity which included: (1) groundwork and immersion, (2) divergent exploration, (3) selection, (4) focused exploration, (5) initial articulation of a potential solution, (6) development and transformation, and (7) implementation. It should be noted that the last two stages are typically defined as steps in the *organizational innovation* process, following the generation of the creative idea as defined by their first five stages. Finally, Shapero (1985) defined the creative process as made of: preparation, incubation, illumination, and verification.

In summary, there are several different approaches to define the process of creativity. Some of those are aligned, and some are not. The focus of this study is not in the process of creativity, but rather in the context that supports it. The literature review in this section was provided as background to understand the creative process that is supported by the appropriate antecedents.

Antecedents of Employee Creativity

A significant body of research exists in the area of factors affecting employee creativity. The categorization of those factors varied among researchers. Amabile (1988, 1998) identified three groups of factors: expertise, creative skills, and motivation (combining personal and organizational context, while separating personal characteristics into expertise and skills). Basadur and Hausdorf (1996) categorized the antecedents of creativity into: personal (cognitive, motivational, and attitudinal), social, and environmental. Oldham and Cummins (1996) simplified and categorized the factors in two: individual level and organizational level.

Figure 3 synthesizes prior research and presents three areas of antecedents of individual creativity (the generation of a creative idea) in the work environment: (1) personal characteristics that exist prior to the involvement in the organizational environment, (2) personal context (outside the organization) that exists while the individual operates within the organizational environment, and (3) the organizational climate, including the team and workgroup setting. The current study investigated the differences in the level of creativity that individuals experience between startup companies and mature companies. For that purpose, the focus of the study was on the three shaded areas: organizational climate, personal context, and the generation of the creative ideas. To eliminate the possible effect of the individual characteristics on the creativity generated by that individual, the participants were individuals who worked in both environments and were therefore in a position to compare their experiences of the three shaded areas, while maintaining similarity of their own individual characteristics.

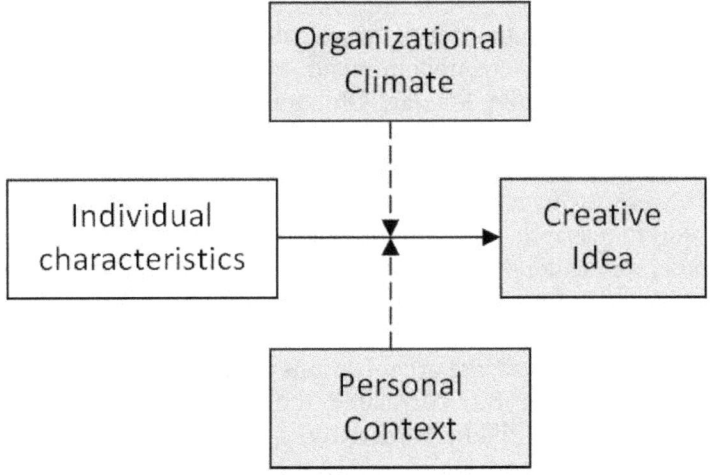

Figure 3 – Antecedents of individual creativity in the work environment.

Individual Characteristics

Many studies were conducted and models created that linked individual characteristics to individual creativity. Review of 43 years of research produced the following list of characteristics found to positively affect creativity: being a hobbyist; persistence; curiosity; broad interests; attraction to complexity; intuition; high energy; proactivity; openness to experiences; unconventionality; originality (although it can be argued that originality is really creativity); outcome driven; honesty; self-motivation; self-confidence; creative self image; cognitive abilities (genius, brilliance, general intellect, divergent thinking style, ideational fluency, ability to find problems, associational, analogical and metaphorical, imaginative); risk orientation; ambiguity tolerance; prior relevant job experience (including startup experience); expertise; education; domain knowledge (and being at the forefront of technology); practicality; independence; resourcefulness; opportunistic; being an achiever; passion; strong will; joyfulness; strength; compassion; irreverence for the status quo; explanatory style; social skills; naiveté (being new to the field); commitment to the project, the organization, and ownership; strong desire to innovate (Ahuja et al., 2008; Amabile, 1988; Ancona & Caldwell, 1987; Anderson et al., 2004; Barron & Harrington, 1981; Cutler, 2000; Devanna & Tichy, 1990; Elkington & Hartigan, 2008; Engle et al., 1997; Farr & Ford, 1990; Galbraith, 1982; George & Jing, 2007; Hamel, 1998; Isaksen & Lauer, 1999; King, 1990; Kirton, 1976; Leifer et al., 2000;

Mathisen & Einarsen, 2004; Mauzy & Harriman (2003; Ray, 1987; Ripple, 1989; Runco, 1993; Scott, 1965; Scott & Bruce, 1994; Shalley, 1995; Solomon, 2007; Taylor, 1990; Thompson, 1965; Turnipseed, 1994; Woodman & Schoenfeldt, 1989).

Baldridge and Burnham (1975) empirically discovered that biographical characteristics (sex, age, cosmopolitanism, education) did not have strong impact on creativity, while Madjar, Oldham, and Pratt (2002) concluded through research that married people exhibited higher levels or creativity, and Woodman and Schoenfeldt (1989) found that sex, family position, and birth order were influencing personal creativity. Barron and Harrington (1981) reviewed research and summarized that thought disorder (such as schizophrenia, manic depression, and brain damage) may have had a positive effect on creativity. Anderson (1992) criticized the *knowledge* element, and proposed that MBAs have all the traditional business knowledge, and therefore it cannot differentiate organizations anymore.

Carne and Kirton (1982) correlated the Myers Briggs Type Indicator (MBTI) dimensions to individual creativity, specifically the Kirton Adaption-Innovation (KAI) inventory, and found that creative people are significantly more intuitive, perceiving, and moderately extroverted. Montuori and Purser (1995) claimed that even the loneliest geniuses (giving Einstein as an example) operated within historical context with social, historical, and environmental factors. Madjar et al. (2002) suggested that the role of creative personality was in *moderating* the creative outcome to the environmental context, and not directly affecting the creative outcome. Runco (1993) stated that the "motivational and attitudinal contributions to creative performance are without a doubt important, but they may merely help to determine how cognitive skills are used.... Cognitive potential might determine the range of what an individual can do—defining his or her potential—with motivation determining exactly how much of that potential is used" (p. 354).

Born Creativity

Personal characteristics can be genetic or acquired. Of all the authors cited in this section, Ripple (1989) was the only one who acknowledged that there is a controversy whether creativity can be improved through training, without suggesting an opinion. Cutler (2000) claimed that creative people were creative early in life. Scott (1965) identified rich early life experiences and even parent-child relationships as antecedents of individual creative ability. Taylor (1990) determined that innovation could not be taught, as it is an emotional experience, coming from the genes, early life, and early education. Ray (1987) claimed that creativity is idiosyncratic to the individual, suggesting it cannot be learned, and also that people have individual and different ways of being creative.

Conversely, Dormen and Edidin (1989) summarized a six decade longitudinal research starting in the early 1920 that selected 1,528 genius school children (with IQ above 135) and found that very few made notably creative contributions to society, supported by other research that showed no correlation between creativity and IQ. This finding was also reported by Gough (1979) and Kirton (1976). Drucker (1985b) claimed that "[a]bove all, innovation is *work* [italicized] rather than *genius* [italicized]. It requires knowledge, it often requires ingenuity, and it requires focus. There are clearly people who are more talented as innovators than others but their talents lie in well-defined areas" (p. 72). At the same time, he tied innovation to people, and their "pre-existing conditions", and did not discuss conditions conducive to innovation or creativity. Farr (1990) claimed that all individuals are capable of being innovative in their work roles. Ripple (1989) stated that "the potential for creative thinking and behavior exists to a greater or lesser degree in everyone" (p. 189) and that creativity occurs on a daily basis, calling it "ordinary creativity". West and Farr (1990) stated that "far from being an isolated indication of genius, creative expression in the world of work is manifested by almost everyone, given the appropriate facilitating environmental conditions" (p. 4). There was overall agreement that appropriate training has a positive impact on individual creativity (Anderson et al., 2004; Basadur & Gelade, 2006; Bharadwaj & Menon, 2000) and that creativity can be learned and practiced (Cutler, 2000; Drucker, 1985a; Mauzy & Harriman, 2003). King (1990) agreed that training could enhance creativity, but only addressing the *strategic* blocks (lack of creative skills), and not the other *personal* blocks (values, perceptual, and self image). Farr (1990) did not focus on creativity training, but rather on creativity enhancing techniques such as brainstorming, morphological analysis, and lateral and divergent thinking. Finally, Scott, Leritz, and Mumford (2004) conducted a meta-analysis of studies addressing the effectiveness of creativity training and reached the following conclusions: (1) creativity training is effective, mostly on divergent thinking and problem solving; (2) there were differences for different populations, where creative training was less effective for gifted children and women; (3) the strongest and most effective element of creativity training is cognitive processing activities; (4) the cognitive capabilities that had the biggest impact on the effectiveness of training were: new idea generation (problem finding, conceptual combination, and idea generation); (5) the training techniques that worked the best were: critical thinking, convergent thinking, constraint identification, and use of analogies; (6) lecture based instructions were the most effective on divergent thinking; and (7) training effectiveness improved when it included an explanation of the cognitive processes that occurred, and when training was lengthy and challenging.

In summary, there is still debate whether personal characteristics supportive of creativity are born or acquired, and whether creativity training can improve the creativity capabilities of individuals. This study attempted to isolate personal characteristics (creativity capabilities) through using a sample of individuals who worked for both environments (startup and mature companies), assuming their personal characteristics and creativity capabilities have not significantly changed upon the transition. As a result, further discussion of personal characteristics was not required beyond this background, and the focus will now shift to personal context and organizational climate.

Personal Context

For this study, the term *personal context* was used to include the factors that could not be directly controlled by management. Three sub categories were defined for personal context: affect (mood), job satisfaction, and support and pressure outside of work.

Affect (Mood)

Elkington and Hartigan (2008) claimed that "unreasonable entrepreneurs" (their term for highly creative people) were fueled by emotions more than others. The relationship between affect and mood on individual creativity was studied by several researchers, but different conclusions were reached. Earlier literature assumed and studied the intuitive hypothesis that *positive* mood has a positive effect on the level of creativity. However, later research showed the positive effect of *negative* mood on creativity, and most recent research focused on the coexistence of negative and positive moods (emotional ambivalence), and the effect the interaction between them has on creativity (King, 1990). Amabile et al. (2005) defined affect as *feeling of emotion*. They identified prior studies that showed mostly a positive relationship between affect and creativity, but also studies that showed a negative relationship. They observed a reciprocal relationship between creativity and mood, where creativity could also affect mood, and not only the other way around. In a longitudinal study of 222 members of 26 project teams they found a strong and linear positive relationship between positive affect and creativity. They found: (1) affect as an antecedent to creativity (immediately or through incubation), (2) affect as a direct or indirect consequence of creativity, and (3) affect occurring simultaneously with creativity. Madjar et al. (2002) claimed that positive mood did not have a direct effect on creativity, but was rather a moderator of the relationship between other factors (such as non-work support) and creativity. They also claimed that negative mood was not proven to have any contribution to creativity. Anderson et al. (2004) reviewed creativity research and found that most studies showed a positive correlation between negative mood and level of creativity. Davis (2009) conducted a meta analysis of 62 experimental and 10 non-experimental studies evaluating the relationship. He defined affect as made of emotions (relationship with an object or event) and mood (experienced over longer period than emotions). His analysis concluded that positive mood has a positive impact on the *ideation* component of creative thinking, and a less obvious impact on the other elements of creative thinking. The contrast of positive and negative or neutral mood intensifies the impact on creativity. The benefits of positive mood were shown to be context related in (1) mood attributions, (2) mood intensity, and (3) the type of creative task. Finally, he found no effect of mood on problem solving tasks. George and Zhou (2002) positioned negative and positive moods on two extremes of a single continuum, opposite to one another and not interacting with one another. They found that negative mood was positively related to creativity when perceived recognition and rewards for creative performance and clarity of feelings were high. Fong (2006) supported the notion of the reciprocal relationship between emotions and creativity. He studied the impact of emotional ambivalence—the ability to experience positive and negative emotions simultaneously. He claimed that there was evidence that emotional ambivalence exists in the workplace, and his study showed that individuals experiencing emotional ambivalence demonstrated increased sensitivity to associations, an important aspect of creativity. George and Jing (2007) adopted the "mood as information" theory, claiming that moods have pervasive effects on cognition, and provide information about changes in the environment and thus can be supportive of creativity. They further stated that there is evidence of how both positive mood and negative mood enhanced creativity, and specifically that:

> In a work context that supports creativity, positive and negative mood states interact to promote creativity. Negative moods promote problem identification... and a dissatisfaction with the status quo that can promote opportunity identification.... Positive moods promote confidence and divergent thinking. Both moods likely contribute to creativity in the workplace through their differential tuning effects.... creativity in ongoing organizations likely benefits from both kinds of strategies being utilized at different times. (p. 607)

They claimed that supervisors played a key role influencing employee creativity (the role of supervisors in affecting creativity is discussed later in this literature review) in the effect they had on employee mood which, in turn, affected employee creativity. This effect was achieved through providing developmental feedback, displacing interactional justice, and being trustworthy, all three of which interact with employee mood. They concluded that (1) when positive mood was low—negative mood did not affect creativity, and (2) when positive mood was high—negative mood affected creativity and the supervisory behavior (developmental feedback, interactive justice, and trust) affected the direction of the relationship: when those were high—the *magnitude* of the negative mood positively affected creativity, and when those were low—the magnitude of negative mood negatively affected creativity. Examples: if positive mood is low, then negative mood would have little effect on creativity. If positive mood is high but trust is low—negative mood would cause lower creativity. If supervisor feedback is high—negative mood would cause higher creativity. In summary—mood is a factor that may affect individual creativity, and therefore was one of the factors considered for comparison in this study.

Job Satisfaction

The link between job satisfaction (or dissatisfaction) and creativity was also researched by many. In general, there were two approaches to the impact that job satisfaction has on creativity. The classical approach claimed that job *satisfaction* leads to creativity, suggesting that happy employees are more creative (Ekvall, 1996; Isaksen & Lauer, 1999; Pierce & Delbecq, 1977; Roethlisberger & Dickson, 1939; Turnipseed, 1994). This approach was aligned with claiming a positive link between positive mood and creativity. A less intuitive approach claimed that job *dissatisfaction* led to creativity, and that employees who are *not* satisfied with the status quo are more prone to change it, and are therefore more creative (Anderson et al., 2004; Pierce & Delbecq, 1977; Zhou & George, 2001). This approach was aligned with claiming a positive link between negative mood and creativity. Pierce and Delbecq (1977) had a somewhat ambivalent attitude towards satisfaction, claiming that both *job* satisfaction and *performance* dissatisfaction had a positive effect on creativity and innovation. According to them, to maximize creativity, an employee must be satisfied with his or her job, and dissatisfied with performance, at the same time. Finally, Turnipseed (1994) expanded satisfaction to include satisfaction in personal life, beyond job satisfaction, in claiming a positive effect on creativity. The significance of the relationship between job satisfaction and creativity as emerged from prior studies warrants making it a factor of comparison between startup companies and mature companies in this study.

Support and Pressure outside Work

The effects of work related factors on workplace creativity were researched comprehensively. However, little research was done to show the relationship between non-work factors and creativity at work. Madjar et al. (2002) included non-work sources such as family and friends in their study of antecedents to creativity. They studied 265 employees of three companies, and used six items to measure support of friends and family. They found that non-work support for creativity was stronger than support at work, positive mood made a positive impact on the relationship between support (including non-work) and creativity, and that less creative individuals responded more positively to support from family and friends, thus concluding that the effect of the support of family and friends on workplace creativity is stronger for less creative individuals, whereas more creative individuals would be less affected by non-work support. The support and pressure outside work could be different when the individual is working for a startup company versus a mature company, so these factors were included in this study.

In summary, personal context is made of three major factors: mood (affect), job satisfaction, and support and pressure from home. Research has evolved from claiming positive effect of *positive* mood on creativity, to positive effect of *negative* mood on creativity, eventually to positive effect of *mood ambivalence* on creativity. Research was more consistent claiming that job *satisfaction* had a positive effect on creativity, although few researchers claimed that job *dissatisfaction* had a positive effect on creativity, through the desire to change the status quo. Finally, prior research showed that support from home had a positive effect on creativity, whereas pressure from home had a negative effect.

Organizational Climate for Creativity

The most studied category of antecedents for individual creativity was the *organizational* context of creativity. It could almost be grouped to show that *psychology* researchers focused on personal characteristics and context affecting creativity, whereas the *organizational* and *management* researchers focused on the organizational context affecting creativity. The latter seems only logical, as the organization can be more effective in controlling the factors within its control (organizational context) than the factors outside of its control (personal characteristics and personal context). None of the researchers investigated the *entire* list reviewed here, and not all of them agreed on the amount (or even the direction) of impact of each one of the factors on individual creativity. The following review is of the antecedents that achieved consensus among researchers. Organizational climate is defined as an "attribute of the organization, a conglomerate of attitudes, feelings, and behaviors which characterizes life in the organization, and exists independently of the perceptions and understandings of the members of the organization" (Ekvall, 1996, p. 105). Isaksen et al. (2000) defined climate as "the recurring patterns of behavior, attitudes, and feelings that characterize life in the organization" (p. 172). It was also defined as the shared perceptions of "how things are like around here" (Anderson & West, 1998). For the purpose of this study, organizational climate means the aggregation of factors that would potentially affect creativity of individuals within this organization.

Extrinsic and Intrinsic Motivation

Amabile (1998) developed a model of the context for creativity, including three components: expertise (personal), creative thinking skills (personal), and motivation (external). She included two types of motivation: extrinsic and intrinsic, and claimed that motivation (both types) is the easiest for management to influence, and that it is the most important component of the three (Amabile, 1988). Extrinsic motivation was defined as external to the task environment, while intrinsic motivation is contained within the task and the person conducting the task. Shalley (1995) categorized the conditions for creative behavior relatively similarly, including ability, certain cognitive activities, and intrinsic motivation (not considering extrinsic motivation at all).

Extrinsic motivation is easier for management to influence than intrinsic motivation because it is easier to measure and implement. It is made mostly of financial rewards and promotions, and in general *contingent rewards* (Benabou & Tirole, 2003). King (1990) claimed that in the *need hierarchy theory*, the state of being motivated is the equivalent of self actualization—the highest level in the need hierarchy. The following discussion reviews two opposing schools: one claimed that intrinsic motivation is conducive to creativity while extrinsic motivation is detrimental to creativity, and the other claimed that extrinsic motivation promotes creativity. No position was found that claimed that intrinsic motivation is detrimental to creativity.

Amabile (1988) posited that *"the intrinsically motivated state is conducive to creativity, whereas the extrinsically motivated state is detrimental"* (Amabile, 1996, p. 107). Benabou and Tirole (2003) contrasted the economic belief that incentives promote effort and performance with the psychological controversy on the topic. Their paper, supported by economical mathematics, concluded that "explicit incentive schemes may sometimes backfire, especially in the long run, by undermining agents' confidence in their own abilities or in the value of the rewarded task. This side of social psychology has been largely neglected by economists" (p. 516). They further claimed that contingent rewards, due to cognitive dissonance, may be negative reinforcers, especially in the long run, and that employees find contingency rewards an alienating and dehumanizing way of control. Cummings, Hinton, and Gobdel (1975) characterized the bureaucratic organization as, among other things, heavily reliant on extrinsic rewards which, together with the other characteristics, inhibit creativity. Cummings (1965) explained this by stating that the extrinsic reward system (money, promotions, status) promoted conformity and not novelty. A similar statement was made by Thompson (1965), who claimed that extrinsic rewards stimulate conformity rather than innovation, while creativity is promoted by intrinsic rewards. Roethlisberger and Dickson (1939), in their report of the Hawthorne experiments, stated that "none of the results... gave the slightest substantiation to the theory that the worker is primarily motivated by economic interests" (p. 575-576). They concluded that most dissatisfaction with wages was based on fairness—differences from other employees, and that wage incentives failed to work when they were not aligned with social values, thus making both *fairness* and *social value alignment* more important than the rewards themselves. Taylor (1990), too, concluded that individual recognition (component of intrinsic motivation) is more important than salaries, bonuses, or promotions (components of extrinsic motivation) to maintain creativity. Anderson et al. (2004) focused on the importance of motivation for individual level creativity, but extended the definition of intrinsic motivation to include internal sources such as determination to success and personal initiative. Based on the work of Amabile et al. (1996) and Amabile and Gryskiewicz (1987), the *Center for Creative Leadership* developed a handbook to help managers create the environment to intrinsically motivate employees to be creative (Gryskiewicz & Taylor, 2003). Pierce and Delbecq (1977) segmented the innovation process into three sequential components: initiation (creativity), adoption, and implementation. They found that intrinsic motivation had positive impact on all three.

On the other hand, not all researchers agreed that extrinsic rewards inhibit creativity. Farr and Ford (1990) suggested that the reward-performance link and financial rewards in general influence the perceived payoff from change, thus promoting change (where change is associated with creativity). Freeman and Engel (2007) stated that one of the two central elements of innovation is the alignment of incentives. Galbraith (1982) stated that the functions of the reward system are to attract and retain people, motivate to innovate, and reward successful performance. He added that rewards are a combination of intrinsic and extrinsic motivators: opportunity to pursue one's ideas, promotions, recognition, and special compensation, and even suggested "percentage of take" (royalties) as a possible motivator. George and Zhou (2002) concluded that perceived rewards for creative performance acted as a moderator on the positive link between negative mood and creative performance. The rewards they identified seemed to be extrinsic, although not contracted, made of pay raises and promotions. Tellis et al. (2009) found in their multi-national study that incentives for enterprise (innovation, new business creation) were important practices that allowed engendering and sustaining radical innovations.

A few additional positions on intrinsic and extrinsic motivation are also worth mentioning. Basadur and Gelade (2006) claimed that there is a cyclical relationship between creative activity and motivation. Creative activity increases motivation which, in turn, increases the interest in more creative activity. Finally, several authors identified the transition in the organization from an innovative, entrepreneurial organization, to an operationally oriented one. Katz (2004b) suggested that through the life cycle of a long job tenure, even the employee goes through a transition from the socialization stage (becoming part of the organization), through the innovation stage (challenging job, improved skills, contribution, and influences), to stabilization (routinization, preservation, minimizing vulnerability), a transition parallel to the transition the organization goes through. Ray (1987), too, identified the transition in the type of motivation. As the organization grows, individual commitment is diluted. Extrinsic motivation replaces intrinsic one, and people are drawn to the organization for different reasons.   Amabile (1988) initially stated that extrinsic motivation can influence algorithmic problem solving, whereas intrinsic motivation can influence heuristic problem solving, and that extrinsic motivation can be effective for some people and under certain conditions, thus recognizing the value of both types of motivation.   However, later she became more definitive in her position that extrinsic motivation is detrimental to creativity (Amabile, 1996; 1998).

In conclusion, the consensus position that only intrinsic motivation is conducive to creativity was adopted for this study, and intrinsic motivation factors were studied in the transition between startup and mature companies.   Following are the intrinsic motivators that through research were shown to affect individual creativity.

Autonomy and Freedom

Autonomy, freedom, independence, discretion, and self-managing were terms used interchangeably in the literature to describe a situation where the employee is given latitude to design his or her task execution without intervention, specifically from management.   Ekvall (1996) defined it as the "independence in behavior exerted by the people in the organization" (p. 107). Autonomy was claimed theoretically and found empirically to be one of the most influential antecedents of individual creativity in work setting (Abbey & Dickson, 1983; Amabile, 1988; 1998; Anderson et al., 2004; Burnside, 1990; Cummings, 1965; Ekvall, 1996; Engle et al., 1997; Isaksen & Lauer, 2002; Isaksen et al., 2000; Kanter, 1989; King, 1990; Mathisen & Einarsen, 2004; Peters & Waterman, 1982; Shapero, 1985; Thompson, 1965; Turnipseed, 1994).   Burgelman's (1983, 1984) model of corporate entrepreneurship emphasized the importance of the autonomy of the entrepreneurial system in the organization, and explained the "tolerance" of management towards autonomous strategic behavior as extending corporate capabilities to find new opportunities, and allowing to avoid increasing competitive pressures in the core business.   Farr and Ford (1990) suggested that autonomy is one of the factors influencing perceived payoff from change, thus making autonomy the desired end state, and change (and creativity) as the way to get there, a reverse link between the two constructs.   McCoy and Evans (2002) claimed that physical work design (architecture) that is conducive to creativity is that one that instills feeling of freedom. Thompson (1965) included the term *security* in the definition of autonomy.   Careful consideration of the link between those terms showed that employees are, in fact, free to do as they choose, but may not feel secure (from consequences) to do so. Therefore, the term autonomy should imply freedom *and* security. Turnipseed (1994) defined autonomy as an area of personal growth.   Kanter (1989) identified factors supporting autonomy and factors restricting autonomy.   Supporting autonomy: physically separated space between existing business (mainstream) and innovation groups (newstream), acceptance of distinctive newstream culture, design of own systems and procedures, and freedom to use or ignore mainstream services. Restricting autonomy: confusion between newstream and mainstream territories, uniformity requirements, and insistence that newstream projects go through mainstream channels and services.

Support and Encouragement for Creativity

Another important factor affecting individual creativity is the support the employee is receiving, encouraging him or her to be creative. The employee needs to feel that being creative is a desired behavior. Different authors focused on different sources of such support: (1) non-specific organizational support (Abbey & Dickson, 1983; Anderson et al., 2004; Anderson & West, 1998; Basadur & Gelade, 2006; Burnside, 1990; Engle et al., 1997; Farr, 1990; McCoy & Evans, 2002; Scott & Bruce, 1994; Stokols, Clitheroe, & Zmuidzinas, 2002; Zhou & George, 2001); (2) support from management in general and executive management in particular (Amabile, 1988; 1998; Andrew et al., 2008; Burnside, 1990); (3) direct supervisor's support (Amabile, 1998; Burnside, 1990; Ekvall, 1990; Farr & Ford, 1990; Madjar et al., 2002; Oldham & Cummings, 1996; Stokols et al., 2002; Turnipseed, 1994); (4) support from other team members (Ekvall, 1996; Farr & Ford, 1990; Isaksen & Lauer, 2002; Isaksen et al., 2000; Madjar et al., 2002; Stokols et al., 2002; Zhou & George, 2001); and (5) support from family members, outside the organization (Madjar et al., 2002). Mathisen and Einarsen's (2004) definitions of support through the review of different creativity environment instruments included idea support as used in CCQ: "the ways new ideas are treated. In the supportive climate managers and colleagues receive ideas and suggestions in an attentive and receptive way and there are possibilities for trying out new ideas." (p. 122); organizational support as used in KEYS: "Encouragement of risk taking and idea generation, fair, and affirmative evaluation of new ideas, valuing of innovation from all levels of management, reward and recognition of creativity, and a cross-fertilization of ideas that resulted from participative management and decision making." (p. 126); and supervisory encouragement as used in KEYS: "Supervisors who provide goal clarity, give support of the team's work and ideas, and engage in open interactions with [subordinates] and [supervisors]" (p. 126).

Challenge

One of many dictionary definitions for the word "challenge" is: "difficulty in a job or undertaking that is stimulating to one engaged in it." (challenge, n.d.). Ekvall (1996) defined it slightly differently, as the "emotional involvement of the members of the organization in its operations and goals" (p. 107). Defining challenge as an antecedent of individual creativity suggests that facing difficulties in a job forces individual employees to find a creative solution. Sometimes, simply telling someone that something cannot be done is incentivizing enough to have it done. The positive impact of challenge on creativity was identified by many researchers (Amabile, 1988; 1998; Burnside, 1990; Ekvall, 1996; Farr, 1990; Isaksen & Lauer, 2002; Isaksen et al., 2000; Mathisen & Einarsen, 2004; McCoy & Evans, 2002; Turnipseed, 1994). Amabile made challenge one of the top six antecedents of creativity that were implemented in the KEYS instrument (Amabile et al., 1996). Burnside (1990) developed a model for improving creativity, focused on goal clarity, assisted by challenge, one of three other factors. Isaksen and Lauer (1999) disagreed with a previous proposition that challenge and conflict are two opposites of the same dimension, claiming these are two separate dimensions. Oldham and Cummings (1996) did not specifically identify challenge as a factor affecting creativity, but nevertheless linked the complexity of the task with employee creative performance. Mathisen and Einarsen's (2004) review of creativity climate instruments provided the following definitions for challenge: "The degree to which the people of the organization are emotionally involved in its operations and goals and find pleasure and meaningfulness in their job" (p. 122) and "A belief that tasks [are] important and therefore [provide] a source of motivation, work that is intellectually challenging" (p. 126).

Recognition

Recognition has many forms, but in general it is a positive statement made by one person on another person's work product, also associated with appreciation. The recognition is important and impactful when it comes from a peer, a supervisor, a senior executive, a respected industry authority, and the more public it is. Users are motivated to innovation through recognition they get (Ahuja et al., 2008; Amabile, 1988; Burnside, 1990; Galbraith, 1982; King, 1990; Taylor, 1990). Amabile (1988) included within the term recognition other components such as feedback (positive) and rewards (extrinsic motivation). Ahuja et al. (2008) added that the recognition is important not only as a temporary feeling, but also as a link to reputation that helps in the job market in the future. Burnside (1990) added that evaluation pressure (from inappropriate evaluation, feedback, criticism, and external evaluation), the opposite of positive recognition, are obstacles to creativity. George and Zhou (2002) learned that perceived recognition acts as a moderator of the link between (negative) mood and creativity. Taylor (1990) claimed that individual recognition is more important than salaries, bonuses, or promotions to maintain creativity. Research on the importance of recognition was focused on peer and supervisor recognition. Although recognition was not part of the leading organizational creativity climate instruments (Mathisen & Einarsen, 2004), it was supported by a significant body of research as a positive antecedent of creativity, and was therefore included as one of the factors explored in this study.

Resources

Different approaches were taken as far as how resources affected creativity and innovation. The importance of resources to company success was emphasized in the resource based view theory: "firms obtain sustained competitive advantages by implementing strategies that exploit their internal strengths, through responding to environmental opportunities, while neutralizing external threats and avoiding internal weaknesses" (Barney, 1991, p. 99). Christensen (1997) reminded that companies depend on their customers and investors for the resources they need to support disruptive innovation.

The availability of resources, and specifically sufficient *time for ideation*, promotes individual creativity, whereas insufficient resources inhibit creativity (Amabile, 1988; 1998; Burnside, 1990; Engle et al., 1997; Farr & Ford, 1990; Isaksen & Lauer, 1999; King, 1990; Mathisen & Einarsen, 2004; Scott & Bruce, 1994; Skarzynski & Gibson, 2008; Staw, 1990). Amabile et al. (1996) included scales to measure availability of resources in the KEYS instrument.

Different types of resources were addressed in the literature: financial and budgetary, materials, time, personnel, tools, facilities, geography, and manufacturing (Amabile, 1988; Andrew et al., 2008; Barney, 1991; Bharadwaj & Menon, 2000; Isaksen & Lauer, 2002; Isaksen et al., 2000; Thompson, 1965). Andrew et al. (2008) suggested that *key people* need to be allocated to innovation, and not just anyone. This ties well with the notion that some people are more creative or innovative than others. Barney (1991) specified a slightly different slate of strategic resources: physical capital resources (technology, plant, equipment, geography, access to raw material); human capital resources (training, experience, judgment, intelligence, relationships, and management insight); organizational capital resources (formal reporting structure, planning, controlling, and coordinating systems, and informal relationships with the environment).

Some of the authors discussed *slack resources*, thus identifying a situation in which the organization allows a certain amount of resources to be available when innovation projects need them, and not be fully allocated all the time. The innovation process is significantly less consistent and steady in its use of resources, and only keeping a resource slack allows the innovation team access to resources when those are required (Anderson et al., 2004; Andrew et al., 2008; Burgelman, 1983; Leifer et al., 2000; Mone et al., 1998). Damanpour (1991) defined slack resources as those beyond the minimum required to maintain operations. Freeman and Engel (2007) noted that a central element of innovation is the organization's ability to mobilize resources. March (1991) identified a dilemma in the competition between the innovative and operational parts of the organization over scarce resources, forcing the organization to make tradeoff decisions between them. Prahalad and Hamel (1990) claimed that the organizational business units imprison resources and therefore bound innovation. Rosenfeld and Servo (1990) observed that as the innovative idea grows through the process, the organization becomes more committed and invests more resources. Thompson (1965) claimed that bureaucracy prevents the accumulation of free resources required for innovation.

Abbey and Dickson (1983) used data about research and development budget as a measure of innovation. Ekvall (1996) considered organizational climate a moderator on the effect that resources (people, buildings, machinery, know-how, patents, funds, material, products, and concepts) have on quality, productivity, innovation, job satisfaction, well-being, and profit. He referred to *idea time* as an element of the organizational climate, and not a resource.

The conclusion is that the availability of resources (specifically funding, facilities, materials, people, information, and time) has a positive impact on creativity, as emerged from prior research. As such, the availability of resources in startup and mature companies was explored as a factor affecting creativity in this study.

Team Dynamics

Several factors associated with the dynamics of teamwork were identified by different studies as antecedents of individual creativity: team cohesion, internal competition, trust and openness, supportive presence of coworkers, team support, conflicts and debate, internal communications, and play, humor, and fun.

Anderson and West (1998) reported the development of the Team Climate Inventory (TCI), the only creativity measurement instrument addressing the workgroup level found in this review of literature. They argued that the workgroup is the appropriate level to measure organizational climate, and defined the proximal team as "the permanent or semi-permanent team to which individuals are assigned, whom they identify with, and whom they interact with regularly in order to perform work-related tasks" (p. 236).

Isaksen and Lauer (2002) studied team creativity, stating: "Teams are one of the basic building blocks of every organization.... considered the most important resource in any organization." (p. 75). The purpose of their study was to explore the climate for creativity within the team. Their study concluded that the *most* creative teams were characterized by respect, communications, clear roles and responsibilities, freedom to develop ideas, "play hard, work harder", reaching the goal, pitching in, enthusiasm, commitment; comfortable discussing everything, brainstorming to improve others' ideas without feelings hurt; leading by example, encouraging new ideas, sharing best practices, leader provided guidance, support, encouragement, and secured support and resources from outside the team; common, clear, compelling, open, and challenging goals. In contrast, the study found that the *least* creative teams were characterized with lack of communication, animosity, jealousy, political posturing; lack of motivation, initiative, ideas, inability to recognize the value of the end result; individuals placing their own interests above the team's, not listening to other opinions than own, wanting to finish as quickly as possible; leaders causing confusion, fear, distrust, kept control; conflicting agendas, different missions, and no agreement on the end results.

Amabile (1988, 1998) identified the qualities of the team as a factor promoting individual creativity. She further claimed that the intrinsic task motivation, domain relevant skills, and creativity skills model that applied to individuals also applied to small teams. Farr (1990) consolidated all three levels, claiming that the methods used to increase individual creativity will also work at the workgroup level.

Burnside (1990) developed the Work Environment Inventory (WEI) to measure organizational climate for creativity, but identified coworkers (teamwork, willingness to help, commitment, and trust) as stimulants to creativity, and political problems (lack of cooperation, turf battles) as obstacles. Zhou and George (2001) found that coworker feedback, help, and support had a positive effect on creativity.

Several theories and research showed the importance of the physical separation of teams of creative individuals from the rest of the organizations (Amabile, 1998; Andrew et al., 2008; Cummings et al., 1975; Cummings, 1965; Devanna & Tichy, 1990; Drucker, 1985a; Ekvall, 1997; Farr & Ford, 1990; Freeman & Engel, 2007; Galbraith, 1982; Kanter, 1989; Leifer et al., 2000; Pierce & Delbecq, 1977; Prahalad & Hamel, 1990; Rosenfeld & Servo, 1990; Taylor, 1990; Thompson, 1965). Zhou (2003) used the social cognitive theory (claiming that individuals tend to exhibit the same type of behaviors that they observe others exhibiting), and in two studies learned that the presence of creative coworkers moderated (increased) the relationship between supervisory close monitoring and the level of creativity. In summary, several elements of team dynamics were shown through research to affect individual creativity of team members, including conflict and debate, internal competition, trust and openness, and internal communications. As a result, team dynamics was a factor further explored in this research. The dimensions of team dynamics that prior research has shown to be most influential over creativity were: conflict and debate, internal competition, trust and openness, and internal communications.

Conflict and debate

Rickards and Moger (2006), in a content analysis of articles published by the *Creativity & Innovation Management Journal* found that conflict was one of the top nine factors affecting (here—hindering) creativity. Ekvall (1996) defined conflict (a negative phenomenon) as "the presence of personal and emotional tensions (in contrast to conflicts between ideas) in the organization" (p. 108), and debate (a positive phenomenon) as "the occurrence of encounters and clashes between viewpoints, ideas, and differing experiences and knowledge" (p. 108). Cummings et al. (1975), without distinguishing between negative conflict and positive debate, stated that one of the characteristics of the bureaucratic organization that inhibits creativity is the perceived illegitimacy of conflict (here—the lack of open debate), which followed an assertion made by Thompson (1965) that bureaucracy stifles debate (of the positive kind). Ekvall (1996) included debate in the CCQ instrument, claiming that debate is important to radical innovation, more than for incremental innovation. He later (Ekvall, 1997) claimed that the existence of innovators (radical) and adaptors (incremental developers) causes conflict in the negative sense. Freeman and Engel (2007) provided additional insight, claiming that there was a conflict between innovation and execution, and as a result of a clash of personal styles between creative people and execution oriented people. Kanter (1989) made similar statements as to the conflict between newstream projects and the organization's mainstream operations. Isaksen and Lauer (2002) suggested that what makes conflict hamper creativity is the personal and emotional nature of it between team members, whereas debate, or open discussion and questioning of ideas, promotes creativity in the team. Mauzy and Harriman (2003) recommended that companies encourage "conflicts of ideas" (as opposed to personal conflicts) to build an inventive organization. Emphasizing the importance of dealing with conflict of the negative nature, Ripple (1989) indicated that the ability to tolerate and resolve conflict is an important personality attribute associated with creativity. Rosenfeld and Servo (1990) claimed that innovation involves a battle between numerous people, but failed to make it clear whether they were describing an unfortunate consequence of life, or a positive factor affecting innovation. Souder (1988) suggested that R&D and marketing personnel depend on each other for the creation of new product innovation, and through a study of 289 new product innovation projects discovered three main categories of relationships between them, along with the success rate of projects under those relationships: harmony (52% successful projects and 13% failures), mild disharmony (45% partially successful projects), and severe disharmony (68% failures and only 11% successes). Stokols et al. (2002) were more specific, stating that the conflicts with coworkers that were negatively affecting the social environment for creativity were about priorities.

Internal competition

While conflicts might be temporary episodes, internal competition can be long lasting. Amabile (1988) noted that internal competition was a negative team dynamic, inhibiting creativity. Isaksen and Lauer (2002) added animosity, jealousy, and political posturing. Shalley (1995) studied several factors affecting individual creativity, one of which was the presence of coactors (coworkers working on the same task). She concluded that working alone was more conducive to creativity than in the presence of others working on the same task, due to feeling of competition.

Trust and openness

Trust and openness were two additional team dynamics factors listed as important to creativity climate (Burnside, 1990; Ekvall, 1996; Isaksen & Lauer, 2002; Isaksen et al., 2000; Mathisen & Einarsen, 2004; Turnipseed, 1994). Ekvall (1996) defined trust among team members as: "the emotional safety in relationships" (p. 107). Isaksen and Lauer (2002) gave examples of team openness that promote creativity: comfortable discussing everything, and brainstorming to improve others' ideas without feeling hurt.

Internal communications

Internal communications was identified as a key element of creativity within the team. Three types of internal communication channels were identified: availability of information, communication between team members, and communication with the team leader, or supervisor (Burnside, 1990; Cummings et al., 1975; Cummings, 1965; Isaksen & Lauer, 2002; Rosenfeld & Servo, 1990; Shapero, 1985; Skarzynski & Gibson, 2008l; Stokols et al., 2002; Turnipseed, 1994). Cummings (1965) indicated that secrecy (the opposite of open communications) inhibits creativity. Damanpour (1990) was more specific and identified the importance of the manager's communication of innovation expectations, and not just "general" communications. He later found (Damanpour, 1991) that the extent of internal communications between units or groups (not only within group) significantly and positively affected creativity. Farr (1990) identified persuasive communications as part of social cognition that contributes to creativity. Farr and Ford (1990) also identified the existence of information systems as an element influencing perceived efficacy for implementing change. Rosenfeld and Servo (1990) blamed the "communication gap" for the reason the innovation process gets dropped in the organization in many places. Among other types of communication breakdowns, they blamed the inventor's inability to communicate the value of his or her creative idea. Skarzynski and Gibson (2008) indicated that fostering connection and conversation is especially important for *radical* innovation, as one of three preconditions (along with diversity and the creation of time and space for innovation).

Structure, Bureaucracy, and Formalization

Abbey and Dickson (1983) researched the link between 10 work climate dimensions and perception of innovativeness. Decentralization was one of those dimensions, but the study was inconclusive with respect to this dimension. Ahuja et al. (2008), in a literature review, claimed that bureaucracy stifled innovation. Dormen and Edidin (1989) suggested that *conformity* stifled creativity. Amabile (1988) identified good project management as a factor promoting creativity, but later (Amabile, 1998) added that "creativity is undermined unintentionally every day in work environments that were established-for entirely good reasons-to maximize business imperatives such as coordination, productivity, and control" (p. 77), essentially contradicting her earlier statement. Burgelman (1983, 1984) claimed that organizations maintain a dichotomy of autonomous strategic initiatives (chaos), as well as maintaining order through imposing the concept of strategy on the organization. He developed the model of strategic behavior that included both initiatives simultaneously. However, his approach separated the innovative part of the company from the highly structured "standard" business. This dichotomous approach was supported by Galbraith (1982), though. Some of the characteristics of the bureaucratic organization that inhibit creativity include hierarchical, authoritative structure, limited span of control, priority of production and control objectives, over-specification and specialization of human resources, all parts of the organizational structure. It should be noted, though, that research only showed *partial* effect of procedures and organizational controls on creativity (Cummings et al., 1975). Cummings (1965) specified the features of the bureaucratic organization that inhibited creativity: discouragement of diversity and conflict, division of labor that prevents cross-fertilization, intolerance for instability (bi-product of creativity), whereas the features of the creative organizations included low formalization, high flexibility, low human resource specificity, and flexible power-authority-influence structure, all opposite characteristics to the bureaucratic organization. Damanpour (1991) in a meta-analysis claimed that formalization does not affect organizational innovativeness. If creativity is a necessary part of innovativeness, then this finding goes against the belief that formalization stifles creativity. He did conclude, though, that decentralization, functional differentiation, and professionalism have positive effects on innovation. Dougherty and Hardy (1996) found that innovation was linked to organizational configurations, but suggested that the existence of processes supporting innovation allowed the organization to maintain sustained innovation. Ekvall (1996), through the development of the CCQ, found that (1) formalization had a strong negative impact on organization innovativeness, (2) centralization had a negative impact on innovativeness, while (3) professionalism had a positive impact. He later (Ekvall, 1997) added that while decentralization was supposed to promote creativity, it only promoted incremental (adaptive) innovation, and not radical innovation. He identified three dilemmas of radical innovation: (1) organizational principles, systems, and procedures that on one hand protect the organization's stability—on the other hand stifle creativity; (2) the large amount of resources required to deliver new and radical products also require structure, coordination, and control which, at the same time, prevents radical innovation; and (3) highly competitive markets require operational efficiency, which requires processes and structures that prevents radical innovation, which is required to be competitive in highly competitive markets. Engle et al. (1997), using two measurement instruments (KAI and LOC), found that entrepreneurs were more innovative than employees of mature companies, and also less conforming than employees, thus tying innovation with anti-conformity. Freeman and Engel (2007) identified the opposite relationship: disruptive innovation causes "creative destruction" not only to the industry, but also to the company structure itself. This suggests that the company structure serves as a self-preservation mechanism against innovation. Galbraith (1982) suggested that innovation requires certain structure and processes, especially once transitioning from innovation to operation. Ireland, Kuratko, and Covin (2003) were not specific in stating that corporate entrepreneurship strategy required pro-entrepreneurial organizational architecture, including structure and systems. Isaksen and Lauer (1999) positioned the organizational policies, structures, and systems within the psychological climate for creativity. Jennins and Lumpkin (1989) in a study of entrepreneurial and conservative organizations showed significant differences in decentralization and participative decisions making between the two types of organizations. Jones, Edwards, and Beckinsale (2000) found in a six year longitudinal study that the innovation process was a result of the social interaction between the individual (agency) and the organizational rules and structures (structure). They used the "structuration" theory: a process in which systems are produced through actors' usage of rules and resources. Khan and Manopichetwattana (1989) claimed that formalization and centralization had a negative effect on innovation, and found that locus of control was an important factor for innovative companies. Kirton (1976) concluded that adaptors needed bureaucracy, whereas innovators did not. He did not go further to state that bureaucracy stifled the innovators, though. Although the term "process" is associated with bureaucracy (thus assumed to be stifling creativity), some processes (such as brainstorming and predicting technology trends) are used to fuel creative thinking (Leifer et al., 2000; Solomon, 2007). Mone et al. (1998) conducted a literature review and concluded that concentrated power structure served as a moderator that causes organizational declines to have a positive effect on innovation. Pierce and Delbecq (1977) segmented the innovation process into three stages: initiation (creative idea generation), adoption, and implementation. They then measured the impact of structural, contextual, and individual factors on the different stages, and found that the different factors had different effects on the different stages. Specifically— differentiation, professionalism, and decentralization had positive effects on initiation, while formalization and stratification had negative effects on initiation. It should be noted that formalization had a positive effect on the adoption and implementation stages, whereas decentralization had a negative effect on implementation. Ray (1987) found that there was a conflict between attempts to improve the organizational structure, and increasing individual creativity. Rickards and Moger (2006) found that resource and activity coordination, symptoms of formalization, were barriers to creativity. Rosenfeld and Servo (1990), in defining "the office of innovation", suggested that the more decentralized it was—the more successful it would be. Scott (1965) stated that creative people could not be redirected. Shapero (1985) characterized the creative organization as less specialized, more generalized, decentralized, loosely controlled, and implementing participative decision making. Staw (1990) explained the negative effect of formalization on creativity in that organizations attempt to reduce variation, which is in conflict with innovation, which requires increased variation. Tellis and Golder (1996) claimed that "large bureaucracies either discourage innovations or are slow in bringing them to market" (p. 72). Thompson (1965) stated that bureaucratic conditions are driven by productivity and control, and are inappropriate for creativity, and that innovation requires decentralization.

Based on all the literature reviewed that addressed the relationship between structure, bureaucracy, and formalization, it was concluded that the more structured, bureaucratic, and formalistic the organization is—the less innovative it would be. There was no conclusive agreement on whether centralization contributed to innovation and creativity positively or negatively. Structures and processes sometimes operate as mechanisms to protect the organization from innovation that might "destroy the old and bring the new". Structurization might be appropriate for later, more stable stages of the organization life cycle, but the consensus from this review was that highly structured and process-oriented organizations inhibit creativity. Amabile et al. (1996) defined "organizational impediments" as "internal strife, conservatism and rigid, formal management structures" (Mathisen & Einarsen, 2004) and included it as one of the dimensions measured by the KEYS instrument. Formalization, bureaucracy, and processes were therefore a factor explored in the current study.

Organizational Climate for Creativity—Summary

In summary, the organizational climate was the most studied area of influence on individual creativity in organizations. It was separated to extrinsic and intrinsic motivational factors, and it was claimed that intrinsic factors had significant impact on creativity, although there was disagreement in prior research on whether a few extrinsic factors have positive, negative, or influence on individual creativity. Autonomy was one of the strongest factors positively affecting creativity. Support and encouragement (supervisor, organizational, and work group) were shown to have positive effect, although not as strong as autonomy. Challenges, and specifically those who can stimulate individuals were also described as driving creativity. Recognition was described as having several forms, and the informal form of recognition was described as supporting creativity. Overall, prior research was consistent in claiming that the availability of resources has a positive impact on creativity. Prior research also showed a strong impact of team dynamics on individual creativity, describing positive team dynamics sub-factors that positively affect creativity such as open idea debate, trust, and open internal communications, and negative team dynamics sub-factors that negatively affect creativity such as personal conflict and internal competition. Finally, formalization, bureaucracy, "heavy" processes, and other internal organizational impediments were shown to have significant negative impact on individual creativity in organizations.

Prior Employee Creativity Research Methodology

This section reviews the research done on employee creativity, and focuses on methodology, rather than the results and conclusions that were already discussed above. It shows that four types of studies were done: (1) exploratory studies, seeking to find new factors affecting creativity (whether organizational factors, individual factors, or external factors); (2) confirmatory studies, seeking to confirm an established conceptual framework and hypotheses (typically for the purpose of developing new creativity and climate measurement instruments); (3) creativity assessment studies, using the existing quantitative instruments to assess organizational climate, and (4) correlation studies, correlating different creativity assessment instruments.

Ancona and Caldwell (1987) conducted a comparative case study to explore the creativity and innovation process in large organizations, using qualitative interviews with new product team managers and members in seven high tech corporations. Amabile and Gryskiewicz (1987) conducted a qualitative interview study of 120 R&D scientists, using open-ended interview questions, in a semi-structured format, lasting 20 minutes each, exploring the factors affecting motivation for creativity. Amabile (1988) conducted another research, this time interviewing marketing people (as opposed to R&D professionals in the previous study). This study too was qualitative, and used the critical incident technique, asking the participants to focus on events they considered highly creative, and events they considered of low creativity. Both studies were exploratory and qualitative, and resulted in a set of factors later used in the development of the KEYS instrument, used to measure the organizational climate for creativity (Amabile et al., 1996), as well as the Work Environment Inventory (WEI) instrument, developed by Burnside (1990). Other prominent exploratory-qualitative studies included Jones et al. (2000) six-year longitudinal study of a single manufacturing company, focusing on two "critical episodes" using narrative, critical incident research designs; Lynn et al. (1996) case study of creativity and discontinuous innovation in organizations; and Leifer et al.

(2000), who concluded their six-year longitudinal case study of 12 radical innovation projects in 10 companies using interviews (in person and over the phone). Zien and Buckler (1997) conducted a cultural anthropological research design using interviews to study how mature companies created a culture of innovation. They sought insight and diversity, and became cultural anthropologists when they observed experiences within their own company. Amabile et al. (2005) conducted one more longitudinal study of 222 members of 26 project team from seven companies in three industries. This was an exploratory qualitative narrative data collection and coding, and quantitative data analysis aimed at creating a conceptual framework for the effect that affect has on individual creativity in the workplace.

While the KEYS and WEI instruments were developed following exploratory, qualitative research, other instruments were developed through confirmatory studies based on a theoretically developed conceptual framework. One example was the development of the Creative Climate Questionnaire (CCQ) by Ekvall (1996), who described climate as an objective attribute, hinting towards the use of an objectivistic tradition. Isaksen et al. (2000) then developed the Situational Outlook Questionnaire (SOQ) instrument, based on the CCQ instrument, reducing the number of dimensions from ten to nine, eliminating *dynamism*. They reported that SOQ seemed to perform similarly to its parent measure, CCQ. However— SOQ also provided narrative data, and therefore allowed qualitative data analysis to provide further insight. The developers proposed future research to analyze the narrative data and create new items as a result. Finally, Kirton (1976a, 1976b) developed the Kirton Adaption-Innovation (KAI) instrument with a single dimension, varying from adaptive to innovative, as an individual inventory quantitative survey instrument.

Examples of the use of existing instruments included Isaksen and Lauer (2002), who used an existing instrument to assess a "new" environment. They conducted a study of team creativity, and used the Situational Outlook Questionnaire (SOQ) with 170 participants, in the first attempt to use SOQ with teams. The study was quantitative in essence, but the inclusion of a qualitative part enhanced the quantitative part of the study significantly and added dimensions/granulation that did not exist in the quantitative part. Turnipseed (1994) used existing instruments (the Climate for Innovation Questionnaire—CIQ and the Work Environment Scale—WES) to examine relationships between social environment in the organization, employee satisfaction (work-related and personal), and perception of a creative work environment.

The fourth type of creativity research included studies that investigated correlation between dimensions and scales of different instruments. Although this was not the focus of his study, Turnipseed (1994) found a strong correlation between the WES and CIQ: seven out of ten variables were found to be strongly correlated. Isaksen and Lauer (1999) tried to determine a relationship between cognitive style and individual perceptions of climate for creativity and change, through a correlation of the KAI and SOQ/CCQ instruments. Carne and Kirton (1982) found a correlation between the Myers-Briggs Type Indicator (MBTI) and the Kirton Adaption-Innovation Inventory (KAI).

In summary, when researchers attempted to explore new *factors* or new *environments* in the past, interview based narrative case studies were used. Those typically resulted in the development of quantitative measurement instruments, but only after the conceptual frameworks have emerged from the qualitative studies. Some of the survey instruments, though, were developed through confirmatory research, based on a theoretical conceptual framework rather than exploratory narrative studies. Once instruments were developed, they were then used to assess different environments (whether organizations or teams). In some of the reviewed studies, those instruments were taken away from their "natural environment" (for which they were developed), but while assuming the existence of same conceptual model of those instruments in the original setting.

Summary and Conceptual Framework

This review of the literature showed consistency around the finding that startup organizations were more innovative than mature ones. It further showed that creative ideas that originated in the minds of creative people, being creative, were the fundamental building block of the innovation process. The relationship between the individual creativity and organizational innovation, along with the differences in the innovation created by startup companies and mature companies suggested an exploration of the differences in creativity between the two types of organizations, the focus of the current study. The conceptual framework (Figure 3) that emerged from the review of prior creativity research illustrated three categories of antecedents for individual creativity in the workplace: individual characteristics (the creativity of an individual before entering the organizational setting), personal context (factors that are not directly related to the organization that may affect creativity), and the organizational climate. Figure 4 expands the high level conceptual framework and adds the details of the four concepts.

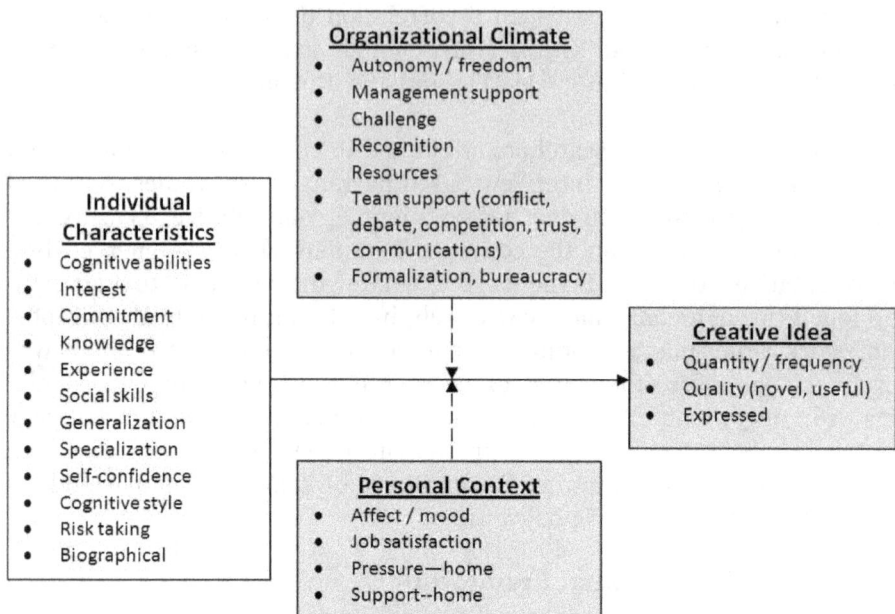

Figure 4 – Comprehensive model of antecedents of individual creativity.

The personal characteristics concept is detailed, although it was not researched in this study, and was controlled through the use of the same people to described both environments. It was included since it was important to remember what individuals bring with them into the organizational setting to be creative.

The organizational climate includes the factors that prior research consistently associated with affecting creativity. The personal context includes all the factors that are external to the task at hand, and outside of the organization. Finally, the creative idea concept is expanded to include the characteristic of creativity according with Amabile's (1988) definition (novelty and usefulness) as well as the quantity and frequency of such ideas, and whether those ideas were expressed (filed, submitted, discussed) beyond their generation in the creative person's head.

Table 1 is a compilation of all the research studying the antecedents of individual creativity that was reviewed here. Its main value is in listing all the individual factors affecting individual creativity, regardless of their source. For each factor, several attributes were listed, as emerged from this review of the literature. The first attribute was the domain within which the factor exists, including personal characteristics that are determined before the employee begins working for the organization, organizational context that is affected by the organization and the immediate team or workgroup, and personal context that is determined outside of the workplace and may still affect creativity at work. The second attribute was the effect that the specific factor had on individual creativity. This effect was listed as positive or negative, if the overwhelming majority of literature reviewed concluded that it had a positive or negative effect on creativity, respectively. The effect was listed as "mixed" whenever the literature was in disagreement regarding the direction of the effect or whenever the effect did not have a simple positive or negative impact on creativity.

Table 1 – Summary of Factors Affecting Individual Creativity

Factor	Domain	Effect	Organizational Control
Cognitive abilities	Personal characteristics	Mixed	Through hiring
Interests	Personal characteristics	Mixed	Through hiring
Commitment	Personal characteristics	Positive	Through hiring
Domain Knowledge	Personal characteristics	Positive	Through hiring
Experience	Personal characteristics	Positive	Through hiring
Social skills	Personal characteristics	Mixed	Through hiring
Generalization	Personal characteristics	Positive	Through hiring
Specialization	Personal characteristics	Mixed	Through hiring
Self-confidence	Personal characteristics	Positive	Through hiring
Cognitive style	Personal characteristics	Mixed	Through hiring
Risk taking	Personal characteristics	Positive	Through hiring
Biographical	Personal characteristics	Little to none	Through hiring
Autonomy/freedom	Organizational context	Positive	Direct supervisor
Management support	Organizational context	Positive	Management/Supervisor
Challenge	Organizational context	Positive	Indirect
Recognition	Organizational context	Positive	Direct supervisor
Resources	Organizational context	Positive	Management
Team support			
Conflict / debate	Organizational context	Mixed	Team
Internal competition	Organizational context	Mixed	Team
Trust / openness	Organizational context	Positive	Team
Internal communications	Organizational context	Positive	Team
Formalization / bureaucracy	Organizational context	Negative	Management
Affect / mood	Personal context	Positive	Indirect / None
Job satisfaction	Personal context	Positive	Indirect
Pressure—home	Personal context	Negative	None
Support—home	Personal context	Positive	None

The last attribute was the control that the organization has over this factor. In some cases (mostly in the domain of personal traits) the only control the organization has over the factor is through hiring of employees with the "right" personal characteristics or training. In other cases, the organization has a more direct control (such as in the case of resource allocation) and it simply needs to exercise that control to affect the factors and spark creativity.

3. Methodology

The purpose of this study was to explore the perceived changes in the level of creativity of employees who moved between mature companies and startup companies, and their perception of the organizational climate and personal context that may have affected those changes. The research questions were:

1.   *How do employees who worked in both startup and mature companies experience the differences in their own creativity between the two types of organizations?*
2.   *How do employees who worked in both startup and mature companies experience the differences in the organizational climate for creativity between the two types of organizations?*
3.   *How do employees who worked in both startup and mature companies experience the differences in their personal context between the two types of organizations?*

Research Design

The focus of the study was on individual creativity and the factors affecting it through individual transitions. Several criteria were used to select the research methodology and design: the researcher's theoretical perspective, the exploratory nature of the study, the richness of information sought, and the research questions wording.

Crotty (1998) and Creswell (2003) linked the research design to theoretical perspective. Morgan and Smircich (1980) explained that positivists seek knowledge by constructing positivistic science and prefer quantitative survey designs, whereas the subjectivists consider reality as viewed and interpreted by the participant, within its context. Amabile (1996) claimed that social and contextual factors play a crucial role in performance, hinting towards the use of qualitative methodology and, in fact, used qualitative research to develop the KEYS instrument (Amabile & Gryskiewicz, 1987; Amabile, 1988) and in later research (Amabile et al., 2005). Crotty (1998) emphasized the importance of the researcher identifying bias and theoretical stance. In the current study, the researcher assumed that different individuals under the same circumstances may have interpreted the organizational climate differently, and would therefore prefer to let the individuals provide their own perspective. The researcher's acknowledged subjectivistic-interpretivistic theoretical perspective thus drove the use of qualitative methodology.

The nature of this study was exploratory. This study was not seeking to confirm the relationship between different factors and creativity. Instead, it sought to explore the contextual differences that individuals who transitioned from one type of organization to another type (startups and mature companies) experienced through this transition. The study explored the meaning of those differences to the participants, and how they perceived the differences in their own creativity as a result. While the study began with a conceptual framework (as illustrated in Figure 4)—it was open to explore exceptions to this framework. Such an exploratory study was thus best served by a qualitative methodology (Creswell, 2003, 2007; Yin, 2003).

Amabile and Gryskiewicz (1987) chose loosely structured interviews to develop the initial framework leading to the development of the KEYS instrument, claiming that loosely structured interviews allowed maximum flexibility and range of responses, as well as elaboration and clarification. Creswell (2003) brought another element—richness: the standardization of measurement used by quantitative survey methods versus the ability of themes and theory to emerge from the open ended qualitative interview research. Rubin and Rubin (2005) claimed that surveys do not "tell a story" or convey "the richness and complexity that make research realistic" (p. 2), whereas "qualitative interviewing projects are especially good at describing social and political processes' that is, how and why things change" (p. 3). The position of *creativity as a process* suggested the use of qualitative interviews for this study to achieve the desired richness.

Creswell (2003) stated that quantitative research focuses on "relating or comparing variables or constructs" (p. 93) and Yin (2003) made the distinction between case study and quantitative surveys by the type of questions answered by each. Case study is the preferred strategy to answer *how* or *why* questions (exploratory), whereas a survey is the preferred strategy when answering *who, what, where, how many,* or *how much* questions (confirmatory). The current study explored through "how" questions, and was therefore best served through qualitative research. It was supplemented with numerical coding of the narrative that was then used in a confirmatory quantitative analysis.

In summary, based on the four criteria (the researcher's subjectivistic-interpretivistic theoretical perspective, the richness of information sought, the exploratory nature of the study, and the research question wording) this study used primarily a qualitative research methodology, supplemented with quantitative confirmatory analysis. The case study method could be used to provide description and detail, to test a theory, or to generate a theory (Eisenhardt, 1989). The current research project used the case study method to explore how employees experience the differences in their creativity, organizational climate, and personal context between startup and mature companies. Although the study began with theoretical framework illustrated in Figure 4, the researcher allowed new themes to emerge from the narrative analysis to add insight to its conclusions. A further description of the specific interview research design is provided in the section "Instrumentation / Measures" below.

The Researcher

The researcher worked in both startup and mature companies. He joined a small company in 1988 and worked there for seven years as the head of the research and development group. He left that company to start a startup company, where he served as the CEO for three years, until closing the company. He then joined another small company as a Vice President of Marketing, and participated in selling this company to another startup company that went through an initial public offering (IPO) and became a public company. He stayed with the acquiring company as a Vice President for two more years, until he left that company to join a mature, Fortune 500 company, where he filled various marketing, business development, and general management roles. In 2008, the researcher left that company to join a medium size public company. As such, the researcher is very aware of the environment in startup companies as well as mature companies.

Through his wide professional network, developed over the years, the researcher learned to know the participants, the companies they worked for, and most of the technologies they work on. While the researcher avoided offering personal insight into the participant experiences, it was easy for him to understand their stories. The researcher avoided guiding the participants in the study, and did not offer them his personal opinion during the interview, to avoid potential bias.

The Sample

The conclusion from the literature review (Chapter 2) was that there are three categories of antecedents to creativity in organizations: individual characteristics, personal context, and organizational climate. This study attempted to answer the following research questions: (1) how do employees who worked in both startup and mature companies experience the differences in the organizational climate for creativity between the two types of organizations? (2) How do employees who worked in both startup and mature companies experience the differences in their own personal context between the two types of organizations? And (3) how do employees who worked in both startup and mature companies experience the differences in their own creativity between the two types of organizations? The interviewees had to be experienced and knowledgeable in the topic of the study, and offer a variety of perspectives (Rubin & Rubin, 2005). For that purpose, the participants had to be people who were exposed to the environment under study. In order to control the effects of individual characteristics on the study results, the participants in the study were selected such that they worked for both environments (large companies and startup companies) at different times. The sampling was therefore purposive, theory driven, with the following criteria:

The participant would have worked for both a startup and mature company. This allowed controlling the effect of individual characteristics.

Each participant had to have filled relatively similar positions in both companies (did not transition from engineering to marketing, for example), to control for the impact of such a potential change.

The participant had to have filled an individual contributor role (or functional manager) in both companies, such that he or she would have been expected to be creative with respect to product innovation.

Both companies that the participant has worked in had to be in the electronic product hardware or software industry.

Although achieving generalizability of the study to all companies might have required selecting participants who worked for companies in diverse industries—the differences between those industries could have inhibited the ability of themes to emerge from the study, and introduce more *cross industry* differences than *cross company* differences (Baldridge & Burnham, 1975; Stevens & Burley, 1997). For that purpose, this study balanced generalizability with consistency, and the participants were selected from the electronic product industry only. However, the participants were chosen from different companies, to eliminate the potential effect of specific company climates on the study results. Individuals move between the two types of companies for many reasons, some of which are: acquisition, divestiture, seeking opportunity, seeking stability, and reduction in force or termination. Potential participants who appeared biased against one of the companies due to the circumstances of the departure from that company (for example, due to termination) were not considered for this study due to such bias.

The sample included 20 participants, recruited through theory driven, purposive, convenience sampling. The researcher was well connected with individuals in many companies in the electronic hardware and software industry, through participation in many industry trade associations, standardization organizations, trade shows, and professional networks in that industry, which allowed him to access the required sample directly. Eisenhardt (1989) recommended the use of theoretical and not random sampling for case study, as well as implementing an iterative process of data collection as new themes emerge during the interviews and data analysis. This iterative process included following up with interviewees to ask additional questions, as well as expanding the sample. However, Eisenhardt also recommended not adding more cases when reaching theoretical saturation—when new cases do not add new information.

Variability of the sample

This study focuses on the electronic product industry in the technology sector. Participants were selected across all the different components of this industry as much as possible. An electronic product (e.g., a navigation system) is made of four major components: semiconductor integrated circuits (e.g., a microprocessor), hardware system (e.g., the navigation system itself), application software (e.g., user interface with the device), and content (e.g., the map and navigation information). The development of the product also involves development tools (e.g., tools that allow for software development and testing). The participants in the study worked (or were still working at the time of the interviews) in companies that produced all five components: semiconductor companies, hardware system companies, application software companies, content creation companies, and development tool companies. Overall, the 20 participants worked for 19 different startup companies and 8 different mature companies in the different areas. All startup companies were private, ranging from 10 to 150 employees. All mature companies were public, with annual revenue ranging from $1 billion to $75 billion, and ranging from 5,000 to 125,000 employees.

One assumption made in this study was that the participants themselves have not evolved during the period. That assumption was not strong since employees, like all people, evolve over time. They mature, they gain more experience, their personal circumstances change, and they do not stay the same. However, to control this evolution as much as possible, two things were done: (1) the sample included employees who moved from startup companies to a mature ones, as well as employees who moved in the opposite direction, so that evolution existed in both directions; and (2) the participants have moved directly between the two companies, with no time gap between them, whether employed by a third company or not. With the exception of four participants—all participants made the transition between the companies between the years 2000 and 2007, and spent at least two years in each company, so their experience is considered recent and relevant. Only four participants made the transition from one company to the other in 1997, 1998, 1999, and 2008. Only two participants spent less than two years in one of the companies: one spent one year and eight months, and the other spent one year and three months in a company. Only two participants had an employment gap between the two companies of interest in this study: one had a six month unemployment gap, and the other had a ten year gap in which he worked for a medium size company.

Table 2 summarizes four attributes of the sample participants. The participants were chosen so that their distribution across the different combinations of attributes will be maximized.

Table 2 – Variability of the Sample

Nature of Role	Order	Still working	Related	Participants
Business	Mature to startup	No	No	P3, P5, P20
Business	Mature to startup	No	Yes (team left)	P15
Business	Mature to startup	Yes	No	P9, P11
Business	Mature to startup	Yes	Yes (team left)	P7
Business	Startup to mature	No	No	
Business	Startup to mature	No	Yes (internal)	P13
Business	Startup to mature	Yes	No	P2, P10, P18
Business	Startup to mature	Yes	Yes	P19
Technical	Mature to startup	No	No	P8, P14, P17
Technical	Mature to startup	No	Yes (team left)	P16
Technical	Mature to startup	Yes	No	P12
Technical	Mature to startup	Yes	Yes	
Technical	Startup to mature	No	No	
Technical	Startup to mature	No	Yes (acquisition)	P1, P6
Technical	Startup to mature	Yes	No	
Technical	Startup to mature	Yes	Yes (acquisition)	P4

Twelve participants filled business roles in both companies they worked for, from marketing, to business development, to general management. Eight of the participants filled technical and operational roles in both companies. In each case, the participant filled very similar roles in both companies. None of the participants filled a technical role in one company and a business role in the other. Twelve participants made a transition from a mature company to a startup company, while eight participants made the opposite transition—from a startup company to a mature one. Seven of the participant made a related transition, either through an acquisition of the startup company by the mature company, or through a team that left the mature company as a whole to start or join the startup company. Thirteen of the participants made a transition between two unrelated companies. Finally, ten of the participants were still working for the company they transitioned into at the time of the interview, whether startup or mature company, while the other ten participants no longer worked for any of the two companies.

Instrumentation / Measures

The exploratory, qualitative part of this study used *investigative interviewing*, a sub category of *responsive interviewing*—a research design that acknowledges the fact that both the interviewer and the interviewee are human beings, with biases. Specifically, the researcher needed to conduct *self reflection* during the interview (Rubin & Rubin, 2005). The researcher in the current study worked in both types of companies, startup and mature, and therefore self reflected on those experiences, while avoiding influencing the participants' responses. This study used open ended interviews, using the critical incident techniques, and using comparative questions. The following sections describe the rationale behind each one of these selections.

Open Ended Interviews

To get to the desired depth of understanding, the research design must be flexible and have a conversational nature (Rubin & Rubin, 2005). The researcher, although personally involved in the topic, avoided voicing any opinion during the interview, as well as through the way the questions were constructed or asked. During the interview, it was important to ask for narratives and stories, which allowed for the extraction of subtle insights. The preferred interview was conducted face-to-face. A telephone interview was not a preferred way for depth interviews, but was unavoidable when the participants are geographically distributed (as done by Leifer et al., 2000). In this study, and given the participant selection criteria—the target sample was distributed across the US (with one participant in China), and therefore telephone interviews were used in many cases.

Rubin and Rubin (2005) recommended using the interview questions to achieve depth, detail, vividness, nuance, and richness. Depth is achieved through asking follow up questions that explore additional meaning and implications of an answer. Detail is achieved through asking for additional information at a greater level of detail, to better understand an answer. Vividness is achieved through getting additional background information, emotions, and other context information that, when conveyed at the final report, allowing the reader to feel he or she was there. Nuance highlights the subtlety of meaning—the understanding that there are many shades of gray between black and white. Finally, richness adds themes to the narrative, sometimes in unexpected directions.

When the interview is fully structured with specific questions and a closed list of possible answers—it becomes a survey rather than an interview (Fowler, 2002). Choosing a survey research design allows for a highly effective interview process, but at the expense of richness and insight. Choosing this design would have allowed getting data on all creativity factors, but at very low detail, insight, and richness. At the other extreme is the use of a completely open ended interview, with very high level questions, allowing for follow on questions to take the interview in different directions (Rubin & Rubin, 2005). Choosing this design would have provided richness and new themes to emerge, but might have caused the interview to miss creativity factors because the interviewee did not remember them without being specifically asked. The semi structured interview was therefore the best compromise in the context of this study. It allowed keeping the interview focused on factors that prior research showed had impact on individual creativity, but at the same time allowed for increased depth, detail, nuance, and richness. Furthermore—it allowed comparing the two types of organizations (and the transition between them) along all the factors in the theoretical framework.

For example, one of the main questions in this study was: "How would you describe the freedom (or autonomy) you had in your job?" Detail could be achieved through asking a follow on question such as: "what did it make you feel?" or "what did the mature company do to make you feel less autonomous?" Depth could be gained through a follow on question such as "how did that affect your creativity?" Nuance could be obtained through a follow-on question such as: "how different was your autonomy in the two companies?" Finally, richness could be gained through asking the participant to elaborate more, and then simply continuing down new paths that were not anticipated upfront. Rubin and Rubin (2005) suggested that the researcher should not be as concerned with the exact wording of the questions, as long as what is being asked is clear enough and no bias or examples are introduced through them. The main questions in the current study were prepared upfront, and are included in Appendix A. The participants were asked to compare how they experienced their personal level of creativity at the two types of organizations. Then, they were asked how they experienced the differences between the organizational climate and their personal context between the two environments, and how did those differences affect their creativity. To be successful, a research project must be manageable (Creswell, 2003). To make this study manageable, only the factors supported by prior research the most (illustrated in Figure 4) were included: (1) creativity, (2) autonomy, (3) support from management, (4) challenge, (5) recognition, (6) availability of resources, (7) team dynamics, (8) formalization and bureaucracy, (9) affect and mood, (10) job satisfaction, and (11) pressure and support outside the workplace. Follow on questions were used to elaborate and gain detail, depth, nuance, and richness for the factors identified. Some of the follow on questions are also listed in Appendix A.

Critical Incident

When Amabile and Gryskiewicz (1987) conducted their initial qualitative research that led to the development of the KEYS instrument, they used the critical incident technique, and asked each participant to contrast a high creativity event with a low creativity event. Ronan and Latham (1974) defined the critical incident technique (CIT) as "a systematic interview procedure for recording behavior that has been observed to lead to success and/or failure regarding the accomplishment of a specific task" and defined *incident* as "any observable activity that is sufficiently complete in itself to permit inferences and predictions to be made about the person performing the act" (p. 53). CIT was widely used since 1954 for performance appraisals, perceived determinants of satisfaction and dissatisfaction, and other purposes (White & Locke, 1981). Webster and Mertova (2007) discussed the use of the critical event strategy in detail. They claimed that "an event becomes critical in that it has some of the following characteristics. It has impacted on the performance of the storyteller in a professional or work-related role." (pp. 72-73). Critical events help focus people's recollection.

The more time that passed since the event or situation, the more important the focus on the critical even to recollect memories is. While the recollection of the participants of events in the company they have worked in most recently might be vivid enough, their recollection of events that happened less recently might be less vivid, and the use of the critical event technique would help refresh their recollection. Webster and Mertova (2007) claimed that critical events exist in a particular context, have impact on people involved, have life changing consequences, are unpredicted and unplanned, may reveal patterns and stages, can only be identified *after* they happen, and are intensely personal with strong emotional involvement. In this study, the life changing impact of a project on its participants could be questioned, but even a less impactful event would still help focus the participants' recollection of the climate during those events, which was the focus of this study. The critical incident technique has its critics. White and Locke (1981) studied the factors which individuals perceive as directly influencing their productivity, using the critical inquiry (CI) strategy, but cited critics of CI claiming that defensive bias may occur—good outcomes will be attributed to self while bad outcomes attributed to others. Schneider and Locke (1971) proposed a new method for CI that separated events from agents, but at the same time admitted there might be some bias in the agent responses, although event data appeared to be free of bias. White and Locke (1981) identified a drawback with CI, in that it identifies factors that are present at the critical incidents themselves and not all factors. This might have caused participants in the current study to ignore some of the factors studied simply because they did not exist in one of the companies at the recollected critical incident. To avoid that—the interview schedule was semi structured, asking about specific factors in the specific companies, rather than asking for a general description of the climate and context in each company. This way—the participants had to discuss all factors and compare them between companies.

Amabile and Gryskiewicz (1987) were not alone in using CIT in creativity research. Isaksen et al. (2000) used it to compare organizational climate for creativity when developing the SOQ instrument, asking people to think about the best and worst climates for creativity they experienced. Isaksen and Lauer (2002) used CIT in their study too, asking participants to compare their most creative team experience with their least creative team experience, and Jones et al. (2000) study of the process of idea creation asked the participants to focus on "critical episodes" of creativity. The validity and reliability of the use of CIT was analyzed by Ronan and Latham (1974) and is provided in the "Validity and Reliability" section of this chapter.

While Amabile and Gryskiewicz (1987), Isaksen et al. (2000), and Isaksen and Lauer (2002) asked participants to recollect events of high creativity and low creativity in the *same* organization, the current study asked the participants to recollect *typical* projects in different companies. Asking the participants to recollect events of high or low creativity in different organizations might have skewed the results of this study, causing participants to focus on high creativity events in the startup company and low creativity events in the mature company, or vice versa. While the *typical* project might not be a "life changing event" for the participants—it might still be used to focus their stories.

CIT was used in this study by asking the participants to focus on specific projects they worked on, when they compared their creativity and the environment conducive to or inhibiting creativity.

Comparative Questions

The research was based on case studies of individuals who moved from a mature company to a startup company (or vice versa) and was therefore able to compare the two environments, rather than independently measure the factors and their influence on an absolute scale. This comparison provided a more reliable comparison of both types of organizations. During the interviews, the participants were asked to compare the two organizations along the dimensions of the different creativity climate and context factors, and their own level of creativity. Comparative questions are a valid interview design, allowing the extraction of subtle differences, and can be used to allow the participants to contrast different situations and immediately ask about the implications of such differences (Rubin & Rubin, 2005). These subtleties might have been lost using a survey instrument with 4-point Likert type scales such as KEYS or CCQ.

Like the critical incident technique, the use of comparisons is not new to creativity research, and was used by Amabile and Gryskiewicz (1987), asking participants to compare projects of high creativity with projects of low creativity; and by McCoy and Evans (2002), asking participants to compare two physical environments to find how they are perceived to affect creativity. Cooper and Schindler (2006) advocated the use of comparative scales when the manager is interested in benchmarking (in this study: perception of the climate, context, and creativity in a startup versus a mature company). Tversky (1977) claimed that the order in which two items (here—the two companies) are compared may result in different judgment of similarity. Wanke and Schwarz (1995) conducted four studies and further claimed that reversing the order of the comparison might even result in reversal of the ordinal ranking. The conclusion was that care had to be taken when asking the participants to compare the two organizations, and that the order in which they were asked to compare might affect their answers. For that purpose, approximately half of the participants were chosen such that they have worked more recently at the startup company while the other half was made of participants who worked more recently at the mature company.

Field Test and Pilot Test

To assure clarity and deliverability of the interview schedule, a field test was conducted. The original interview schedule was sent to a panel of three academic experts in qualitative research, interview design, and the field of innovation. The comments received from the panel members were integrated into a second draft of the interview schedule, which was sent to the panel a second time. More comments were received, and were integrated into the interview schedule again. The changes made to the original interview schedule based on the comments from the field study panel included the following.

First, the experienced creativity question only asked if the participants felt creative in both environments, but did not ask *how* they experienced creativity and how they defined creativity. The interview question about creativity was modified to include the participant's definition and experience. Second, the interview included questions that were not directly related to the conceptual framework, and at the same time omitted questions that should have been directly related to the conceptual framework. The interview schedule was modified, and factors not related to the conceptual framework (for example: "why did you leave company A and join company B?") were eliminated, while factors related to the conceptual framework that were not represented in the interview schedule were added (for example: recognition was omitted from the original interview schedule). Third, few questions were not clear enough for participants (for example: "compare the task related challenges you faced..."). The questions were corrected for clarity. Fourth, the personal context was originally assumed to be constant across both companies for the same participant. Based on comments received from the panel, this assumption was dropped and questions addressing the elements of personal context were added to the interview schedule to explore whether personal context has changed. Fifth, the original interview schedule asked the participants to compare the two companies without asking them to describe the projects in greater detail such that themes could emerge from the project description. The questions were modified to ask the participants to describe the projects in their own words. Sixth, to avoid a possible bias toward the first company in a pair that participants are asked to compare (Tversky, 1977; Wanke & Schwarz, 1995), the order of companies was originally flipped across questions in the original interview (in some questions, the participant was asked to compare the startup company to the mature company while in other questions the participant was asked to compare the mature company to the startup company, reversing the order). One panel member commented that the benefit of eliminating such potential bias could be overshadowed by possibly confusing the participant. The interview questions were corrected such that they all ask to compare in the same order. Finally, one comment suggested that it might be better to ask the participant to describe one company across *all* factors of the conceptual framework, and only then to ask the participant to describe the other company, rather than ask the participant to compare the two companies one factor at a time. This comment was not accepted by the researcher initially as the researcher felt that it might have reduced the ability to compare the factors as described in Figure 5 and have the research questions drive data collection, rather than the other way around (Howe & Eisenhardt, 1990). This issue was further explored during the pilot test.

Once the field test feedback was gathered and implemented and once the Institutional Review Board (IRB) approved the study, a pilot test was conducted. Wengraf (2001) recommended to conduct a pilot test of the interview on "somebody or a couple of somebodies" (p. 187) before conducting the real interview, and suggested that such test will almost certainly improve the design and offer practice such that the interview will be more effective. Cooper and Schindler (2003) defined one form of pilot test as "pretesting" the instrument (here, the interview schedule) with colleagues or friends who can comment on issues that were not identified by the academic panel during the field test. Conducting the field test and pilot test before "entering the field" to conduct the real interviews could save time and effort that could be incurred by entering the field with a problematic interview schedule. For the pilot study, the researcher chose two people from his professional network who met the criteria of being part of the target sample in general. Both participants were interviewed as if they were part of the target sample. The pilot study was done to assure validity and reliability of the interview schedule, although it focused on the validity and reliability of two cases only, rather than the entire study (cross case analysis is a significant factor affecting reliability and validity of the entire study and will not be achieved at the pilot study). During the pilot study interview, the researcher looked for clarity of the information provided by the participants (thus assuring interpretive validity), and the knowledge and depth that the participants provided upon answering the interview questions (assuring descriptive validity). The interview was recorded, noted, and transcribed like the "real" research interviews, and the researcher analyzed the transcript and field notes to evaluate the interview. Specifically, the researcher looked for evidence that the research questions guided the interview, and not the other way around (Howe & Eisenhardt, 1990). Furthermore, since detailed field notes and accurate transcription of a high quality recording significantly contribute to reliability (Creswell, 2007), the researcher evaluated the quality of the recording, the accuracy of transcription, and the consistency of the researcher's field notes and transcription. The interview schedule was modified to assure such validity and reliability. The insights from the pilot study with the first participant suggested changing the order of the questions slightly. Instead of the original order (creativity, autonomy, management support, challenges, recognition, resources, team support, formalization, mood, job satisfaction, pressure from home, and support from home), the order was changed to assure a better flow that will allow the participants to move from one topic to the other smoothly. For this purpose, the flow was changed to have autonomy, management support, and recognition, all related to supervisor in one section, and then challenges, resources, and formalization in a second section. The second pilot study interview provided additional insights. First, it provided the realization that participants viewed two different main types of challenges: internal (in the company) and external (not related to the company). Second, the participants focused on the companies themselves, and made generalizations and assumptions based on what they perceived other people's experiences were, and the researcher learned to make sure that participants focus on their *own* experiences. Finally, the field notes were initially descriptive of almost everything the participants said, which created a redundancy with the transcript. The researcher learned to avoid such copious note taking, and diverted note taking to add additional insight that could not be captured by the recording (body language, hand gestures, etc.) to add subtlety to the interview transcripts. After two pilot study interviews, the researcher felt ready to enter the field. The final modified interview schedule is included in Appendix A.

Data Collection

The data collection was interview based, with the researcher acting as the data collection instrument. The interviews were semi structured, using the critical incident technique with comparative questions. There could be two approaches to the order of questions: (1) asking the participants to "tell the whole story" of their experience in the startup company, then "tell the whole story" of their experience in the mature company, and then asking them to compare the two; and (2) asking the participant about their experiences in the startup company, the mature company, and asking them to compare the two along each element of the conceptual framework (experienced creativity, organizational climate, and personal context)—one at a time. Since the focus of this study was in the comparison between the two environments, using an existing conceptual framework as a starting point—the second option was selected: focusing on each of the conceptual framework elements in both environments. This allowed for more focused comparisons, while still allowing for new themes to emerge and for the conceptual framework to be modified. The flow of the interview is illustrated in Figure 5. For each factor, the participant was asked to "tell the story" of the startup company, then the mature company, then to compare them, and from that comparison— meaning was derived during the data analysis stage.

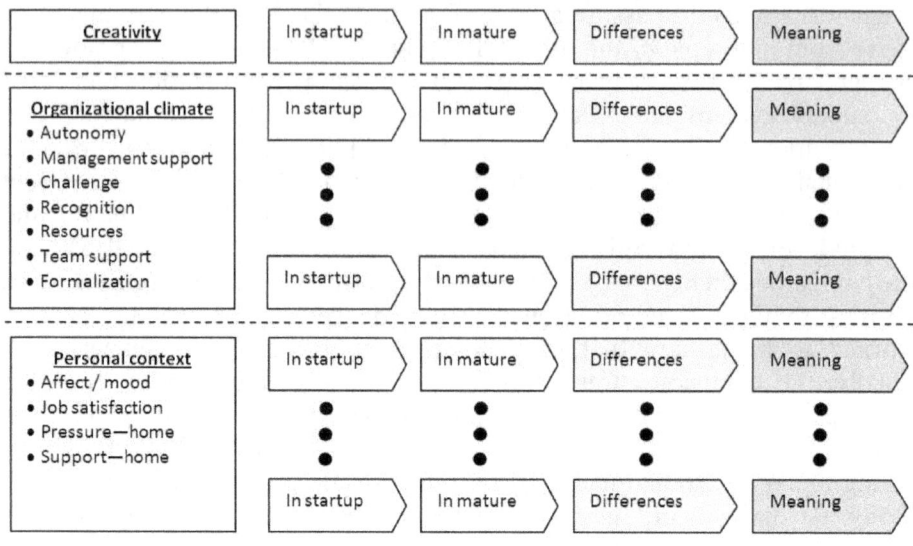

Figure 5 – Data collection flow.

Most interviews were conducted over the telephone, to reach participants across the US, and were approximately 60 minutes long. The interview schedule in Appendix A was used as a guide for the interview, although the researcher explored certain avenues in depth where appropriate through follow on questions. The interviews were recorded and transcribed by the researcher. Although every action taken by the researcher could potentially introduce bias, the transcription process allowed the researcher to objectively convert the voice recording into text. The researcher, knowledgeable in the field, was able to better transcribe field related terms than a transcription service. The researcher also took notes during the interview in case of a recording malfunction, and to complement the recording and transcription, and capture non verbal responses such as intonation and body language. Useful notes include impressions, avoid sifting important information, and identify what is new and different than other cases (Eisenhardt, 1989).

The pilot study helped refine the questions and the pace of the interview. However, as more interviews were conducted, the process improved. It was important during the interview to ask for examples, and to repeat to the participants what they said, to assure that the true meaning was captured. This allowed the increase of *interpretive validity* (Maxwell, 1992). While the main questions remained the same, the probes were changing throughout the interviews as some probes were found to be more effective than others. For example: the question whether the participant received support from his or her spouse differently during his or her employment in the two companies was hard to answer. But a probe such as "if I asked your spouse which company did he/she liked that you worked at more" would have focused the answer better since through this probe the participant was more reflective of the support he or she received from that spouse. Although addressing focus groups, Krueger and Casey (2000) suggested several probes (pause, ask "say more") that proved to be very effective during the interviews since they forced the participants to add depth, subtlety, and insight, which are significant advantaged of the interview based qualitative research methodology (Rubin & Rubin, 2005). In few cases, after a pause or a request for example or more depth, the participants were surprised to find that when they thought about the question more, their answer was the opposite to the one they gave initially. In few occasions, repeating what the participant said caused the participant to change his or her mind and realize that at some point they stated the opposite to what they really experienced, or to differentiate between the two situations in a way that added more depth.

Eight interviews were conducted face-to-face in convenient locations, ranging from a restaurant, coffee houses, to the researcher's home or the participant's home. The other twelve interviews were conducted over the telephone, with the participants located in Texas, California, New York, Oregon, Washington, and China.

Data Analysis

Qualitative Data Analysis

The purpose of this study was to compare the organizational climate, the personal context, and individual creativity in the startup companies and the mature companies as perceived by participants who worked in both. While the data collection was done through semi structured interviews, data analysis could be supported through the theoretical framework in Figure 4, along the 11 factors described in it: (1) creativity, (2) autonomy, (3) support from management, (4) challenge, (5) recognition, (6) availability of resources, (7) team dynamics, (8) formalization, (9) affect and mood, (10) job satisfaction, (11) pressure and support from home. Collected data was coded to indicate the participant, the type of company, and the factor discussed. While those codes helped in sorting the data—they were not a closed list, and additional factors or insights added additional coding. Two tactics are most useful for the generation of meaning: making contrasts / comparisons, and noting relationships between variables. This study focused on contrasting the two types of organizations with respect to the creativity of the participants, the organizational climate for creativity, and the personal context. The differences that emerged through those comparisons were therefore expected to be the main source of generating meaning.

To increase the generalizability of the data, *within case* analysis was performed as well as *cross case* analysis (Miles & Huberman, 1994). Within cases, analysis was done to explore how the differences in the organizational climate and personal context impacted the self-reported creativity differences of a single individual. Cross case analysis assisted in the emergence of consistent themes experienced by multiple individuals who worked for multiple organizations. Based on a software review done by Lee and Esterhuizen (2000) and a more recent comparison and assessment of available qualitative data analysis software tools, QSR's Nvivo8 was chosen to provide code generation and code-based theorizing functions to the data analysis phase.

Quantitative Coding and Analysis

The narrative data offered an opportunity for coding the participants' responses *by the researcher* such that statistical procedures could be used for quantitative data analysis to confirm the findings from the qualitative data analysis. Since no survey instrument was used during the interviews, it was impossible to code the responses on a similar scale. The researcher felt that coding the different factors in a comparative manner with only three ordinal options (1: factor is stronger at the startup company, 0: factor is equal in the startup company and in the mature company, and -1: factor is stronger at the mature company) would provide relatively accurate coding that could be performed by a single rater, the researcher. All 11 factors (creativity, autonomy, supervisor, recognition, challenges, resources, team dynamics, formalization, job satisfaction, mood, and support and pressure from home) were coded according to the scheme described above. During the interviews it became apparent that the *challenges* factor could be separated into two sub factors: internal challenges and external challenges. In a similar manner, some of the participants discussed resources in terms of their *quantity* and *quality*. Finally, some of the participants separated the *support* their received from their families from the *pressure* they felt. Three additional factors were discussed by the participants enough to provide coding information too: "big picture" view, impact on company success, and respect they felt towards their supervisor. Table 3 shows the guiding questions that allowed the researcher to code the different factors at the different cases. As a result, the total number of factors that were quantitatively coded increased to 17.

In many cases, the participants specifically stated that a certain factor was stronger in one of the companies, and did not contradict that in the narrative they provided. In other cases, the participants did not provide such specific comparative evaluation, but it was clear from the narrative they provided that they experienced a specific factor more in one of the companies than the other. Only in few cases the initial comparison conflicted with the narrative, or it was hard for the researcher to evaluate whether this factor was experienced by the participant more in one company versus the other. In those cases the researcher did one of four things: (1) asked the participant to confirm one way or the other without guiding, (2) marked the factor as equal between the two companies, (3) used subjective judgment to extract the comparative result from the narrative, or (4) marked the item as missing value.

There were a total of 20 participants who interviewed for this study, but participant P5 provided two comparisons: one between the traditional business unit in the mature company and the internal startup there, and one between the mature company and a real startup company she worked in. As a result, P5 was coded for quantitative analysis purposes as two cases, resulting in a total of 21 coded cases.

Table 3 – Guiding Questions for Coding the Different Factors in the Different Cases

Factor	Question
Creativity	Did the participant experience more creativity in one of the companies (either through stating that, or experiencing more novelty, usefulness, or quantity of creative ideas)?
Autonomy	Did the participant experience more autonomy in one of the companies?
Supervisor	Did the participant feel more support from his/her supervisor?
Recognition	Did the participant feel more recognized or rewarded (formally, informally, or financially) in one of the companies?
Internal challenges	Did the participant experience more internal challenges in one of the companies?
External challenges	Did the participant experience more external / technological / intellectual challenges in one of the companies?
Resource quantity	Did the participant have more resources available to his/her projects in one of the companies?
Resource quality	Did the participant experience resources of higher quality in one of the companies?
Team dynamics	Did the participant feel that the team dynamics were better in one of the companies? (more friendships, more debate, less conflict, less politics, less internal competition, more communications, more trust)
Formalization	Did the participant experience more formalization, bureaucracy, or processes in one of the companies?
Job satisfaction	Did the participant experience higher job satisfaction in one of the companies?
Mood	Did the participant experience a more positive mood while working in one of the companies?
Support from home	Did the participant feel more support from home while working in one of the companies?
Pressure from home	Did the participant feel more pressure from home while working in one of the companies?
Big picture	Did the participant feel he/she had a view of the "big picture" in one of the companies?
Impact on success	Did the participant feel he/she had more impact on the success of one of the companies?
Respect supervisor	Did the participant feel more respect towards his/her supervisor in one of the companies?

After coding the interview transcripts according to the 17 factors, it was concluded that the *quality of resources* factor could be reliably coded only in three cases and therefore this factor was eliminated from quantitative analysis, and the resources factor was limited to the *quantity of resources* available to the participants in their projects.

Validity and Reliability

Trochim (2006a) defined *credibility* as the believability of the conclusion by the participants. To increase credibility, therefore, the participants were asked to provide feedback on the initial conclusions of the study. *Transferability* is the equivalent of Maxwell's (1992) *generalizability*, which is the applicability of the conclusions to similar circumstances. For this study, generalizability was increased by increasing the variability of the participants, conducting a multiple case study, investigating the outliers and surprising results (Miles & Huberman, 1994), and describing the research environment as much as possible to allow readers to assess the similarity to a new set of circumstances, and therefore the applicability of this study to the new environment. *Dependability* is defined as the replicability of the study, or how likely are the same conclusions to result from the same data. Dependability was increased through cross case explanation that accounted for all the differences in the cases, and thus their results. Finally, *confirmability* is defined as the level that this study can be confirmed by others. Confirmability for this study was increased through maintaining an audit trail, allowing additional researchers to verify that the conclusions are a natural result of the study, and assuring that data collection and analysis are free of biases. Assuring a bias free study can be done by first identifying the potential sources of bias, and compensating for them. In this study, one bias could be that participants might have preferred to portray their current company as more conducive to creativity (not willing to state that they are currently working in a less creative climate), as well as their own creativity. However, identifying this bias through the interview process, and mitigating this by, as an example, separating the questions about startup companies from those about mature companies and forcing the participant to focus on each one separately, achieved that goal.

Additional aspects of validity that needed to be addressed were found in Maxwell's (1992) framework. *Descriptive validity* is the factual accuracy of the data. The use of transcripts and repeated "immersion" in the data will assure factual accuracy. The researcher has immersed himself in the transcription and notes through creating the transcription himself, coding it in several levels, and conducting within case and cross case analysis. *Interpretive validity* is important as qualitative research, mostly of the interpretivistic tradition, is concerned with the meaning of the environment to the participants and to the researcher. To increase interpretive validity, the researcher asked the participants to confirm that the interpretation of their words was done appropriately during the interview. *Theoretical validity* is the sense that the theory or conceptual framework makes. It was increased through a well founded conceptual framework that was built upon proven and valid prior research. This current study was founded on a well researched conceptual framework that was validated substantially. Finally, *evaluative validity* refers to the validity of the process of evaluating the data to create meaning. Using rigorous and well documented method to analyze the data into conclusions increased evaluative validity.

Webster and Mertova (2007) suggested rethinking validity and reliability in the context of narrative research, and that the "standard" definitions of validity and reliability should not apply without appropriate changes. Reliability should refer to the dependability of the data, and validity should refer to the strength of analysis, trustworthiness of the data, and ease of access to it.

Trochim (2006a) was concerned that qualitative researchers sometimes rejected the quantitative term *validity*, as they were not concerned with the absolute truth or false of an observation, thus hurting its generalizability. Merriam (1998) stated that case study is less descriptive of a large population, and less predictive in nature. Due to the limited data collection, a case study is limited in its generalizability, reliability, and validity. However, Yin (2003) claimed that case study could be generalizeable, even if it was a single case study.

Ronan and Latham (1974) evaluated the reliability and validity of the critical incident technique (CIT) that was used in this study. They conducted a study of 440 cases, aimed at assessing the reliability and validity of the technique, and measured *inter-judge reliability* (the only reliability measure that was lower than 80%), *intra-observer reliability*, *inter-observer reliability*, *content validity* (the degree to which the number of recorded incidents represented the total number of incidents that could have been collected), *relevance* (the cause-and-effect link between the observed behavior and the dependent variable), *construct validity* (through factor analysis), and *concurrent validity*. Their conclusion was that the reliability and content validity of the CIT design were satisfactory. Their main concern in their study was with inter-observer reliability that was attributed to the scales used in the specific data analysis, and not an inherent flaw of the CIT strategy itself.

Finally, the quantitative coding scheme used a three point scale. Churchill Jr. and Peter (1984) found that the reliability of a survey instrument increased as the number of points increased, but the researcher felt that attempting to code on more than the three-point scale proposed above would have jeopardized the reliability of the coding, and might have required multiple raters.

Ethical Considerations

Miles and Huberman (1994) addressed several specific ethical considerations for the study, some of which were also addressed by the Academy of Management (2002) code of ethical conduct. The most important consideration is the informed consent, which assures that participants are aware of potential risks of their participation, potential benefits, and the voluntary nature of their participation. Acknowledged informed consent forms that meets all the requirements in the Capella University IRB application checklist were kept by the researcher. The participants were made aware through the form of the voluntary nature of their participation, and of their right to refuse to answer any question or withdraw from participation altogether without any consequences to them. The researcher committed to maintain the confidentiality and anonymity of the participants in the study. The participants were not asked to disclose any confidential information about themselves and the companies they were working for. The interview recordings and transcript files were encrypted and will be kept for seven years on the researcher's computer and external backup drive. Only the researcher will have access to those files. The study report only included codes and aliases to identify the participants and the companies they worked in. Another ethical consideration is the integrity and quality of the research. Reaching the appropriate conclusions while considering all the data is another ethical issue, beyond one of good research practice, as people could be relying on those conclusions to make business and personal decisions. Finally, the intellectual property rights of the data and the complete report will be maintained by the researcher, and the report could be used to advance theory and practice appropriately.

Summary

This study explored the experiences of individuals who moved from startup companies to mature companies (or vice versa) in terms of their individual creativity, organizational climate, and personal context that could have affected their creativity. The focus on individual creativity was derived from the relationship between individual creativity and organizational innovation (Zhou, 2003), and prior research that showed that startup companies are more innovative than mature companies (Christensen, 1997). Seeking to explore those experiences as seen from the perspective of the participants, searching for the richness of those experiences, and admitting the researcher's interpretivistic tradition drove the selection of a case study design, with 20 participants, deploying semi structured interviews using the critical incident technique and comparative questions. Data collection was preceded by a field study with a panel of experts, and a pilot study with two participants who qualified to be part of the sample, both to improve the clarity and deliverability of the interview, as well as improve the validity and reliability of the results.

4. Research Findings

This research was based on the combination of three premises supported by prior research: (1) startup companies are more innovative than mature companies; (2) innovation is based on a creative idea that gets implemented; and (3) there are different factors, organizational and personal, that affect employee creativity. Based on this combination of premises, the purpose of this study was to explore the perceived changes in creativity of individuals who moved between mature companies and startup companies (in both directions), and how they experienced the differences in the organizational climate and in their personal context that may have affected those changes in their creativity. The purpose was not to confirm or reject any of the prior premises, but to explore how participants who worked for both types of companies, startup and mature, experienced the different factors in the different organizations, and understand how the differences between the companies in each factor could be explained by the type of companies, startup or mature, versus simply by differences between the companies (unrelated to type) or other circumstances.

Within Case Analysis

Each of the 20 cases was analyzed according to the 11 factors included in the conceptual framework in Figure 4: creativity, autonomy, supervisor, recognition, challenges, resources, team dynamics, formalization, job satisfaction, mood, and home pressure and support. Additional insights that did not fit any of the factors were also gathered in the interviews. Since the discussion of pressure and support from home were highly integrated, they were covered under the same heading in the different cases narrative. However, they were separately analyzed. For each of the factors in each case, the analysis included the participant's description of this factor in both companies, and the comparison of this factor between the companies. A total of 235 single spaced narrative pages and 120 handwritten researcher note pages were distilled to the text which is included in Appendix B. The cases are titled with the participant code, P1 through P20. It is recommended to read the individual cases in Appendix B before proceeding to read the cross case analysis.

Cross Case Analysis

Even though the qualitative narrative analysis was the foundation of this study and was conducted first, this section begins with the quantitative tables that will be referenced later, within the text describing the individual themes that emerged to confirm them.

Table 4 shows the descriptive statistics of the different factors. In Table 4, a positive mean indicates that this factor appeared more in startup companies, and a negative mean indicates that this factor appeared more in mature companies. However, Table 4 does not provide the statistical significance of those differences.

Table 4 – Descriptive Statistics of Differences in Creativity and Factors Affecting it

One-Sample Statistics

	N	More in startup	Equal	More in mature	Mean	Std. Deviation	Std. Error Mean
Creativity	21	12	7	2	.48	.680	.148
Autonomy	21	14	3	4	.48	.814	.178
Supervisor	18	9	4	5	.22	.878	.207
Recognition	21	9	7	5	.19	.814	.178
Internal Challenges	21	1	0	20	-.90	.436	.095
External Challenges	21	16	3	2	.67	.658	.144
Resource Quantity	21	3	2	16	-.62	.740	.161
Team Dynamics	21	15	5	1	.67	.577	.126
Formalization	20	1	0	19	-.90	.447	.100
Job Satisfaction	21	13	4	4	.43	.811	.177
Mood	11	2	8	1	.09	.539	.163
Support from Home	20	4	15	1	.15	.489	.109
Pressure from Home	20	5	9	6	-.05	.759	.170
Big Picture	17	16	1	0	.94	.243	.059
Impact on success	19	15	3	1	.74	.562	.129
Respect Supervisor	16	7	6	3	.25	.775	.194

To provide the statistical significance of the results in Table 4, a one sample t test was conducted on the remaining 16 factors (Table 5). Since the code 0 was used to describe a factor as equal between the startup and the mature companies, and was also the average of 1 (factor in favor of startup company) and -1 (factor in favor of mature company)—the reference test value used was 0. The question that each of those t tests answered was whether the observed sample mean is likely to be from a population where the mean is 0 (similar in both companies). Wherever this null hypothesis could be rejected—this factor was related to the size of the company (startup or mature).

Table 5 – One Sample t test of Differences in Creativity and Factors Affecting it

One-Sample Test

	T	df	Sig. (2-tailed)	Mean Difference	95% Confidence Interval of the Difference	
					Lower	Upper
Creativity	3.211	20	.004	.476	.17	.79
Autonomy	2.682	20	.014	.476	.11	.85
Supervisor	1.074	17	.298	.222	-.21	.66
Recognition	1.073	20	.296	.190	-.18	.56
Internal Challenges	-9.500	20	.000	-.905	-1.10	-.71
External Challenges	4.641	20	.000	.667	.37	.97
Resource Quantity	-3.833	20	.001	-.619	-.96	-.28
Team Dynamics	5.292	20	.000	.667	.40	.93
Formalization	-9.000	19	.000	-.900	-1.11	-.69
Job Satisfaction	2.423	20	.025	.429	.06	.80
Mood	.559	10	.588	.091	-.27	.45
Support from Home	1.371	19	.186	.150	-.08	.38
Pressure from Home	-.295	19	.772	-.050	-.41	.31
Big Picture	16.000	16	.000	.941	.82	1.07
Impact on success	5.715	18	.000	.737	.47	1.01
Respect Supervisor	1.291	15	.216	.250	-.16	.66

As Tables 4 and 5 show—the following factors were not related to whether the company was startup or mature: supervisor, recognition, mood, support from home, pressure from home, and respect that the participants felt towards the supervisor. The following factors were stronger in startup companies: creativity, autonomy, external challenges, team dynamics, job satisfaction, big picture view, and impact on success. The following factors were stronger in mature companies: internal challenges, resource quantity, and formalization. These factors are discussed in greater detail and subtlety in the following cross case analysis.

Five additional attributes of the participants were recorded and coded to check correlation: (1) which of the two companies (startup or mature) did the participant work for earlier; (2) whether there was there a gap between the participant's work in the first company and the second company; (3) whether the participant held a business or technical position in the companies; (4) whether the two companies were related (through an acquisition, a spin-off, or a team that left together); and (5) whether the participant is still working for the later company. No correlation was expected or supported by prior research, but a cursory correlation was tested in this study for these attributes.

A correlation table was created for the 16 different factors and 5 attributes. In the first run, three factors were found not to correlate with statistical significance with any other factor or attribute and were thus removed from the final table for clarity: mood, support from home, and pressure from home. Those three factors were also not related to the size of the company, as Table 5 shows. Furthermore, four of the five attributes did not have any statistically significant correlation with any of the factors or attributes, and were thus eliminated too: first company, employment gap between companies, relatedness of companies, and whether the participant is still employed in the second company. The correlation between the remaining 13 factors and one attribute (position) is summarized in Table 6.

A few correlations observed in Table 6 are highlighted here:

Creativity is positively correlated to autonomy, external challenges, "big picture" view, perception of ability to impact success, respect felt toward the supervisor, and job satisfaction.

Creativity is negatively correlated to internal challenges and formalization.

The correlation that job satisfaction has with the factors affecting creativity (positively and negatively) is relatively similar, even if in some cases the cross the statistical significance boundary.

Recognition, external challenges, positive team dynamics, job satisfaction, and ability to see the "big picture" were all correlated to respect felt towards the supervisor.

Formalization and internal challenges are perfectly correlated.

"Big picture" view and formalization, as well as "big picture" view and internal challenges are perfectly negatively correlated.

Both creativity and job satisfaction had the highest correlation with the perceived impact the participants had on the success of the company or project.

These correlations and others are discussed in detail within the appropriate sections of the cross-case narrative analysis.

Table 6 – Correlation Table of the Differences in Creativity and Factors Affecting it Between Startup Companies and Mature Companies

Correlations

		Position	Creativity	Autonomy	Supervisor	Recognition	Internal Challenges	External Challenges	Team Dynamics	Formalization	Job Satisfaction	Big Picture	Impact on success	Respect Supervisor
Position	Pearson Correlation	1	.176	-.100	-.074	-.065	-.175	-.051	.116	-.168	.443*	.185	.367	.210
	Sig. (2-tailed)		.445	.666	.770	.781	.447	.827	.616	.478	.044	.478	.122	.435
	N		21	21	18	21	21	21	21	20	21	17	19	16
Creativity	Pearson Correlation	.176	1	.474*	.411	.280	-.498*	.596**	.425	-.513*	.609**	.575*	.657**	.513*
	Sig. (2-tailed)	.445		.030	.090	.219	.022	.004	.055	.021	.003	.016	.002	.042
	N	21		21	18	21	21	21	21	20	21	17	19	16
Autonomy	Pearson Correlation	-.100	.474*	1	.174	.083	-.416	.218	.461*	-.427	.433*	.493*	.501*	.105
	Sig. (2-tailed)	.666	.030		.490	.721	.061	.343	.035	.061	.050	.044	.029	.698
	N	21	21		18	21	21	21	21	20	21	17	19	16
Supervisor	Pearson Correlation	-.074	.411	.174	1	.755**	-.347	.325	.601**	-.347	.508*	.468	.362	.874**
	Sig. (2-tailed)	.770	.090	.490		.000	.158	.188	.008	.158	.031	.079	.154	.000
	N	18	18	18		18	18	18	18	18	18	15	17	16
Recognition	Pearson Correlation	-.065	.280	.083	.755**	1	-.335	.311	.248	-.333	.477*	.432	.331	.645**
	Sig. (2-tailed)	.781	.219	.721	.000		.137	.170	.278	.151	.029	.083	.167	.007
	N	21	21	21	18		21	21	21	20	21	17	19	16
Internal Challenges	Pearson Correlation	-.175	-.498*	-.416	-.347	-.335	1	-.580**	-.661**	1.000**	-.404	-1.000**	-.318	-.430
	Sig. (2-tailed)	.447	.022	.061	.158	.137		.006	.001	.000	.069	.000	.185	.096
	N	21	21	21	18	21		21	21	20	21	17	19	16
External Challenges	Pearson Correlation	-.051	.596**	.218	.325	.311	-.580**	1	.219	-.579**	.281	.748**	.167	.539*
	Sig. (2-tailed)	.827	.004	.343	.188	.170	.006		.340	.007	.217	.000	.493	.031
	N	21	21	21	18	21	21		21	20	21	17	19	16
Team Dynamics	Pearson Correlation	.116	.425	.461*	.601**	.248	-.661**	.219	1	-.700**	.534*	.809**	.296	.608*
	Sig. (2-tailed)	.616	.055	.035	.008	.278	.001	.340		.001	.013	.000	.218	.013
	N	21	21	21	18	21	21	21		20	21	17	19	16
Formalization	Pearson Correlation	-.168	-.513*	-.427	-.347	-.333	1.000**	-.579**	-.700**	1	-.401	-1.000**	-.318	-.430
	Sig. (2-tailed)	.478	.021	.061	.158	.151	.000	.007	.001		.079	.000	.185	.096
	N	20	20	20	18	20	20	20	20		20	17	19	16
Job Satisfaction	Pearson Correlation	.443*	.609**	.433*	.508*	.477*	-.404	.281	.534*	-.401	1	.575*	.815**	.661**
	Sig. (2-tailed)	.044	.003	.050	.031	.029	.069	.217	.013	.079		.016	.000	.005
	N	21	21	21	18	21	21	21	21	20		17	19	16
Big Picture	Pearson Correlation	.185	.575*	.493*	.468	.432	-1.000**	.748**	.809**	-1.000**	.575*	1	.350	.636**
	Sig. (2-tailed)	.478	.016	.044	.079	.083	.000	.000	.000	.000	.016		.168	.014
	N	17	17	17	15	17	17	17	17	17	17		17	14
Impact on success	Pearson Correlation	.367	.657**	.501*	.362	.331	-.318	.167	.296	-.318	.815**	.350	1	.447
	Sig. (2-tailed)	.122	.002	.029	.154	.167	.185	.493	.218	.185	.000	.168		.082
	N	19	19	19	17	19	19	19	19	19	19	17		16
Respect Supervisor	Pearson Correlation	.210	.513*	.105	.874**	.645**	-.430	.539*	.608*	-.430	.661**	.636**	.447	1
	Sig. (2-tailed)	.435	.042	.698	.000	.007	.096	.031	.013	.096	.005	.014	.082	
	N	16	16	16	16	16	16	16	16	16	16	14	16	

*. Correlation is significant at the 0.05 level (2-tailed).

**. Correlation is significant at the 0.01 level (2-tailed).

Following is the data analysis of the different factors across the different cases and themes that emerged from the data analysis. The combination of qualitative narrative analysis and quantitative analysis of the coding of the information strengthened the conclusions reached in this study.

Creativity

The first research question in this study was: *How do employees who worked in both startup and mature companies experience the differences in their own creativity between the two types of organizations?*

To answer the first research question, participants were asked to determine how they experienced creativity in either company, and whether they experienced more creativity in the startup company, the mature company, or equal in both. The interviews began typically by asking the participants to define "being creative", or to define creativity. In most cases, the participants defined creativity consistently with Amabile's (1988) definition. In all cases, the researcher probed the participants to compare the *novelty* and the *usefulness* of their creative ideas, to assure a consistent comparison between their experiences of creativity in startup and mature companies that allowed drawing conclusions about the differences in creativity between the two types of companies. When participants felt that their creative ideas were as novel and useful in one company as they were in the other—a third element was added: the frequency or quantity of creative ideas in both companies. If a participant had ideas that were both novel and useful equally in both companies, but generated creative ideas more frequently or in larger quantity in one company—the participant was considered more creative in that company.

P1 felt that his creativity was a natural thing for him, regardless of the company he worked in. His creativity did not necessarily take place at the office—it could take place in the shower, or while driving. In those places, the work environment was not very influential on him. P1 felt that in the startup company his creativity was basic and "low tech", whereas at the mature company it was more radical and constituted a technological breakthrough. He described filing more patents and publishing more technical papers in the mature company because his creative ideas were more novel there. At the same time, he felt that his creativity in the startup company was broad, while his creativity in the mature company was narrow and linked to a very specific domain area.

P2 defined creativity as "being able to find a solution that is differentiated in the market to a particular product, a particular customer problem". He later added the elements of novelty, radical ideas, and usefulness to the definition. P2 felt more creative in the startup company due to starting with a clean slate, and felt that the existing framework in the mature company was "baggage" that reduced his creativity. He claimed that novelty of ideas was not necessarily perceived as positive in the mature company. In fact, he felt that what was considered radical in the mature company, might not have been considered radical in the startup company. This position is supported by Abernathy and Utterback (1978).

P3 defined creativity as "the formulation and process of putting ideas into action that benefits the company, its employees, and shareholders." P3 felt consistently creative at the startup company, where he felt that creativity was required and instrumental. He felt creative in the mature company in cycles—more creative at the beginning of a cycle, and less creative at the end (the life cycle of job tenure and its effect on employee creativity were supported by Katz, 2004b).

P4 defined creativity as "decisions made in the absence of prior precedents, in pursuit of a defined goal." This definition included the novelty and usefulness elements of the standard definition of creativity. He claimed that since he did everything in the startup company for the first time—he felt more creative there. He felt that the peak of his creativity was similar in both companies, but in the startup company his creativity was consistently high, whereas in the mature company his feelings of creativity were very spiky, with prolonged intervals of feeling less creative.

P5's definition of creativity was very similar to Amabile's (1988) definition. Based on that definition, she felt more creative in the internal startup at the mature company since she felt that her ideas were novel to the market, and represented breakthrough technology. She experienced low creativity at the traditional business unit in the mature company because she had very little freedom to be creative. Her creativity at the real startup company was driven by the company being in survival mode: "they were dying, thirsty, wanting anything, because they had essentially nothing", but felt limited to her specific role in her creativity, more so than in the internal startup at the mature company.

P6 felt initially as creative in both companies, but felt that his ideas were embraced by the startup company, whereas only one in four of his ideas where implemented in the mature company. Eventually, he felt discouraged by that low percentage.

P7 focused on the uniqueness and novelty of his ideas. He felt that the startup company had to have radical ideas to succeed since it could not succeed with "me too" products. In the mature company, on the other hand, radical ideas were often shot down, discouraging him from generating more radical, creative ideas.

P8 described creativity in terms of novelty (differentiation) and usefulness of ideas. He felt creative in both companies, but more so in the startup company, where he felt the company was willing to try new things, and he started with a clean slate. In the mature company he felt that "things had to be done in a certain way" and the company rejected new approaches. He felt that more of his ideas in the startup company were worthy of being patented. He also associated creativity with the stage in the product development cycle that lent itself to creativity more in the early stages.

P9 initially felt more creative in the mature company. However, when asked about the novelty of his ideas—he felt more creative in the startup company where he started with a clean slate and his ideas were more radical and "out of the ether", whereas in the mature company there were a lot of assumptions and constraints that limited the novelty of his ideas. He also felt his ideas were more useful in the startup company because, as a software company—ideas reached fruition much faster than in a semiconductor company, were the development cycle is in excess of three years.

P10 experienced "full artistic creativity" in both companies. He felt that his ideas were more radical and novel in the mature company because of the breadth of technologies and applications he was involved with, compared to the limited and focused application he was involved with at the startup company. He filed patents with both companies and felt that the rate of ideas and patents were relatively similar.

P11 thought of creativity as a discipline that involves passion and emotion. He believed his ideas in the startup company were more novel because he started with a clean slate and as a result he claimed that the product based on his ideas was disruptive to the market. He felt less creative in the mature company because nothing there was really new, and he was limited by rules, policies, procedures, and culture. He felt that his ideas in the startup company were more useful simply because it was easier to measure their impact on the company, which was hard in the mature company.

P12 felt creative in both companies. He could not distinguish whether his ideas in one company were more novel or radical than his ideas at the other company. However, he felt that his ideas in the startup company were more useful, simply because they got implemented, whereas he believed that almost none of his ideas in the mature company ever saw the light of day, consistent with Oldham and Cummings (1996).

P13 felt creative in both companies but, like others, felt that a much smaller percentage of his ideas reached fruition in the mature company, compared to the startup company. At some point, he stopped feeling creative at the mature company as a result.

P14 felt more creative in the startup company than in the mature company, but associated that with the product life cycle. When he worked in the startup company, the product was in the definition phase, which allowed a lot of creativity: "Figuring out completely new ways to do those things nobody actually knew how to do before." However, when he worked for the mature company, the product there was in the productization phase, where the work was more mechanical and routine, with fewer opportunities to be creative. This position was supported by Katz (2004b).

P15 worked remotely and felt that creativity was a prerequisite for remote employees. He did not feel that his ideas in one company were more novel than in the other, but felt that his ideas in the startup company were more useful than the mature company, simply because they got implemented at a higher rate.

P16 felt more creative in the startup company than in the mature company because he was responsible for the big picture, which allowed more creativity than when he was responsible only for a narrow niche in the mature company. He also felt that his ideas were radical in the startup company and incremental in the mature company. He filed a very similar number of patents in both companies.

P17 felt creative in both companies. However, he felt his creativity was more radical in the startup company and more incremental in the mature company since it was hard to push radical ideas against organizational inertia in the mature company. In the startup company, creativity meant new products, whereas in the mature company it also meant solving problems creatively, and convincing the company to move in a certain new direction.

P18 felt his ideas were more novel in the startup company because he started with a clean slate there. In contrast, there was an existing framework in the mature company that created resistance to new ideas, thus making his creativity there incremental.

P19 described a limiting environment in the mature company that included existing frameworks and requirements for business justification. However, he felt more creative in the mature company than in the startup company because in the latter he was very involved with tactical "fire fighting" that did not allow him to be strategic and creative.

P20 felt more creative in the mature company where he felt that the management embraced his creative ideas, as radical as they might be. He felt pockets of acceptance for his creativity in the startup company, but those were the exception to the rule, resulting in discouraging his creativity.

Of the 21 cases, 12 participants reported being more creative in the startup company, 2 participants felt more creative in the mature company, and 7 participants felt equally creative in both companies. Table 5 shows that a hypothesis that this sample came from a population in which employees felt equally creative in both of those companies could be rejected ($p < 0.01$). Table 4 shows that they felt more creative in startup companies than in mature ones. The correlation analysis in Table 6 supported the Amabile et al. (1996) or Ekvall (1996) models of organizational and personal antecedents of creativity in most part. As Table 6 shows, based on coding of the narratives in this study, creativity was positively correlated to autonomy (0.474, $p < 0.05$), external challenges (0.596, $p < 0.01$), job satisfaction (0.602, $p < 0.01$), big picture view (0.575, $p < 0.05$), impact on success (0.657, $p < 0.01$), and respect towards the supervisor (0.513, $p < 0.05$). Creativity was negatively correlated to internal challenges (-0.498, $p < 0.05$), and formalization (-0.513, $p < 0.05$). Neither the narratives nor the correlation analysis of the coding suggested a significant correlation between creativity and supervisor support, recognition, or team dynamics. No evidence was also found to support a correlation of experiencing creativity and any of the five attributes reported for participants.

In summary, most participants felt more creative in the startup companies than in the mature companies. They felt that both the novelty and usefulness of their ideas were stronger in the startup company than they were in the mature company. The novelty of their ideas was mostly described as *new to the company*, and often described as *new to the market*, too. Novelty in the startup company was mostly described as a result of starting with a clean slate, whereas the resistance to novelty in the mature company came from existing frameworks and organizational inertia, leading to participants reporting more radical ideas in startup companies and more incremental ideas in the mature companies. The participants described the usefulness of their ideas in terms of whether they were implemented. This was consistent with Oldham and Cummings (1996), who defined usefulness as the willingness of the organization to further develop a creative idea. The participants reported a higher implementation rate of their ideas in the startup company than in the mature company. Few participants described the lower implementation rate as discouraging their future creativity. Some participants offered a metric to creativity in terms of patentability of their ideas (whether they were qualified to be patented) and the eligibility of their ideas to be published in peer reviewed journals and presented in professional conferences. Few participants described the creativity in the startup company as driven by the survival instinct of those companies. Several participants claimed that creativity took place in other settings than the office, where they were less exposed to organizational factors, making creativity more of an individual trait than something that could be affected by the organization. Finally, creativity was shown to occur more in startup companies, and correlated positively to autonomy, external challenges, job satisfaction, big picture view, impact on the success of the company, and respect towards the supervisor, and negatively correlated to internal challenges and formalization.

Autonomy

The second research question in this study was: *How do employees who worked in both startup and mature companies experience the differences in the organizational climate for creativity between the two types of organizations?* To answer this question, the organizational factors were compared across all cases. The first factor, autonomy, is discussed in the following.

All twenty participants in the current study commented on their autonomy in both companies. Fourteen of the participants indicated having more autonomy in the startup company, four experienced more autonomy in the mature company, and three felt they had a similar level of autonomy in both companies.

Founders in startup companies

Founders of startup companies felt different levels of autonomy than regular employees in any company. P1 was one of the founders of the startup company, and as such experienced a high degree of autonomy: "if I said that something was a good idea—that was typically automatically generally accepted". P2, as the CEO of the startup company, felt the board of directors gave him free reign to run the business. P12 felt he had all the autonomy he could have as the founder of a startup that was created based on *his* idea. P16 had a higher level of autonomy in the startup company because he was one of the founders: unless something was outrageous and he needed to get the CEO approval—he had complete freedom.

More autonomy in startup companies

Most non founders experienced more autonomy in the startup company too. P3 explained that since the startup company was low on resources—people were given more autonomy to do what was needed. In the internal startup, P5 felt she had very high autonomy, with her supervisors saying: "just go do something and don't hurt anybody". P13, also working in an internal startup, described having an oversight committee, but with the exception of periodic reviews and the occasional study request from someone—he had full autonomy. That autonomy diminished considerably when the product matured and large customers became involved, causing the management team to begin micro managing the team. This phenomenon is supported by Ray (1987). In the true startup company, P5 felt she had high autonomy for a different reason—nobody there knew how to perform her job. P6 felt his autonomy in the startup company was a function of reliance on him, and his autonomy was kept intact as long as he was aligned with his peers. P8 attributed his freedom to being given a clean slate with no restrictions. P11 felt more autonomy in the startup company because he had the freedom to create the *charter* to which his group would perform.

Less autonomy in mature companies

The participants who experienced more autonomy in the startup company also explained how they experienced less autonomy in the mature companies. P1 felt that when his ideas went against his supervisor in the mature company—they would be overruled. P3 felt that the autonomy in the mature company was limited to doing things "the [mature company]'s way". P7 and P9 felt less autonomy in the mature company because their jobs overlapped with others' ("coactors, as described by Shalley, 1995), and because they had to coordinate their actions with others in the organization. P8 felt that his autonomy in the mature company was restricted by the unwillingness of the company to deviate from "standard operating procedures". P10 highlighted the potential legal exposure to a large company as a limiting factor on what he could do before "getting in trouble". P16 felt that the restrictions on his autonomy came from having four layers of management that needed to be convinced in order to act. P2, P6, and P16 felt that autonomy was mostly limited in their respective mature companies with respect to radical ideas, whereas incremental ideas were much easier to get autonomy for.

More autonomy in mature companies

Few participants experienced more autonomy in the mature companies. To some extent, P1, P6, and P12 felt they had less autonomy in the startup company through the scope of their work—in the startup company everything had to be aligned with the objective of the company, while in the mature company they were allowed to make "side trips" and investigate things not directly aligned with their objectives, and that was where creativity sometimes occurred. P14 felt he had "almost complete autonomy" in the mature company, including the freedom to step outside the established processes. He felt that since the startup company was driven by the marketing and sales group—it limited his autonomy as an engineer. P20 described the mature company as having an entrepreneurial spirit, and experienced high autonomy and accountability for his work style, methods, and prioritization, subject to delivering the ultimate deliverables.

Equal autonomy or unrelated to startup vs. mature

P1 felt that he carved his own autonomy. While natural at the startup company—he sometimes did what he felt was right at the mature company even if his supervisor thought otherwise. P4 felt "extreme autonomy" in both companies, but distinguished between them as *group* autonomy in the startup company and *individual* autonomy in the mature company. P8 felt that autonomy was related to the product development cycle. In the early stages—there was a lot of autonomy to use multiple architectures and be creative, whereas in later stages, especially during the productization stage—there is a narrow range of freedom to do things (supported by Katz, 2004b). Like P1, P17 felt he defined his own autonomy, and behaved as if he "didn't have a boss". He felt that the size of his "sandbox" (as defined by the domain area) was limited in the mature company, but not too much. P18 described limited autonomy due to being a generalist in a very narrow domain area in the startup company, versus being a specialist over a wide domain area in the mature company, but claimed that it was unrelated to the company size. P20 described lower autonomy in the startup, but it was associated with a very narrow job definition and responsibilities, and not with the company size.

Remote site and autonomy

Few participants worked from a remote site, or from their home office. P4 stated, half jokingly, that his autonomy resulted from: "nobody cares where I am". P5, working from a remote site from the company's headquarters in a different country felt that the work was highly directed from the remote headquarters and she had very little autonomy. P7 attributed his feeling of high autonomy in the startup company to working from a remote site in a different state across multiple time zones with little to no supervision, and being in charge of the marketing function, reporting only to the CEO. P15 was a remote employee for both the startup and mature companies, but felt less connected to the business unit in the mature company, thus feeling more autonomy, whereas he received more guidance from the startup company headquarters, thus limiting his autonomy somewhat.

Autonomy—summary

Autonomy was experienced by participants generally in startup companies more than in mature companies. Founders of startup companies felt the ultimate autonomy. Generally, in startup companies there was not a lot of redundancy in resources that caused management to trust employees and give them autonomy. On the other hand, participants experienced more overlap with other employees, unwillingness to deviate from "the way things are done around here", and supervisors who disliked ideas opposite to theirs. Few participants felt that the restrictions on their autonomy came from the narrow scope of their specific job. This happened in both startup and mature companies. Other participants felt that the autonomy they enjoyed in one company and missed in the other was related to the stage of the product development cycle. This position was supported by Abernathy and Utterback (1978) and Katz (2004b). Finally, few participants enjoyed autonomy by working from a remote site or from home, but also described it cynically as "nobody cares where I am".

Table 6 shows correlation of autonomy with creativity (0.474, $p<0.05$), team dynamics (0.461, $p<0.05$), job satisfaction (0.433, $p=0.05$), big picture view (0.493, $p<0.05$), and impact on success (0.501, $p<0.05$). Tables 4 and 5 show that the likelihood that there is a positive link between high autonomy and startup companies coming from a population where such a link does not exist could be rejected ($p<0.05$).

Supervisor and Management Support

In the current study, nine of the eighteen participants who commented on supervisory support and encouragement indicated they received more support from supervisors in the startup company, five indicated receiving more support and encouragement in the mature company, and four indicated no significant difference in supervisory encouragement. Table 5 shows that a hypothesis that this sample was taken from a population where there was no difference between supervisors support in both types of companies could not be rejected. Through the interviews, fifteen participants described the respect they had towards their supervisors. This information was coded too, and the hypothesis that this sample was taken from a population in which the participants respected both supervisors equally could not be rejected either. Not surprising, though, was the high correlation (0.874, $p<0.01$) between the respect that participants had towards their supervisors and the support and encouragement they perceived to have received from them (Table 6). This finding is supported by George and Jing (2007) who claimed that the trustworthiness of the supervisors had direct impact on creativity.

P1 was a technical person, and as such felt respect towards his supervisors in the mature company, who were highly technical themselves, more than he did towards his supervisor in the startup company, who he described as very driven to success, willing to "cut corners", but not technical enough. While his supervisors in the mature company supported his continuing education—his supervisor in the startup company dismissed it. P2 described a strategic relationship with his supervisors in the startup company—the board of directors, who never second guessed him, while his supervisor in the mature company supported his creativity as long as it matched with his own position. P3 respected his supervisor in the startup company, the CEO, and felt he was supportive of him. He attributed troughs in his creativity in the mature company to lack of leadership, and was amazed how quickly a leader could kill creativity. P4 claimed that his supervisors in the startup company *encouraged* his creativity, while his supervisors in the mature company *tolerated* it (Burgelman, 1983, believed that "tolerating creativity" is all that he expected from supervisors in mature companies). He also described that many of the top management decisions in the mature company were done in solitude, and appeared arbitrary, creating an atmosphere of uncertainly and dampened creativity. P5 felt the most support from her supervisor at the internal startup, while she received absolutely no support from her supervisor in the traditional business unit in the mature company. She respected her supervisor in the real startup company technically, called him "very bright and technically competent", but also described him as having very little people management skills. P6, a technical person, respected his supervisor in the startup company both as a technical person and as a quick decision maker. He did not respect his supervisor in the mature company, who was not a technical person. P8 appreciated his supervisor in the mature company as one who promoted him, but lacked technical abilities. He respected his supervisor in the startup company (the CEO) more, as someone who learned very quickly and have an overall technical knowledge in a wide range of topics. P9 respected and appreciated the flexibility that his supervisor in the startup company exhibited more than the one in the mature company. P11 felt that his supervisor in the startup company (the CEO) respected and trusted him, and as a result P11 respected his supervisor. He felt that his supervisors in the mature company did not listen to him, and were very directive towards him, and as a result he felt they were less supportive, and he respected them less. P13 described his supervisors in the internal startup as "enablers", whereas in the mature company he felt more distant communications and less encouragement. Rosenfeld and Servo (1990) also noted this depersonalization that occurs when companies mature. P14 described good relationships with both his supervisors (in the mature and startup companies), but felt more respected and listened too by his supervisor in the mature company, whereas he felt like a "second class citizen" by his supervisor in the startup company. P17 had tremendous respect towards his supervisor in the startup company (the CEO). He considered him a friend, as well as "an amazing marketing person, good sales person, a strategist, and even a decent engineer". He felt he could always talk with him, and felt his supervisor expected him to be creative. He described his supervisor in the mature company as a very busy person, unapproachable, and never felt he was on top of his supervisor's priority list. P20 worked for his supervisor in the mature company in a previous company, and had respect for his capabilities, vision, and wisdom. Even though they were not working together after the sale of the startup company—he still described him as a friend.

The findings in the narrative analysis were supported by the coding analysis in Table 6, which showed a positive correlation between the perceived supervisory support and recognition (0.755, $p < 0.01$), team dynamics (0.601, $p < 0.01$), respect that the participants felt towards the supervisor (0.874, $p < 0.01$), and even job satisfaction (0.508, $p < 0.05$).

In summary, the differences between the supervisory support and encouragement and the respect that different participants felt from and towards their supervisors were not related to whether the company was a startup or a mature one. These factors were situational, and related to the specific supervisors. The perceived support and encouragement from those supervisors was correlated to the respect the participants felt towards their supervisors, though, and to whether they felt they could speak openly with their supervisor, and whether their supervisors actually listened to them. For participants in technical positions, it seemed that the technical competency of the supervisor was an important factor for that respect to exist.

Recognition

The participants in the current study provided several insights into their experiences of recognition and rewards. First, they described three types of recognition: (1) formal recognition systems, established in the company, allowing for the promotion and non-financial rewards for them; (2) informal recognition by peers, supervisors, upper management, and the market; and (3) financial rewards (bonuses or stock grants in mature companies, and stock grants and exits in startup companies). The participants discussed which, if any, of those rewards and recognition were important to them, and whether they experienced some of them in one of the companies more than in the other. Some of the special insights follow.

P1 felt that there was no formal or informal recognition in the startup company, and attributed it to the high expectations from him, believing he could only disappoint, but not really exceed the expectations. P2 and P13 described that due to the distributed nature of accountability and responsibility in the mature company, it was hard to know who to recognize there, leading to a lower overall recognition in the mature company. The recognition could come from any supervisor, and not necessarily the direct supervisor. In fact, some of the participants appreciated the recognition they received from much higher levels of management in the mature company than recognition from their direct supervisor. A few of the participants experienced recognition in the form of exposure to VC firms, tradeshows, senior management in the company, media, and analysts.

Many of the participants described having a formal recognition system only in the mature company, with a formal system of identifying, nominating, and winning awards and promotions there. Some of the participants were positively affected by such recognition, while others were not. P8 described how the formal recognition system was abused by the "buddy system" in the mature company, although he experienced that type of recognition himself. P10 described how "self marketing" needed to be done to win any formal recognition.

Some of the participants enjoyed the immediacy of the financial rewards in the mature companies, while others enjoyed the promise of the future financial rewards from a startup company during an exit event. A few of the participants enjoyed those rewards in the startup companies when they were acquired. P13 felt that he received an "extra special" financial recognition at the internal startup in the mature company for an "extra effort" he made there.

Participants who enjoyed informal recognition were typically those who thought highly of their supervisor, and enjoyed encouragement from their supervisor. Table 6 supports this finding and shows high correlation between experiencing recognition and a supportive supervisor (0.755, $p<0.01$) and between experiencing recognition and respecting the supervisor (0.645, $p<0.01$).

However, in general not all of the participants who enjoyed high recognition felt more creative, and vice versa. Table 6 did not show any correlation between experiencing recognition (of any kind) and experiencing creativity, although it showed a correlation between recognition and job satisfaction (0.477, $p<0.05$). P16 described that even small rewards created pride and satisfaction for him. Only P15 described recognition as a strong motivator for him, although did not link it directly to creativity. Furthermore, Table 5 did not allow rejecting a hypothesis that this sample came from a population where recognition was experienced equally between startup and mature companies. The narrative showed that none of the participants felt very passionately about recognition (or lack thereof) as much as they felt about other factors such as autonomy, their impact on success, etc. Many of the participants cared less about recognition in the startup company, and more about the potential success of the company and future significant rewards in the company. P16 described counting the millions he and the other founders in the startup company will receive upon a successful exit (in the late 1990s), thus completely ignoring immediate recognition.

In summary, all participants felt one type or another of recognition in both companies. Formal recognition was more institutionalized in mature companies than in startup companies. However, prior research showed that extrinsic reward systems promoted conformity and not novelty (Cummings, 1965; Thompson, 1965; Roethlisberger & Dickson, 1939). Participants cared about informal recognition more if they respected their supervisors. Participants cared less about recognition in the startup companies, and much more about potential future financial rewards there.

Challenges

The analysis of the narrative from this study suggested several types of challenges: intellectual/technical challenges, external challenges in the marketplace, and organizational challenges. Amabile et al. (1996) categorized the latter under the title of *organizational impediments to creativity*. However, given that participants referred to those as challenges, they were identified and analyzed as such. The main categorization of challenges in this study was into *external* challenges (including intellectual, technical, and market challenges), and *internal* challenges (organizational impediments to creativity).

All but one of the twenty participants associated *internal* challenges with the mature company. P20 did not experience any internal challenges in the mature company, but experienced poor and disorganized management as a challenge in the startup company. Participants described the internal challenges in the mature company as: getting their ideas implemented (P1, P6, P10, P13, P16, and P19); addressing all internal constituencies (P2, P4, P9, P13, P15, and P19); reaching compromises and alignment between people with conflicting agendas and arrogance (P2, P4, P15, P17, P18, and P19); getting management excited about a new project (P3); working from a remote location and staying connected (P5 and P15); promoting radical ideas and challenging "the way we do it here" and organizational inertia (P5, P8, P11, and P16); identifying the decision makers and process (P7, P9, and P14); conflict between engineering and marketing (P11); slow decision making process (P4, P11, P12, and P19); keeping the team cohesive, intact, motivated, and engaged (P16, P17, and P19); and poor and disorganized management (P20). Table 5 shows that the hypothesis that this sample came from a population that experienced internal challenges equally in startup and mature company can be rejected (p<0.01). Table 4 shows that internal challenges were associated with mature companies. Internal challenges were positively correlated (Table 6) with formalization (1.000, $p < 0.01$), supporting Amabile's (1988) categorization.   Internal challenges were negatively correlated with creativity (-0.498, $p < 0.05$), external challenges (-0.580, $p < 0.01$), team dynamics (-0.661, $p < 0.01$), and big picture view (-1.000, $p < 0.01$).

Participants typically felt more passionate about the external, task related challenges. Sixteen out of twenty participants described experiencing more external challenges in the startup company, two experienced more external challenges in the mature company, and three experienced external challenges equally in both companies. The participants described different types of external challenges in both types of companies: the survival of the company (P1, P3, and P9); building a business from scratch (P2); technological problems (P2, P9, and P17); gaining industry support and market acceptance of the new products (P4, P5, P14, P15, P18, and P20); external fierce competition (P13); available resources and funding (P7, P8, P12, and P14); execution and product delivery (P7, P8, P12, P14, P15, P18, and P20); representing a startup company with no brand name (P9, P15, P16, and P17); or representing a large company with potential exposure (P10).

Table 5 shows that the hypothesis that this sample came from a population that experienced external challenges equally in both types of companies can be rejected ($p < 0.01$), and that external challenges were associated with startup companies more than with mature companies (Table 4).   External challenges were positively correlated (Table 6) with creativity (0.596, $p < 0.01$), big picture view (0.748, $P < 0.01$), and respect towards supervisor (0.539, $P < 0.05$).   It was negatively correlated to internal challenges (-0.580, $p < 0.01$) and formalization (-0.579, $p < 0.01$).

Most participants described the *internal* challenges as unproductive, delaying progress, and a waste of time and energy, while describing the *external* challenges as exciting, interesting, and constructive. P15 described the external challenge as a game that he enjoyed playing.

A few special insights: P4 counted at some point 30 people he had to convince in order to get permission to speak with a customer. P9 associated the technical challenges with the type of technology: the semiconductor industry had order of magnitude higher technical challenges than the much shorter design cycle and capital efficient software industry. P14 associated the technical challenges with the stage in the product design cycle: greater challenges in the early stage, and less challenges in the later productization stage. P3 and P20 described their own need for challenges to stay motivated, and felt that when they lacked challenge—they felt the urge to move on to the next challenge, even if it meant moving to another company.   A few participants described an external challenge carrying a small, unknown company's business card, but stated that the more radical and novel the technology was—the less this was a hurdle.

In summary, participants described two types of challenges: internal challenges and external challenges. Internal challenges were experienced in the mature companies, viewed as hurdles, and could meet Amabile's (1988) definition of *organizational impediments to creativity*. External challenges were task related, viewed positively as motivators, and experienced in startup companies more than in mature companies.

Availability of Resources

The participants in the current study were asked about the availability (or lack thereof) of resources to them and their projects, and how did it impact their creativity. While all participants commented on the *availability* and *quantity* of resources to them and their projects, a few participants also commented on the *quality* of those resources. Of all participants, 16 described having more resources available in the mature company, 2 described having equal availability in the startup and mature companies, and 3 described having more resources available to them in the startup company than in the mature company. As Tables 4 and 5 show—this indicates that more resources were available in mature companies, and there is very low likelihood ($p < 0.01$) that those results would exist in a sample from a population in which there is no difference in the availability of resources between startup and mature companies.

Several of the participants stated that even if resources were not directly available to their projects, it was easy to access them either formally (through changing priorities) or informally (through informal influence). P5 stated: "I had to creatively borrow resources, using other people's people... money,... I had to sell internally". Eventually—she obtained the resources she needed. Few participants commented on a resource allocation prioritization system that was too complex and arbitrary in the mature company, which could not provide the *right* resources when needed.

Even though most participants stated that they had more resources available to them in the mature companies—many of them claimed that they had *enough* resources in the startup company.

An interesting result came from the secondary question: how did the lack of resources affect you? Several of the participants claimed they were *more* creative when resource availability was *low*. P7 described:

> ...you have to be more creative when you have less resources, because you have to do more with less and it kind of spurs the creativity process.

P9, commenting on the same, said:

The more resource constrained you are—the more creative you end up being, and I think, when you have more resources, you come up with maybe less efficient ideas, or maybe more resource intensive ideas, whereas when you know you have a lot more *finite* [italics added to emphasize the limitation and not availability] resources, you typically tend to be more creative.

This indicated the opposite to the Amabile et al. (1996) framework that suggested that high availability of resources enables creativity. The correlation test of resource quantity versus creativity could not reject the null hypothesis that there is no correlation between the two. However, the Pearson Correlation factor was negative (-0.401), although with insufficient statistical significance (p=0.072). There is a possibility that with a larger, more representative sample this correlation could be demonstrated with sufficient statistical significance.

P14 distinguished the availability of resources that already existed in the company from resources that needed to be acquired externally. While access to *existing* resources was abundant in the mature company, it was easier to acquire *external* resources in the startup company in comparison.

P12 claimed that due to the focus of the startup company he had more resources available to him in the startup company than in the mature company. P4 worked in a well funded startup company, and did not feel any resource shortage there, compared to the mature company that acquired his startup company. P15 described:

> ...the bigger the organization got, the more dispersed it became, the more political it became, the less I saw the ability for the team and our business to find the resources necessary to achieve its objectives.

P17 described "fierce competition" for resources at the mature company. Although the company had a higher absolute resource quantity—their availability to his projects was very limited.

Four participants commented on resource *quality*, and not only quantity and availability. P4 described a lot of "recycling" of human resources in the mature company, moving people who have not done well in one position into another. P13 described high average resource quality and low resource quality variability in the internal startup, contrasted with low average quality and high variability in resource quality in the traditional business unit in the mature company. He claimed that similar projects took 10 times as many resources and longer time in the traditional business unit compared to the internal startup for that reason. P14 was surprised to see that the quality of the engineering team in the mature company was lower than that in the startup company. Finally, P19 worked with the same team in the startup company and the mature company (post acquisition), but described the team as gaining maturity and experience with time, thus being a higher quality team in the mature company compared to the startup company.

In general, the resources discussed by the participants included the "standard" list identified in prior literature (people, time, funding, equipment, and facilities). A few participants added new resources that were important to them: management mindshare, multi-disciplinary knowledge and expertise, and the ability of the company to influence other companies, markets, and the government.

In summary, most participants claimed they had higher resource availability in mature companies compared to the startup companies, although most of those described having *enough* resources in the startup company, and some of them described lack of resources as a stimulus for creativity, and a few participants described having higher quality and more effective resources in the startup company, and described being able to do more with less in the startup company.

Team Dynamics

Prior research summarized in the literature review showed that several elements of team dynamics affected individual creativity of team members the most, including conflict and debate, internal competition, trust and openness, and internal communications. In the current study, the participants were asked to describe the team dynamics in both companies (startup and mature), and were probed to specifically address conflict and debate, internal competition, trust and openness, and internal communications if they did not bring those factors unsolicited. In general, according to the narrative and supported by the *t* test results (Tables 4 and 5) the participants experienced more positive team dynamics in the startup companies (p<0.01).

P1 hated to work alone, and thus ranked team dynamics high on his priorities. He developed strong personal relationships with team members in the startup company, but never felt he had personal friendships with team members in the mature company. He described lower trust, less open communication, and higher internal competition and negative personal conflicts. He described task related debates at the same level in both companies.

P2, P6, P7, P9, and P15 described the collocation of the team in the startup company as a stimulus for the team to gel quickly, whereas their respective teams in the mature company were geographically distributed across several countries, and cultural differences caused internal competition. In general, P2 felt more internal competition in the mature company because team members wanted to get promoted more than they wanted to see the team succeed.

P3 experienced strong, trusting relationships with good balance in a consistent manner in the startup company. The constant churn in the mature company did not allow trust to be built. P4 had close relationships with the team in the startup company, and as a result had team members support him when he travelled to different countries, even if this was during unreasonable hours for them. He felt that the lack of such friendships in the mature company reduced his motivation. While he stayed away from internal competition—he noticed it in others, causing him to prefer to work from a remote location. P5 described lifelong relationships that were created at the internal startup, where all team members were working towards a similar goal and filling multiple roles. She portrayed an atmosphere of openness, where ideas were debated openly and without fear. She described a cutthroat atmosphere in the traditional business unit in the mature company, mainly due to constant churn that did not allow trust to emerge.

P6 described very open debate of ideas in the startup company, resulting from trust and lack of fear or competition. P7 describe the internal competition in the mature company as "a bunch of people trying to pull themselves out of the pack and get recognition so they can move up the organization". It took him a while to earn their trust. However, when they all left as a team to create the startup company—the trust and experience working together helped create very strong and positive team dynamics. He also described ideological debates in the mature company, based on different technical approaches, but not in a positive way: people were entrenched in their positions, turning ideological debate into personal conflict.

P8 described the open communications in the startup company as resulting *from* the view of the big picture that everybody shared. Although P9 developed stronger personal relationships in the mature company—he still felt the internal competition to get promoted stronger there, which reduced trust. He described the startup company as "too small for politics".

P10 described a high level of political correctness in the mature company that prevented open debate, and slowed progress. Given the size of the mature company he could not earn the trust of everyone he needed to interact with. At the same time, he could not trust everyone because people had conflicting priorities, whereas in the startup company everyone had the same objective.

P11 described the dynamics in the mature company as one of constant conflict. He experienced people stabbing each other in the back just "to get ahead of the pack." In the startup company, he described open communications, idea sharing, listening to different perspective, and benefiting from the diversity of experiences of the different team members. He felt that open debate was restricted in the mature company by senior management. He claimed that his senior management defined teamwork as "agreeing with the boss" and nothing more. If you did not agree with your supervisor—you were not a team player.

P12 explained the lack of competition in the startup company due to the team working together for 10 years, and there was nowhere to get promoted to. He experienced good team dynamics in the mature company simply because the team members were autonomous and worked on individual projects, limiting the interactions between them for better or worse. He did not feel that the team was working together towards the same goal in the mature company.

P13 felt that as the team grew in the mature company, individual members were striving for power, and achieving it by saying "no" to requests from other team members. This was supported by Emerson's (1962, 1964) theory of power in organizations: individuals gain power through controlling resources others depend on. His story is also supported by Ray (1987) who described that as the organization grows—individual commitment to the shared objective is diluted. P13 knew every team member in the internal startup group intimately, and felt bad that as the team grew into a traditional business unit—he did not know everyone by name anymore.

P14 described "massive political conflict" at the management level of the mature company, mainly between different businesses, competing for resources and mindshare. He did not experience that at the startup company, where he felt everyone was working towards the same goal. However, he felt the classical marketing-engineering conflict over direction.

P15 felt comparable levels of communications he had from a remote site with the rest of the teams in the startup and mature companies. However, where he felt the communication in the startup company was productive—he felt that in the mature company he had "communication without action", and discounted that type of communication. Even though both teams were globally distributed, P15 felt that working towards the same goal bridged geographical and cultural differences in the startup company, whereas the geographical-cultural differences caused conflicts and internal competition in the mature company.

P16 compared the teams' level of commitment and felt that the team in the mature company was committed to achieving the individual objectives associated with individual rewards and nothing more, whereas in the startup company he felt that all team members were committed to the company's success. He experienced stronger personal relationships in the startup company that resulted from "brothers in arms" environment, fighting to achieve the same goals.

P17 did not describe intra-team competition, but experienced very strong cross-team competition over resources, to the point of challenging the existence of his team, which was very detrimental to the business. He emphasized the ideological debates in the startup company as driving towards company success, and the lack of interpersonal conflicts and competition there. P18 worked with several different teams within the mature company, and described them as very different from one another, attributing team dynamics to specific teams and personalities of team members, rather than to the startup or mature nature of the company.

P19 joined the mature company through the acquisition of the startup company he worked in. The team remained intact, and he described improved team dynamics and mainly trust, in the mature company. He attributed that to the maturity of the team, the increased experience and competency of team members, and to trust that was built over time. He described a small level of competition over promotions, since there were many more opportunities to get promoted in the mature company.

P20 loved the team he worked with in the mature company. This was a result of the appreciation he had for the team member competencies. He described them as:

> These are all virtually, across the board, really great people, really bright, really motivated, kind of like the all-star team, and you wonder: how did I get so lucky to have such a great group of work colleagues.

He felt he created many personal friendships in the mature company, and enjoyed a lot of trust. More than all—he felt that everyone was working towards the same goal.

In summary, participants described trust as the central piece affecting team dynamics. This concept is illustrated by Figure 6. Trust was positively affected (full arrows and white boxes) by personal friendships, time the team spent together, and perceived competencies of team members, and negatively affected (dashed arrows and grey boxes) by constant churn and geographical distribution and cultural differences. The existence of trust allowed open communications and open (and "safe") debate of ideas, whereas the lack of trust caused internal competition and conflicts.

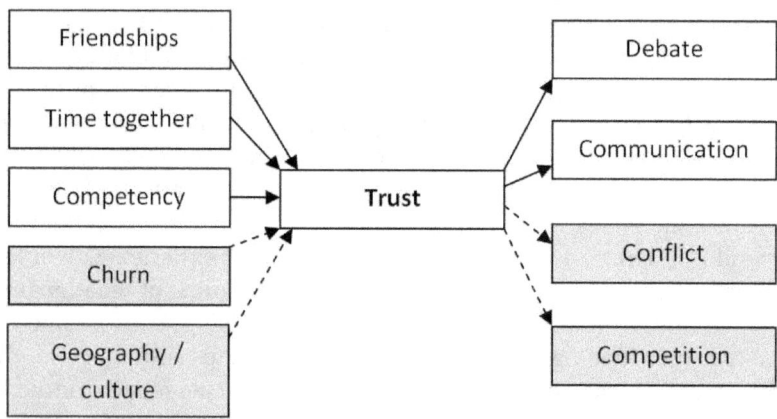

Figure 6 – Team dynamics around trust.

Internal competition was described by the participants almost as a unique factor to mature companies, and explained as follows: in the startup companies, there was nothing to compete for. The probability for promotion was minimal due to the flat organization. However, employees of the startup companies had the ability to significantly affect the success of their companies and, in return, be affected by it (financially, among other effects), and therefore there was no reason for internal competition. In the mature companies, in contrast, the likelihood of a significant impact on the success of the companies was minimal, but there were many positions in a not-so-flat organization to compete over. Table 6 shows that positive team dynamics was positively correlated to autonomy (0.461, p<0.05), supervisory support

(0.601, p<0.01), job satisfaction (0.534, p<0.05), big picture view (0.809, p<0.01), and respect towards the supervisor (0.608, p<0.05), and negatively correlated to internal challenges (-0.661, p<0.01), and to formalization (-0.700, p<0.01).

Formalization, Bureaucracy, and Processes

In the current study, challenge and formalization were treated as two independent factors. The *challenges* factor was further broken into *internal* and external *challenges*. The analysis of the narrative in this study supports the Amabile et al. (1996) categorization: only the *external* challenges met Amabile's definition of *challenges*, while *internal* challenges and formalization met Amabile's definition of *organizational impediments*. Table 6 shows a near perfect correlation (1.000, p<0.01) between formalization and internal challenges. Of the 20 cases, 19 participants experienced higher formalization in the mature company, and only 1 participant reported higher formalization in the startup company. Tables 4 and 5 show that the likelihood that this sample was taken from a population that experienced formalization equally in startup and mature companies can be rejected (p<0.01). However, the analysis of the narrative in this study provided some additional insights on formalization.

P1 accepted the fact that the mature company required more formalization and processes, as it was a large and complex organization. He felt that the processes were cumbersome, and did not stop his creativity, but rather the implementation of his creative ideas. He attributed the lack of formalization in the startup company to the immaturity of the founders. P2 felt that the processes in the startup company were optimized to the single project that the company worked on, whereas the processes in the mature company were generic, attempting to address all possible projects, and thus far from optimized to any specific project. He felt that the processes slowed progress. P3 felt that the processes in the mature company were required for the coordination of many constituencies in the company that had different priorities. P4 described the creation of processes in the startup company, which was less obtrusive to his creativity than the existing processes in the mature company. He, too, accepted the need for processes in the mature company to support the complex coordination, although claimed it delayed decision making significantly. P6 gave specific examples of how the bureaucracy in the mature company reduced his motivation and prevented promotions. P7 experienced mixed emotions towards the processes in the mature company. On one hand, they slowed decision making, but on the other hand—they allowed him to identify potential problems early on and avoid them. P8 participated in the creation of processes in the startup company, and described how those processes were developed by people with experience from mature companies who could choose the best processes to implement. P9 felt he wasted a lot of time in meetings required by the formalization of the mature company. He also described little need for process when people had a big picture view. P10 similarly connected personal accountability to lower need for formalization in the startup company. P11 described how the lack of processes in the startup company caused people to go beyond their official job title and perform whatever was required to get the job done. P13 transitioned from the internal startup to the larger business unit within the same mature company, and was required to comply with the same processes. However, he claimed that the big picture view and the level of autonomy he enjoyed at the internal startup allowed him to "cut corners" in complying with the process, whereas in the traditional business unit the same process was implemented to the letter, and sometimes slowed progress arbitrarily, mainly due to the amount of people that were required to participate in alignment steps in the process. P15 described the tradeoff between longer development time to a "perfect" product through process compliance, and shorter development time to a "good enough" product through skipping process steps consciously. P17 described that some elements of the mature company processes had to be implemented in the startup company, to prevent complete chaos. P20 was the only participant who experienced less formalization in the mature company compared with the startup company. He attributed the loose formalization to the high caliber and professionalism of the people in the mature company, who did not need processes to do the right thing, and had a big picture view of the entire project, whereas in the startup company, he saw more junior people who needed processes to guide them.

Table 6 shows that formalization was positively correlated only with internal challenges (1.000, $p<0.01$). Both were later treated as a single factor, aligned with Amabile's (1998) *organizational impediments* factor. Formalization was negatively correlated to creativity (-0.513, $p<0.05$), external challenges (-0.579, $p<0.01$), positive team dynamics (-0.700, $p<0.01$) and, as described by a few participants—big picture view (-1.000, $p<0.01$).

In summary, almost all participants experienced higher formalization and bureaucracy in the mature company, compared with the startup company. Most of them accepted the fact as "the nature of the beast"— accepting that large and complex companies involved with multiple projects require processes to succeed. Dougherty and Hardy (1996) explained that large companies must have multiple projects to grow. However, the participants also claimed that the high formalization caused delays in decision making and progress, and had a negative impact on their motivation. The participants described the processes in the startup companies as optimized for the single project those companies worked on, as opposed to the "generic" processes in the large companies that were not as efficient and optimized to individual projects. A big part of the negative consequences of high formalization was the need to coordinate and align multiple constituencies with different agendas in the organization. Some of the participants described their ability to bypass the processes, when needed, and especially in an environment of high performance teams and high autonomy. Finally, participants described that when they had a good view of the entire project (big picture view)—they did not need to rely on processes as much.

Job Satisfaction

The third research question in this study was: *How do employees who worked in both startup and mature companies experience the differences in their personal context between the two types of organizations?* The following sections analyze the personal context factors across all cases, stating with job satisfaction.

Many researchers claimed that job *satisfaction* leads to creativity, suggesting that happy employees are more creative (Ekvall, 1996; Isaksen & Lauer, 1999; Pierce & Delbecq, 1977; Roethlisberger & Dickson, 1939; Turnipseed, 1994). Therefore, participants in the current study were asked whether they were satisfied with their jobs in both companies, and whether they were more satisfied with one company over the other. Thirteen participants experienced higher job satisfaction in the startup companies, while four experienced higher job satisfaction in the mature companies, and four participants experienced equal job satisfaction in both types of companies. Table 5 shows that the likelihood that this sample was taken from a population where job satisfaction was experienced equally in both types of companies can be rejected ($p < 0.05$), and Table 4 shows that job satisfaction was experienced in this sample more in startup companies than in mature companies. Beyond being asked *where* did participants experience higher job satisfaction, they were asked *how* did they experience job satisfaction, and *why* did they experience higher (or lower) job satisfaction.

There were many reasons why participants felt more satisfied in the startup companies. P2 was satisfied because of the impact he had on the company's success, building something new, and making a difference. P4 described his experience in the startup company as "the peak experience of my career", driven by teamwork, autonomy challenging the boundaries, rich and meaningful interaction with management, constant learning, filling multiple roles, and ownership and impact on the outcome. P5 described the internal startup as a fun place to work in, because she experienced creativity, informal recognition, and the "bleeding edge technology". P6 attributed his satisfaction to the ability to focus on external challenges that increased shareholder value. P8 was more satisfied in the startup company because of the talented people he worked with, and working with them towards the same goal—the success of the company. P9 felt more satisfied in the startup company due to experiencing more excitement, and feeling his efforts were rewarded better there. P11 was more satisfied in the startup company because of the interaction he had with the board of directors, his involvement in decision making, the external selling, and the impact he made on the company. As a founder, P12 was more satisfied in the startup company because the company was built to implement his idea. P13 described his satisfaction at the internal startup as:

> [Those were] the best days. It was frantic, it was fun, and it was challenging, whatever, but everybody was sort of on the same page, everybody was fighting the same cause, and it goes a long way.

P14 enjoyed having the opportunity to create something new that did not exist before, starting from scratch. P16, too, felt satisfaction because he was building something from nothing, but also because of the potential financial payout to himself when the company goes through an IPO, or gets acquired. P17 was more satisfied in the startup company because he felt he had an impact on the company. The participants who experienced high job satisfaction in the startup company described not minding working 12 or more hours a day. P4, P12, and P16 decided, unsolicited, to measure their satisfaction on a scale, describing the ratio between their satisfaction in the startup company to their satisfaction in the mature company as ten to one (all three participants).

P2 felt less satisfied in the mature company because he spent more time "feeding the internal machine", activity he saw little value add in. P6 echoed that, and felt that he spent a lot of energy on internal challenges that were unproductive. P3 experienced more anxiety and "baggage" that made him feel less satisfied in the mature company. P4 felt less satisfied in the mature company because his role was very narrowly defined, and he did not have an impact on the outcome. P7 enjoyed the dynamic environment in the mature company, but when his role became more operational and routine—he became increasingly less satisfied and eventually left. P8 felt his work in the mature company was sometimes mechanical and boring, leading to lower satisfaction. P11 felt he spent a lot of unnecessary time on developing use cases, scenarios, plans, and recommendations for his management, but was not invited to participate in the decision making, thus having less impact on the results, and lower job satisfaction. P12, too, complained about his inability to participate in decision making in the mature company. P13 was less satisfied in the traditional business unit in the mature company because of the internal competition for power, and people's agendas that were not aligned. He also felt he did not have any impact on the results anymore. P14 was less satisfied in the mature company, but only because his was working on a product at a much more mature stage, in which his work was less interesting. P17 claimed that in the mature company "whatever you do will not move the needle", explaining his lower satisfaction there. Capozzi and Chakravorti (2006) explained that large companies must be engaged in large markets and multiple innovation projects to grow, thus making the impact of each project relatively small, causing the described dissatisfaction.

Few participants experienced higher job satisfaction in the mature companies. P3 "enjoys the finer things in life", and thus the financial rewards in the mature company made him feel satisfied. P5 felt less satisfied in the startup company due to the lack of leadership, whereas she felt a strong and supportive leader, fun technology, and team bonds in the internal startup in the mature company that made her feel more satisfied with her job. P15 attributed his higher satisfaction in the mature company to the higher impact he had on the outcome, and the pervasiveness of the technology he evangelized in the marketplace. P18 felt more satisfied in the mature company because of the weight it had in the industry to support his activity. P19 was more satisfied in the mature company because it was more professional, he had more resources that allowed him to work on more strategic and creative activities, he felt compensated in a way that reflected his contribution, he enjoyed the success of his product line, and the exposure he received inside and outside the company. Finally, P20 described being much more satisfied in the mature company. He was very passionate when he spoke about his experiences in that company. He enjoyed working with "the best and brightest", felt strong team camaraderie there, and the impact on the success of the company, and liked his product.

Few participants felt equally satisfied in both companies. P1 believed he was a happy person by nature, and therefore was as satisfied with his job at both the startup and the mature company. He experienced high and low points in both companies. P10 felt that the environment in both companies was dynamic, and felt empowered in both of them, leading to experiencing equal job satisfaction.

In summary, different reasons were cited by participants for why were they more (or less) satisfied with their work in the startup company versus the mature company. Table 6 shows that job satisfaction was positively correlated to creativity (0.609, p<0.01), autonomy (0.433, p=0.05), supervisor encouragement (0.508, p<0.05), recognition (0.477, p<0.05), positive team dynamics (0.534, p<0.05), big picture view (0.575, p<0.05), impact on success (0.815, p<0.01), and respect towards supervisor (0.661, p<0.01). Table 6 also shows the only correlation between a creativity environment factor and one of the attributes of the participants: job satisfaction was correlated to the position the participants held in the company (0.443, p<.05). As Table 7 shows, technical people were more satisfied in startup companies, whereas business people were satisfied in both types of companies.

Table 7 – Cross Tabulation of Job Satisfaction and Position
Job Satisfaction * Position Crosstabulation

			Position		Total
			Business	Technical	
Job Satisfaction	Higher in mature	Count	4	0	4
		% within Position	30.8%	.0%	19.0%
	Equal	Count	3	1	4
		% within Position	23.1%	12.5%	19.0%
	Higher at startup	Count	6	7	13
		% within Position	46.2%	87.5%	61.9%
Total		Count	13	8	21
		% within Position	100.0%	100.0%	100.0%

Two *t* tests were performed. The hypothesis that the sample of *business* people taken from a population where job satisfaction was experienced equally in startup and mature companies could not be rejected. The hypothesis that the sample of *technical* people was taken from a population where job satisfaction was experienced equally in startup and mature companies was rejected ($p<0.01$), concluding that technical people experienced job satisfaction in startup companies more than they had in mature companies.

Mood and Affect

Only 12 participants in the current study discussed their mood and emotions when they worked in the startup or the mature companies. None of those participants could tell a difference in their mood that was related to things outside of work, and thus could not provide insight on how non-work related mood could affect their creativity. Several of the participants described how their family situation has changed over time, which could have affected their mood, although they did not experience immediate effects. Those changes were completely unrelated to whether they worked for a startup company or a mature company, but rather natural changes over time, creating differences between the *first* company they worked for and the *second* company they worked for. Several of them got married between the different companies, or added children to their family, changing the family dynamics, which might have had some impact on their mood, although they could not identify such impact. Some moved to different states or countries, and one had family health issues. Most of the participants described those family changes as cyclical and equal on average, leading to no significant difference between the two companies.

A few participants (P7, P18, and P19) noticed their own maturity increasing and hypothesized how it could have affected their mood, although they did not provide any specifics to significant differences in mood.

Most participants could not separate their personal mood from their work. The effect that their work had on their mood was very strong. P2 experienced more fear, anxiety, optimism and happiness when he worked for the startup company, compared to comfort, safety, and cynicism when he worked for the mature company. P3 felt constant levels of anxiety at the startup company, versus ups and downs in the level of anxiety at the mature company. This finding was supported by George and Jing's (2007) theory of "mood as information". P4 was euphoric at the startup company and bored at the mature company. P9 felt severe impact when he worked in the startup, and isolation when he worked in the mature company. P13 felt a link with another factor: support from home. When he was more satisfied at work, he was happier, and when he was happier—he received more support from his family. P19 felt the impact of his workload on his mood: when the workload was lighter—he was happier.

Amabile et al. (2005) observed a reciprocal relationship between creativity and mood, where creativity could affect mood, and not only the other way around, supporting the findings of the current study. The conclusion from the literature review was that mood is a factor external to the organization that *may* affect individual creativity, and therefore it was one of the factors considered for comparison in this study. However, the conclusion from this study is that mood was not a factor that varied significantly between startup companies and mature companies. Table 5 supports this conclusion and shows that a null hypothesis that mood was not related to the size of company could not be rejected. In answering part of the third research question, employees who worked in both startup and mature companies did not experience differences in their mood between the two types of organizations.

In summary, most participants could not identify differences in their mood between the two companies that were not related to their work, and thus it was hard to establish that it could have affected their creativity. Participants could describe their mood as a result of their overall job satisfaction. They described experiencing feelings such as happiness, anxiety, fear, euphoria, optimism, safety, cynicism, isolation, and even boredom. Those feelings were associated with either company, and could not be linked to either startup companies or mature companies.

Pressure and Support from Home

The participants in the current study were asked about their support and pressure from home, specifically from their families. Most participants claimed that both pressure and support they received from their families were relatively equal when they worked in both companies. Tables 4 and 5 supported that conclusion and showed that the likelihood of this sample coming from a population where the pressure and support from home were equal between the two companies could not be rejected. No correlation was found between those two factors and any other factor, attribute, or experiences of creativity, or even between the two factors themselves. However, the narrative analysis provided a few interesting insights.

Pressure and support resulting from family stage

P1 described the pressure changes as a result of his family stage. When he worked for the mature company, his wife worked too, and they had no children. However, when his wife stopped working and their children were born—he felt more pressure to be home more. There was some anticipation for potential financial rewards from the startup company that led to slightly more support in the startup company—anticipation that did not exist when he worked in the mature company. P10 was not married when he worked in either company, and described how his own maturity helped him be more considerate and less selfish later, although describing no difference in the support or pressure he received. P13 and P18 described no difference in the support of their growing families, but self imposed travel restrictions to spend more time with their families—resulting in that constant level of support.

Pressure and support resulting from happiness of employee

P2 reported a similar situation, but emphasized that the higher support in the startup company was a result of him being happier, and his family wanted to keep him that way. P3's wife's support, similarly, was a function of his happiness, and he also described that his family was more understanding of the survival nature of the startup company. P6 described the support he received as mainly a function of his happiness, and less as a function of working hours, financial rewards, or job security. P7 described the support in his wife's words:

> When you're happier, you're more pleasant when you're home [laugh], and when you're busy, you're happy, and so, I'd rather have you happier less time than unhappy but here every day.

He, in turn, was considerate of her feelings and the impact his work might have on her, and as a result secured her continuous support. P9 felt that his family's support was a function of his happiness at work, which translated into happiness at home. He experienced pressure from his wife to move on to another company when he was stressed and unhappy. He felt pressure to be home and to spend time with the family after he got married and had children, but stated that this pressure originated with him and not the family. P19's wife's support was higher in the mature company, mainly because he had time to take better care of his health, even though he was traveling more there. Finally, P20 received relatively equal support from his family. His wife was concerned when he was about to leave the stability of the mature company, especially since he was very happy there, and she was concerned with the instability of the startup company, when it was about to run out of money. However, neither of those translated into significant differences in the support or pressure that P20 experienced.

Pressure and support resulting from travel and working hours

P4 experienced pressure from his family when he worked in the startup company due to working during weekends, but at the same time experienced support from the family due to the expected payoff. P11 did not feel more pressure when he worked in the startup company, even though he was commuting to a different state. He assured this by making sure he attended important family functions, took vacations, and spent the holiday season with his family. P12 was traveling much more in the startup company than in the mature company, and could be gone for three weeks at the time. However, he felt that his family got used to the new situation, and were more supportive at the startup company because they saw him happier, realizing his potential, and potentially getting financially rewarded when the startup company succeeds. P14 worked very long hours at the startup company, and felt little pressure from his family for it. P17 was working from home at the startup company, and felt more support from his family because he was more relaxed, less stressed, and was more flexible with his time.

Pressure and support resulting from social relationships

P8 and his family had a social relationship with other families in the startup company, which helped gain more family support there. While his family situation evolved (children were born)—they found ways to balance the family such that it will not induce new pressure.

Pressure and support resulting from the product

P5 received slightly more support from her children when she equipped them with the "cool" products she worked on.

In summary, the support and pressure from home were relatively equal when the participants worked at the startup and the mature companies. The support was mainly a function of the participant's happiness. Since it could not be rejected that the participants' happiness was not related to the size of the company—family support was not considered a function of the size of the company. The support and pressure from home were also related to the stage of the family, number of children, whether the wife worked or not, and even whether the company's products were "cool" or not. The family's involvement with the company (knowing the products, knowing the team, having a social relationship with other families on the team) helped getting family support, regardless of the specific company. In most cases, the participants described the two-way relationship between the support they received from home, and their own balance of home and work, and supporting their family. The participants themselves took action to assure keeping the level of family support, and reducing the level of family pressure. There were slight elements of understanding of the involvement required in the startup company, and the anticipation of the potential rewards there, as well as an expectation of working shorter hours in the mature company. However, those elements were not strong enough to lead to the conclusion that home pressure and support were related to company size.

Dynamism and Involvement

Isaksen et al. (2000) conducted factor analysis of the Creative Climate Questionnaire (CCQ) and as a result eliminated the dynamism factor that was part of it when they developed the Situational Outlook Questionnaire (SOQ) since "the dynamism dimension fell on the challenge factor" (p. 180). As a result, this factor was not included originally in the current study design. However, many of the participants in this study experienced elements of dynamism and other involvement characteristics that warranted bringing back this factor into the analysis. Their descriptions did not separate environmental dynamism factors from individual involvement factors, so those were treated together. Ekvall (1996) defined dynamism as:

> The eventfulness of life in the organization. In the highly dynamic situation, new things are happening all the time and alterations between ways of thinking about and handling issues often occur. There is a kind of psychological turbulence which is described by people in those organizations as "full speed", "go", "breakneck", "maelstrom", and the like. The opposite situation could be compared to a slow jog-trot with no surprises. There are no new projects; no different plans. Everything goes its usual way. (p. 107)

Through the interviews, seven elements of dynamism and involvement were described by participants: (1) diversity, (2) ability to see the "big picture", (3) individual impact on success of the company, (4) "loving" the product, (5) filling multiple roles and participating in multiple projects, (6) a clean slate, and (7) taking risk.

Diversity

Amabile (1988) described diverse experience as an individual factor contributing to creativity. Anderson et al. (2004) described heterogeneity and education level as workgroup factor affecting creativity. Devanna and Tichy (1990) claimed that innovation depends on professional and diverse expertise. Isaksen and Lauer (2002) found in the narrative part of their research that diversity of skills and experience enhanced creativity. Khan and Manopichetwattana (1989) found that a dynamic and heterogeneous environment positively affects innovation. Mauzy and Harriman (2003) found that knowing only one discipline is a hindrance to creativity. Skarzynski and Gibson (2008) claimed that maximizing diversity of thinking is one of three preconditions for radical innovation.

In this study, P1 described interactions with other people in other projects in the mature company as fertilizing, and described examples where such interactions led to creativity. This was supported by Basset-Jones (2005). P2 described the availability of resources with diverse expertise as supporting his creativity in the mature company. P11 was exposed to people from different teams and different discipline in the startup company, as well as people from many different other companies, backgrounds, and experiences, whereas he felt that the people in the mature company "fitted a mold" and reduced diversity.

Big picture

Seventeen participants described their ability to view the "big picture"— all aspects of the project they were working on, as important to their creativity. P2 stated that the ability to view the big pictures in the startup company contributed to the team's open communications. P8 described the opposite relationship: his team's open communication allowed them to see the big picture and address future issues before they occurred. P9 described how the view of the big picture by everyone in the startup company eliminated the need for complex processes, which were required once the company grew beyond 50 employees that could not see the big picture anymore. P13 felt that a big part of the team involvement in the internal startup was due to their ability to see the big picture and to understand the customer development process. Table 4 showed that 16 out of 17 participants associated their ability to view the big picture with the startup company, and Tables 4 and 5 show that the likelihood this result came from a population that does not attribute big picture visibility with startup company could be rejected ($p<0.01$). Table 6 demonstrated that the big picture factor was positively correlated with creativity (0.575 with $p<0.05$), autonomy (0.493 with $p<0.05$), external challenges (0.748 with $p<0.01$), positive team dynamics (0.809 with $p<0.01$), job satisfaction (0.575 with $p<0.05$), and respect towards supervisor (0.636, $p<0.05$). The big picture factor was negatively correlated with internal challenges (-1.000 with $p<0.01$) and formalization (-1.000 with $p<0.01$). In summary, the ability to see the big picture was associated with startup companies, with creativity, and interacted positively with some of the positive factors affecting creativity, and negatively with some of the negative factors affecting creativity.

Impact on success

Nineteen participants identified the impact *they felt they had* on the success of the company or the project as a factor affecting their creativity, or other factors such as job satisfaction. Fifteen of them experienced having more impact on the success of the startup company than on the success of the mature company. Three of them felt their impact on success was similar in both companies, and only one described having more impact on the mature company's success than on the startup company's success. P12 felt he saw immediate impact in the startup company versus never making an impact on the mature company's products. P7 felt that recognition in the mature company was more important because there was so little impact on the company success. P15 described the impact of his work on the company as all the recognition he needed. He was the only participant who experienced having a bigger impact in the mature company than in the startup company. P18, on the other hand, claimed that he received recognition as a result of the visibility of his impact on the company. This ambivalent relationship between the impact that participants experienced and the recognition they received was supported by the fact that the correlation testing in Table 6 shows no statistically significant relationship between the impact on success factor and the recognition factor. P11 felt a relationship between the organizational dependence on him, measured by the impact he had on the company, and the autonomy he experienced there. This finding is supported by Table 6, showing a positive correlation of 0.501 ($p<0.05$) between impact and autonomy. P2 and P13 experienced higher job satisfaction when they felt they had a bigger impact on the company success. This too was supported by Table 6, showing a positive correlation of 0.815 ($p<0.01$) between impact and job satisfaction. Finally, most of the participants experienced having higher impact on the company success in the same environment where they experienced higher creativity. Table 6 shows a high correlation of 0.657 ($p<0.01$) between impact and creativity.

Love the product

After the startup company was acquired by the mature company, P4 realized he was communicating over email with a colleague at 1AM. He then realized that they both felt more than an impact on the company—they felt an impact on society with a product that improved quality of life and safety for many people. P6 described loving what he was doing and the product they were developing in the startup company. He was disappointed when his general manager and supervisor in the mature company told him: "don't fall in love with the product". He considered this a distancing comment. Rosenfeld and Servo (1990) described this phenomenon: "As size increases, there is a tendency towards greater depersonalization" (p. 251). Finally, P5 described how proud she (and her family) was of the products she was responsible for. Only few participants described such feelings towards the products—not enough to establish a statistically meaningful relationship with creativity or with a startup versus a mature company. P20, too, described the good that his product brought to the marketplace, and was proud of that.

Multiple roles and projects

Several participants described filling multiple roles in the startup company and working on multiple projects. P1, a technical person, described working as a development engineer, a technical support person, and even described installing a wireless system on antenna towers. P8, too, described filling multiple roles at the same time in the startup company, and filling multiple roles over a period of time (not simultaneously) in the mature company. He described learning a lot from those different roles. P10 described wearing "different hats" in the startup company, as a result of a more dynamic environment where everyone had to fill multiple roles. P18 felt he filled many more roles in the startup company than in the mature company, including taking out the trash, when needed. He did not feel that was a degrading job, but rather doing his part. P1 also described working on multiple different projects in the mature company, which made him feel that the environment there was very dynamic and less monotonous for him, as well as challenging and stimulating.

Clean slate

Five participants described the environment in the startup company or the internal startup in the mature company as forcing them to start working on a project with a clean slate, or a blank sheet of paper. P2 felt he was more creative in the startup company because he was starting with a clean slate with no prior history, image, conservatism, or business approach. P8 felt that the clean slate approach in the startup company allowed him to try new things, and experienced a higher degree of autonomy as a result. P9 felt his ideas were more novel and radical in the startup company because he started with a clean slate: "you're really starting with a blank board, or a white sheet of paper here at [the startup company], and that allows for creativity on a daily basis." P11 also felt that starting with a clean slate, with no need to conform to rules, policies, procedures, or "anti-innovation" culture allowed his ideas to be more novel. In summary, some of the participants felt that their ability to start with a clean slate and no "baggage" in the startup company (compared with the mature one) allowed them to be more creative, whereas some of them claimed that it caused their creative ideas to be more novel and radical.

Risk taking

Risk taking was one of the factors included in the CCQ creativity culture survey (Ekvall, 1996), independent from dynamism, and later in the SOQ survey (Isaksen et al., 2000). Ekvall (1996) described it as:

> The tolerance of uncertainty in the organization. In the high risk-taking case, decisions and actions are prompt and rapid, arising opportunities are taken and concrete experimentation is preferred to detailed investigation and analysis (p. 108).

Five participants in the current study discussed risk taking. P1 described being expected to take risks at the startup company, while "taking a beating" for taking risk in the mature company. P2 claimed that high differentiation projects always involved taking high risk, and were done only at the startup company, whereas the mature company avoided taking such risks, resulting in developing less differentiated products. He further explained that taking a risk was not the goal of the startup company, but rather a result of the objective of creating a highly differentiated product in the market. He also added that the perception of risk is different between the two types of companies. In the mature company, he observed his supervisors considering certain activities as high risk, whereas in reality those would have been considered low risk in the startup company. P2 felt he took less risk himself in the mature company because he perceived that was the amount of risk his supervisor would accept. P10 described willingness in the startup company to assume risk that would not otherwise be accepted in the mature company, just to shorten the time to market and speed the development up. P14 and P20 discussed the personal financial risk he decided to take when he went to work in the startup company.

Dynamism—summary

Ekvall (1996) claimed that dynamism and risk taking were two dimensions that are more important to radical innovation than to incremental innovation. Khan and Manopichetwattana (1989) posited that dynamism and heterogeneous environment are positively affecting innovation. Isaksen and Lauer (1999), using KAI and SOQ/CCQ as instruments, conducted discriminant analysis and showed significant differences for both perceptions of dynamism and risk taking dimensions (in CCQ) between adaptors (incremental innovators) and innovators (radical innovators), and suggested that innovators were driven more by challenge, dynamism, and risk taking. The participants in the current study supported this position. Across the dimensions of diversity, ability to see the "big picture", individual impact on success of the company, "loving" the product, filling multiple roles and participating in multiple projects, starting with a clean slate, and taking risk—they showed that the startup environment was characterized by higher dynamism and individual involvement driving them to be more creative there. The ability to see the big picture and the impact the participants felt they had on the company success was correlated to their experiences of creativity.

Source of Differences other than Startup vs. Mature

The participants described significant differences between their creativity in the two different companies, and the factors affecting creativity. However, the narrative of the interviews showed that there were several different sources that affected those differences in factor intensity, unrelated to whether the company was a mature company or a startup company: (1) the stage in the product life cycle (reported by P3, P14, and P15); (2) personal maturity (reported by P9, P18, and P19); (3) the specific company, regardless of size (reported by P18); (4) the type of technology involved (reported by P9); (5) the participant's personal financial situation (reported by P1); (6) the participant's family stage (reported by P3 and P4); and (7) the overall business cycle (reported by P3).

Summary of Findings

A purposive, theory driven sample of 20 participants who worked in both startup and mature companies at different times was used for this study. Interviews were conducted with participants in business and in technical positions, participants who worked in the startup company first and participants who worked in the mature company first, participants who are still working in the second company and participants who no longer work there, and participants who moved between two related companies (through acquisitions or spin offs) and participants who moved between two unrelated companies. The interviews were conducted in person or over the telephone.

Within case analysis was done, that described each case in detail using the terminology and points of interest in this study (Appendix B). Furthermore, the narrative was coded into the original 11 factors, expanded to 17 factors based on further detail provided in the interviews. This coding was then analyzed using SPSS, and t tests and correlation procedures were performed on the data, which generally supported the conclusions drawn from the narrative analysis.

Cross case analysis was then conducted to summarize themes that emerged from the data, with the support of NVivo8. Twelve themes were analyzed: creativity, autonomy, supervisor, recognition, challenges, resources, team dynamics, formalization, job satisfaction, mood, support and pressure from home, and finally *dynamism and involvement*—a factor that emerged from the data analysis although not considered in the initial conceptual framework. In few cases, different participants worked in the same companies (but not the same pairs of companies), and described different experiences in the same companies. Few participants felt that their case was unique. However, the data analysis showed high consistency in the finding across cases.

Creativity

Most participants felt more creative, and that their ideas were more novel and useful in the startup companies than in the mature companies. Novelty was mostly described as *new to the company*. Novelty in the startup company was a result of starting with a clean slate, whereas the resistance to novelty in the mature company came from existing frameworks and organizational inertia. Participants reported a higher implementation rate (hence—usefulness) of their ideas in the startup company than in the mature company. Some participants measured their creativity by the patentability of their ideas and the eligibility of their ideas to be published academically. Some of the participants described the creativity in the startup company as driven by the survival instinct of those companies. Finally, statistically creativity was shown to occur significantly more in startup companies, and correlated positively to autonomy, external challenges, job satisfaction, big picture view, impact on the success of the company, and respect towards the supervisor, and negatively correlated to internal challenges and formalization.

Autonomy

Autonomy was generally experienced by participants in startup companies more than in matures companies. Participants felt that their autonomy was related to being trusted in the startup company, and lack of freedom was attributed to overlap with other employees, unwillingness to deviate from "the way things are done around here", and supervisors who disliked ideas opposite to theirs in the mature companies. Few participants felt that the scope of their autonomy (or lack thereof) was related to the wide (or narrow) scope of their specific job, or the stage of the product development cycle.

Supervisor

In general, participants felt that the differences between the supervisory support and encouragement were not related to whether the company was a startup or a mature one, but were rather situational, and related to specific supervisors. The perceived support and encouragement from those supervisors was significantly correlated to the respect the participants felt towards their supervisors. For participants in technical positions, it seemed that the technical competency of the supervisor was an important factor.

Recognition

Participants felt that formal recognition was more institutionalized in mature companies than in startup companies, but they cared about informal recognition more if they respected their supervisors. Participants cared less about recognition in the startup companies, and much more about potential future financial rewards there.

Challenges

Participants described two types of challenges: internal and external. Internal challenges were experienced in the mature companies and viewed as hurdles to progress. External challenges were task related, viewed positively as motivators, and experienced in startup companies more than in mature companies.

Resources

Most participants experienced more resource availability in mature companies compared to the startup companies, although most of those described having *enough* resources in the startup company, and some of them described lack of resources as a stimulus for creativity. Few participants described having higher quality and more effective resources in the startup company, and described being able to do more with less.

Team Dynamics

Participants described *trust* as the central piece affecting team dynamics. Trust was positively affected by personal friendships, time the team spent together, and perceived competencies of team members, and negatively affected by constant churn. The existence of trust allowed open communications and debate of ideas, whereas the lack of trust caused internal competition and personal conflicts. Internal competition was described by the participants almost exclusively in mature companies. Participants explained that in the startup company there was nothing to compete for, as the probability for promotion was minimal in a flat organization. However, employees of the startup company had the ability to significantly affect the success of the startup company and, in return, be affected by it financially, which was more important to them than competing for a better position with higher pay. In a mature company, on the other hand, the likelihood of a significant impact on the success of the company (and the potential financial reward from it) was minimal, but there were many positions in the organization to compete over.

Formalization

Most participants experienced higher formalization and bureaucracy in the mature company, and accepted the fact as "the nature of the beast"—large and complex companies required formal and complex processes to succeed. However, they also claimed that the high formalization caused delays in decision making and progress, and had a negative impact on their own motivation. The participants described the processes in the startup company as optimized for the single project the company worked on, as opposed to the "generic" processes in the large company that were not as efficient and optimized to individual projects. Some of the participants described their ability to bypass the processes, when needed, and especially in an environment of high performance teams and high autonomy (in both startup and mature companies). Finally, participants who had a big picture view did not need to rely on processes very much.

Job Satisfaction

Different reasons were cited by participants for why were they more (or less) satisfied with their work in the startup company versus the mature company. Those included experiencing creativity, autonomy, supervisor encouragement, recognition, positive team dynamics, big picture view, impact on success, and respect towards supervisor. Technical people were more satisfied in startup companies, whereas business people were satisfied in both types of companies. The factors participants described as affecting their job satisfaction (positively and negatively) was very similar to the list of factors claimed by prior research to affect creativity, in the same direction. Participants did not describe a direct impact of job satisfaction on their creativity, although the two were highly correlated.

Mood and Affect

Most participants could not identify significant differences in their mood between the two companies that were unrelated to their work, but rather described their mood as a result of their overall job satisfaction. They experienced happiness, anxiety, fear, euphoria, optimism, safety, cynicism, isolation, and even boredom. Those feelings were associated with either company, and could not be linked to one type of company in particular.

Pressure and Support from Home

Participants did not feel significant difference in the pressure or support they received from home in the two different types of companies. The support was mostly a function of the participant's happiness, and sometimes related to travel and work hours versus family time. The support and pressure from home were related to the stage of the family, number of children, whether the wife worked or not, and even whether the products were "cool" or not. The family's involvement with the company helped getting family support. In most cases, the participants described the two way relationship between the support they received from home, and their own balance of home and work, and supporting their family. In other words—the participants were proactive in assuring family support. There were slight elements of understanding of the involvement required in the startup company by the family, and the anticipation of the potential rewards there, as well as an expectation of working shorter hours in the mature company.

Dynamism and Involvement

Across the dimensions of diversity, ability to see the "big picture", individual impact on success of the company, "loving" the product, filling multiple roles and participating in multiple projects, starting with a clean slate, and taking risk—the participants reported that the startup environment was characterized by higher dynamism and individual involvement. The ability to see the big picture and the impact the participants had on the company success were positively correlated to the participants' experiences of creativity.

Sources of Differences other than Startup vs. Mature

The purpose of this study was to explore the effects that the startup company and the mature company had on creativity and the factors affecting in. However, participants also reported other sources affecting those factors: the stage in the product life cycle; personal maturity; the specific company, regardless of size; the type of technology involved; the participant's personal financial situation; the participant's family stage; and the overall business cycle.

5. Discussion, Implications, Recommendations

This research was based on the combination of three premises supported by prior research: (1) startup companies are more innovative than mature companies; (2) innovation is the implementation of a creative idea; and (3) there are different factors, organizational and personal, that affect employee creativity. The purpose of this study was to explore the perceived changes in creativity of individuals who moved between mature companies and startup companies (in both directions), and how they perceive the differences in the organizational climate and in their personal context that may have affected those changes in their creativity.   Understanding those perceived and experienced changes may help understand why startup companies are more innovative than mature ones, as the first framework suggested.

Discussion of the Findings

Creativity

The first research question in this study was: *How do employees who worked in both startup and mature companies experience the differences in their own creativity between the two types of organizations?*

Amabile (1988) defined creativity as "the production of novel and useful ideas by an individual or small group of individuals working together" (p. 126). The purpose of the first research question was to explore whether startup companies are not only more innovative, but also whether people who worked in startup companies felt more creative there. The results of this study showed that few participants felt creative anywhere they worked, and few participants felt more creative in the mature company, but the majority of the participants felt more creative in the startup companies. Participants experienced their creativity through having more novel and useful ideas, and conceiving them more often.   They experienced more *novel* ideas in the startup companies because they started with a clean slate, because creative ideas were desperately needed for the startup company to survive, and because novel ideas were rejected by the mature companies due to organizational inertia. Participants felt that their ideas were more *useful* in the startup companies because they were implemented. After all, how useful was an idea that never got implemented in the mature companies? Finally, participants experienced a correlation between the percentage of their ideas that were implemented (or not implemented) and their continuous creativity. When a company did not implement many of their ideas—the participants experienced less creativity later. The answer to the first research question, therefore, is that participants experienced higher level of creativity in startup companies, along all three dimensions of creativity: novelty, usefulness, and quantity.

Organizational Antecedents for Creativity

The second research question in this study was: *How do employees who worked in both startup and mature companies experience the differences in the organizational climate for creativity between the two types of organizations?*

This question was answered along the different factors that constitute the organizational climate.

Autonomy

Narrative and statistical analysis of the interviews supported the Amabile et al. (1996) and Ekvall (1996) models in the most part, with few exceptions. The participants in this study experienced autonomy as one of the key organizational antecedents for creativity, and felt significantly higher degree of creativity in the same companies where they also experienced higher degree of autonomy. Most participants experienced higher degree of autonomy and creativity in startup companies than in mature companies.

Availability of resources

Oddly enough, the participants described relationship between availability of resources and creativity opposite to the Amabile et al. (1996) model. The Pearson Correlation factor between resource availability and creativity was negative (-0.401), although with insufficient statistical significance (p=0.072). A significant number of participants described lower availability of resources as a stimulus to creativity. P7 commented:

> ...you have to be more creative when you have [fewer] resources, because you have to do more with less and it kind of spurs the creativity process.

Other participants felt that although they had a lower *quantity* of resources in the startup company—they had higher *quality* resources there. Only few participants described a positive relationship between resource abundance and their experiences of creativity. The role of resources was explored in this study only with respect to individual creativity. However, the availability of resources could have an impact (positive or negative) on the implementation phase of innovation, as will be discussed later.

Supervisor and recognition

Supervisor encouragement of creativity and recognition were factors described by prior literature to support creativity. Participants felt slightly more encouraged by their supervisors in the startup companies than in the mature companies. Coding of this factor did not yield a statistically significant difference. Participants slightly felt more recognized in the startup companies than in the mature companies. This factor, too, was not found to show statistically significant difference. A new factor was discussed by participants in this study: the respect that participants felt towards their supervisor. This study showed a strong link (from the narrative analysis as well as statistical analysis of the coded interviews) between the recognition that participants experienced, their perception of their supervisor as supportive, and the respect they reported feeling towards their supervisors. Although not found to be strongly tied to experiences of creativity—participants who respected their supervisors also felt encouraged by their supervisors to be creative, and also described the recognition as more meaningful to them.   Neither one of these three factors (recognition, supervisory support, and respect towards supervisors) was expressed as strongly linked to startup or mature companies. It should be noted that the participants described three types of recognition: formal, informal, and financial. In general—participants described informal recognition as the most meaningful to them. In the startup companies—participants cared less about recognition, but were significantly driven by the potential future financial rewards resulting from the success of the startup company.

Team dynamics

Team dynamics were either explicitly expressed or implied by prior research as an antecedent for creativity. Amabile et al. (1996) catalogued team dynamics under *work group supports*. Ekvall (1996) was more explicit and separated trust/openness (positive), debates (positive), and conflicts (negative) as independent factors affecting creativity. Participants in this study described four elements of team dynamics they felt affected their creativity: open communications (positive effect), idea debate (positive effect), internal competition (negative effect), and personal conflicts (negative effect). These findings supported prior research. However, the participants in this study associated all four to a very fundamental factor: *trust*. In cases where participants described high trust environment—they experienced the positive factors (open communications and idea debate) more, and the negative factors (internal competition and personal conflict) less.   While *trust* was described by Ekvall (1996) along with open communications as a factor affecting creativity—the current study suggested that trust should be treated as a key factor affecting creativity, and that open communications, idea debate, internal competition, and personal conflicts are the *symptoms* of this factor, although they affected creativity. The participants in this study also described the factors that positively affected trust: geographical and cultural differences (negative), time spent by team members together (long time had a positive impact on trust, whereas a constant churn in team members had a negative impact on trust), off work friendships among team members (positive), and perception of competency (positive). In general, positive team dynamics were described as affecting creativity, although this could not be supported with sufficient statistical significance (p=0.055). Participants overwhelmingly described more positive team dynamics in startup companies than in mature ones. This conclusion was supported statistically, too.

Challenges, formalization, and organizational impediments

Prior research showed that formalization and bureaucracy had negative impact on creativity (Abbey & Dickson, 1983; Ahuja et al., 2008; Dormen & Edidin, 1989). Amabile (1988) described organizational impediments to creativity as internal strife, conservatism, and rigid, formal management structures, and showed that those negatively affected creativity. The current study found that the participants described two types of challenges: internal challenges and external challenges. The *internal* challenges described by the participants were in line with Amabile's (1988) definition of *organizational impediments* and with the prior definitions of formalization and bureaucracy. Only *external* challenges reported by the participants met Amabile's definition of *challenging work*. External challenges were described by the participants as intellectually stimulating, technical, external to the company (market competition), and associated with the survival of the company (exclusively associated with startup companies).

The participants experienced more organizational impediments (formalization, bureaucracy, processes, and other internal challenges) in the mature companies, and experienced more *external* challenges (intellectual, technological, external, and survival-related) in the startup companies. Participants accepted the rigid formalization and complex processes in the mature companies as "the nature of the beast", although did not like them. Finally, participants described the processes of the startup companies as optimized for a single project, while the processes in the mature companies were complex and aimed to be "one size fits all" to all projects ongoing in the mature companies, but not optimized to any of those, thus creating inefficiencies.

It is worth mentioning that some of the *internal* challenges described by participants in the mature companies could be explained using Emerson's (1962) theory of power in organizations. Emerson defined *having power* as a person being in a position to grant or deny another person's gratification. "It would appear that the power to control or influence the other resides in control over the things he values, which may range all the way from oil resources to ego-support... *power resides implicitly in the other's dependency*" (p. 32). When participants experienced other groups or individuals in the mature company blocking progress, not releasing resources, or delaying meetings—they observed how others were exercising their power through using the dependency of the participants in those resources.

Dynamism and individual engagement

Throughout the interviews, several themes have emerged from the narrative, describing the important role that dynamism and individual engagement played in affecting creativity. Ekvall (1996) described dynamism as:

> The eventfulness of life in the organization. In the highly dynamic situation, new things are happening all the time and alterations between ways of thinking about and handling issues often occur. There is a kind of psychological turbulence... The opposite situation could be compared to a slow jog-trot with no surprises. There are no new projects; no different plans. Everything goes its usual way. (p. 107)

The current study participants described elements that affected such dynamism and elements of their own involvement and engagement with the organization and its environment. Due to interactions between the different factors—all those elements were described as one combined factor: dynamism and individual engagement. The components of dynamism and individual engagement that emerged from this study are: diversity, impact on the outcome, big picture view, filling multiple roles and working on multiple projects, starting with a "clean slate", taking risks, and "loving" the product. Participants described the diversity of experiences by individuals in the company as fertilizing their own ideas. They described the importance of the impact they felt they had on the outcome (and company success) as intrinsically motivating them and reducing their dependence on recognition and reward. Filling multiple roles and working on different projects was often mentioned very fondly (including "taking out the trash"). Most participants distinguished their radical creativity in the startup companies from the incremental creativity in mature companies and attributed it to the ability to start with a "clean slate" and no "baggage". Finally—participants experienced taking more risks in a startup company and "loved" their product. All of those components of dynamism and personal engagement were described as positively impacting the participants' creativity, and in the majority of cases described more favorably in startup companies than in mature ones.

Personal Context

The third research question in this study was: *How do employees who worked in both startup and mature companies experience the differences in their personal context between the two types of organizations?*

Prior research suggested several personal factors affecting creativity: job satisfaction (Ekvall, 1996; Isaksen & Lauer, 1999; Pierce & Delbecq, 1977; Roethlisberger & Dickson, 1939; Turnipseed, 1994), mood/affect (Elkington

& Hartigan, 2008; King, 1990), and pressure and support from home (Madjar et al., 2002). The current study failed to show any affect that home pressure and support or mood had on creativity. The participants did not describe any significant differences in their mood, or pressure and support from home between the two types of companies. George and Jing (2007) claimed that mood provides information about the environment. Using this framework, the conclusion is that the participants received more information from their work environment than from their personal environment, thus not affecting creativity, but rather affected *by* creativity. High job satisfaction, on the other hand, appeared to exist in cases with stories about experiencing high creativity. However, participants did not clearly describe how job satisfaction affected their creativity, and therefore based on stories told by the participants in this study, it appears that job satisfaction could not only be related to creativity (as described in prior literature), but also affected by the same factors that affect creativity.

The participants in this study described relationships between three factors: when the organizational climate positively affected creativity, it also positively affected job satisfaction. When participants experienced high job satisfaction—they were in a better mood. When they were in a better mood, their families were more supportive of them. Another element that played a role, as described by the participants, was the balance between work and family life that they maintained. This balance allowed for the home support equilibrium to be maintained. In summary—the participants did not experience any personal context factor significantly differently between startup and mature companies. However, few participants reflected on personal changes (maturity, experience, and training) and felt they evolved over time, and became more effective and creative in the second company they worked for, be it a startup or a mature company. This finding contradicts an assumption made initially in this study that the personal characteristics of the participants did not change. However, the research design used 12 participants who transitioned from a mature to startup companies and 8 participants who transitioned from startup to mature companies, allowing to control that evolution of the participants and separate it from the startup-mature factor.

Summary of Differences between Startup and Mature Companies

The summary of the differences in all factors and outcomes between startup and mature companies is provided in Table 8. It is different than the original Table 1, based on the findings of this research. Creativity is listed as an outcome. Six of the organizational factors were found to have strong effect on creativity, and were indicated with bold font. Four of them had positive effect on creativity (autonomy, external challenges, positive team dynamics, and dynamism and involvement). All of those were higher in the startup companies. One of the organizational factors was found to have strong negative effect on creativity, and was found to be higher in the mature companies. Five of the factors were not found to have a significant difference between startup and mature companies. Two of them were organizational (supervisor encouragement and recognition). All three personal context factors were not found to have a significant difference between startup and mature companies, and were thus eliminated from the modified conceptual framework shown in Figure 7.

Table 8 – Factor and Outcome Differences between Startup and Mature Companies

Factor (outcome)	Domain	Effect	Higher in—
Creativity (outcome)	Outcome	N/A	Startup
Autonomy	Organizational	*Strong Positive*	Startup
Supervisor encouragement	Organizational	Positive	Insignificant difference
Recognition	Organizational	Positive	Insignificant difference
External challenges	Organizational	*Strong Positive*	Startup
Organizational impediments	Organizational	*Strong Negative*	Mature
Resource Quantity	Organizational	Negative	Mature
Positive team dynamics (and trust)	Organizational	*Strong positive*	Startup
Dynamism and involvement	Organizational	*Strong positive*	Startup
Job satisfaction (outcome)	Personal context	*Strong Positive*	Startup
Mood and affect	Personal context	Unclear	Insignificant difference
Support from home	Personal context	Positive	Insignificant difference
Pressure from home	Personal context	Negative	Insignificant difference

Sources of Differences other than Startup vs. Mature

The narrative of the interviews in this study, supported by the statistical analysis (Tables 4 and 5) as summarized in Table 8 showed that creativity and the organizational climate factors conducive to creativity were significantly different between startup companies and mature companies. Creativity, autonomy, external challenges, team dynamics, and dynamism and personal engagement were found more in the startup companies, while formalization and internal challenges were found more in the mature companies. However, the participants also described additional sources that affected those differences, other than the companies being startup or mature. Those sources were: the stage in the product life cycle, personal maturity, the type of technology involved, the participants' personal financial situation, the participants' family stage, and the overall business cycle.

Modified Conceptual Framework

The original conceptual framework that was developed as a result of the literature review was presented in Figure 4. It described how individuals, influenced by organizational climate and personal context, generate creative ideas. As a result of this study, and the insights gathered through the narrative analysis, a more elaborated conceptual framework was developed, and is illustrated in Figure 7. Like the original conceptual framework, the "input" to the creativity process is an individual (with individual characteristic), this time illustrated at the top of the diagram. The "output" similarly is the creative ideas, this time illustrated at the bottom of the diagram. However, while the original conceptual framework showed both organizational antecedents and personal context as potentially influencing creativity—the current study could not show a significant impact of personal context items on differences in creativity, so the personal context factors were eliminated from the final conceptual framework.

The only part of personal context that was described in the original conceptual framework that "survived" this study is job satisfaction. However, although participants described higher creativity and higher job satisfaction in the same companies, but an analysis of their responses to "why were you more satisfied" shows that their job satisfaction was affected by the same factors that affected creativity. No participant described being creative as a *result* of experiencing higher job satisfaction. Therefore, based on stories told by the participants in this study, it appears that job satisfaction could not only be related to creativity (as described in prior literature), but also affected by the same factors that affect creativity.

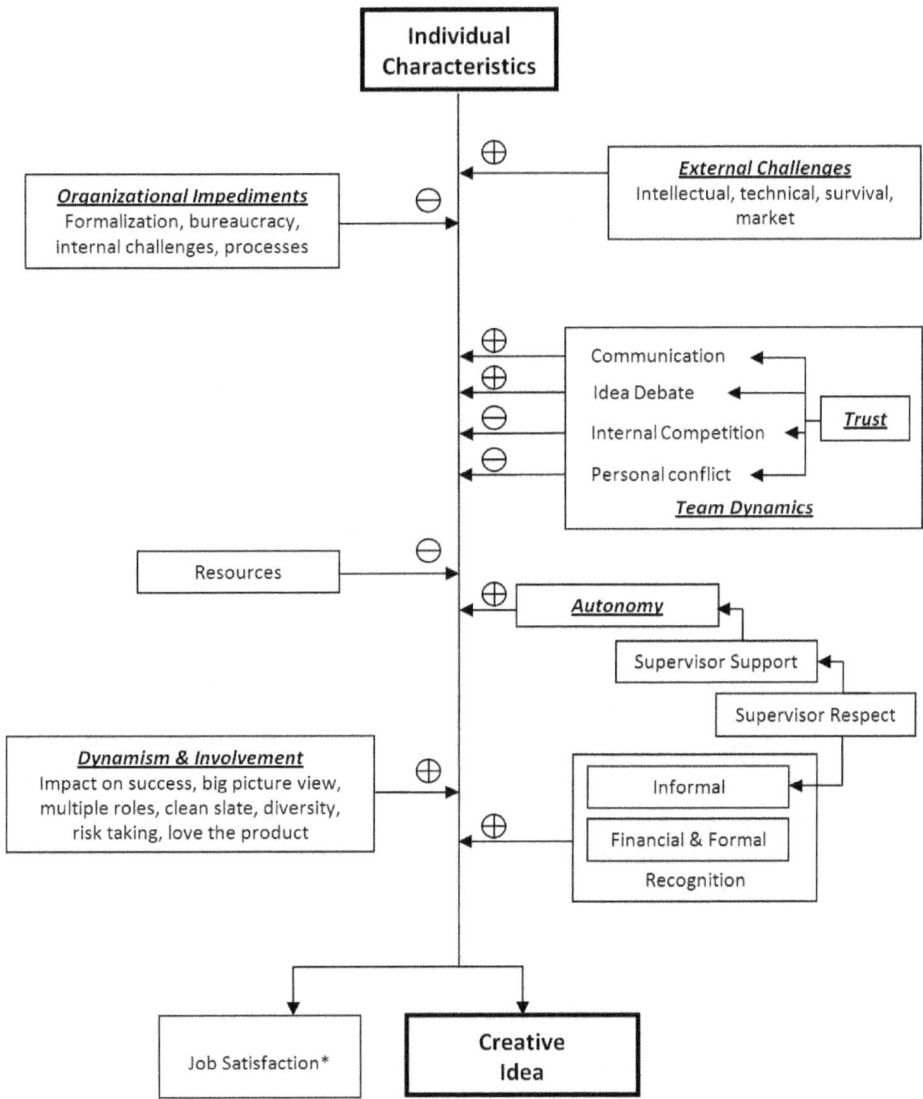

Figure 7 – Modified conceptual framework.

In this modified conceptual framework, the organizational antecedents are described in greater detail than in Figure 4, based on the results and conclusions from this study. Furthermore, Figure 7 illustrates interactions between different factors, which were not part of the original conceptual framework.

Some of the factors in Figure 7 are in a bold and underlined font, indicating that the effect of those factors on creativity, as experienced and described by the participants, was strong. The factors described with standard font indicate that those factors were described by the participants as having lower impact on their creativity. For each factor, there is an arrow going from it to the "spine" (the link between individuals and the creative ideas they generate), indicating a positive (+) or negative (-) impact on creativity, as experienced and described by the participants.

On the right side of Figure 7, the diagram begins at the top showing the *external* challenges, which have a positive impact on creativity. Those challenges have intellectual, technical, survival-related, and market-related elements. Organizational impediments to creativity have a negative effect on creativity, and are made of *internal* challenges, formalization, bureaucracy, and complex and non-optimized processes, and described on the left side of Figure 8. Team dynamics were shown to have a mixed impact on creativity, with open communications and idea debate having a positive effect on creativity, while internal competition and personal conflict having a negative effect on creativity. This study revealed that *trust* was a key element of team dynamics that affected all four, so it was illustrated as a core element in team dynamics. Although not shown in this diagram, trust was shown to be affected by geographical and cultural differences, time together, friendships, churn, and perceived competency of team members.

Resources have a negative impact on creativity (the less resources available to the participants, the more they felt creative), although not a very strong one. Autonomy has a strong, positive effect on creativity, but it is affected by supervisory support which, in turn, is affected by the respect that employees have towards their supervisor. The respect towards the supervisor also affects one of the three types of recognition described by participants— informal recognition. In mature companies, participants who described lack of respect towards their supervisor did not appreciate informal recognition by their supervisor. It should be noted, though, that in startup companies, participants cared less for informal recognition in general, even when they respected their supervisors. All three types of recognition have positive effect on creativity.

Dynamism was a factor that was new to the framework of this study (it is not included in the original conceptual framework in Figure 4), and emerged out of the narratives. As described by the participants—it had seven elements: (1) the impact participants felt they had on the success of the company or project; (2) their ability to view the big picture; (3) filling multiple roles; (4) starting with a clean slate; (5) the diversity of backgrounds, experience and knowledge; (6) risk taking; and (7) loving the product and the positive impact it has on society.

Implications

Implications for Research

Individual creativity in organizations historically began with qualitative, mostly semi structured interviews based studies to develop a list of factors affecting creativity (Ancona & Caldwell, 1987; Amabile & Gryskiewicz, 1987; Amabile, 1988; Jones et al., 2000; Lynn et al., 1996; Leifer et al., 2000; Zien & Buckler, 1997; Amabile et al., 2005). As a result, different creativity climate instruments were developed, such as KEYS, CCQ, SOQ, SSSI (Mathisen & Einarsen, 2004) and others. Most studies following the development of those survey instruments were quantitative and confirmatory in nature, using those survey instruments as a basis for validating or rejecting certain hypotheses about organizational climate for creativity.

The current study revealed several possible limitations in existing conceptual frameworks. The first possible limitation is the relationships between availability of resources and creativity. While prior research claimed a *positive* impact of the availability of resources on creativity (Amabile, 1988)—the current study demonstrated the opposite relationship, in which participants claimed being more creative in face of resource shortage.

The second possible limitation is the relationship between job satisfaction and creativity. While prior research showed a positive relationship between job satisfaction and creativity—the current study suggested that job satisfaction was also affected by the same factors affecting creativity, and therefore the relationship between them might be more complex than described previously.

The third possible limitation is the elimination of dynamism as a factor affecting creativity. Dynamism was not a factor in the KEYS survey instrument (Amabile et al., 1996), and while included in the CCQ instrument (Ekvall, 1996)—it was eliminated in a following instrument, SOQ (Isaksen et al., 2000). The current study demonstrated a strong impact of dynamism (impact on success, big picture view, multiple roles/projects, clean slate, diversity, risk taking, and "loving" the product) on creativity.

The forth possible limitation is the absence of an evaluation of the *level of impact* that different factors had on creativity. The current study demonstrated that autonomy and dynamism, to name only two, had a much stronger impact on creativity than supervisor support and recognition did. Such evaluation would allow organizations that use survey instruments to apply the appropriate weight to different factors when they attempt to improve the organizational climate.

Finally, the fifth possible limitation is the lack of analysis of the interaction between the different factors. Existing survey instruments assumed independent relationships between the different factors and creativity, but not an interaction between factors. For example, no prior research was found to link job satisfaction to mood, and mood to family support and pressure, as discovered in the current study.

Implications for Practice

Christensen (1997) showed that startup companies out innovated mature companies, and cannibalized their markets. The current study demonstrated that employees experienced higher level of creativity in startup companies than in mature companies. Since innovation is the implementation of a creative idea (Figure 2), then the higher level of creativity could, in part, explain why startup companies were more innovative than mature ones. Furthermore, this study revealed that employees felt a climate conducive to creativity more in startup companies than in mature companies, thus explaining their experiences of higher creativity. What do mature companies do to become more innovative, then? Martin (2008) stated that:

> Acquisitions are often efforts to "buy" innovation, folding in a so-called disruptive, or game-changing, technology developed by another firm. Or they represent attempts to bring in a staff known for its consistent and profitable creative output.

However, in 2008 alone, over $800 billion were spent on more than 8,000 acquisitions, with an estimated 60% of acquisitions ending up depleting shareholder wealth and not achieving the goal of "buying innovation" (Martin & Combs, 2009).

At the same time, although most participants in the current study experienced higher levels of creativity and more conducive climate to creativity in the startup companies—two participants experienced higher degree of creativity and more conducive climate for creativity in mature companies than in the startup companies they worked in. It is therefore not inconceivable that mature companies *can* create a supportive environment for creativity. The question is then: what can mature companies do to maintain a climate conducive to creativity? The topic of internal entrepreneurship (often referred to as *intrapreneurship*) was discussed in literature and research. Burgelman (1984) claimed that companies that exploited their incremental opportunities needed corporate entrepreneurship: "extending the firm's domain of competence and corresponding opportunity set through internally generated new resource combinations" (p. 154). He also stated that top management *tolerates* autonomous strategic behavior because it extends corporate capabilities and finds new opportunities, and it allows avoiding increasing competitive pressures in the core business (Burgelman, 1983). He added that "Internal entrepreneurship, on the other hand, involves new resource combinations which remain, to some extent, nested in the larger resource combination constituted by the firm, and thus also retain at least a potential degree of dependence on it" (p. 1354). Kanter (1989) claimed that mature businesses are more comfortable with their existing businesses (mainstream), already generating returns. The rate of change and market disruptions increased in the 1980s such that mainstream businesses did not allow mature companies to compete successfully. "Newstreams grow out of the combination of invention and investment—new ideas and the resources to develop them" (p. 47). The current study could help understand what a mature company *can* do to create conducive climate for creativity, and what it *cannot*.

Resources

From the results of the current study, resource abundance was not a factor attributed to startup companies, while creativity was. The implication is that mature companies do not need to assure abundance of resources to create conducive environment. However, two resources that participants indicated were conducive to creativity and available in mature companies were the availability of expert resources and infrastructure. The mature company needs to assure that experts throughout the organization will be available to advise on different projects, and make the infrastructure available to (and not enforced on) new projects. Furthermore, there are few resources that, while possibly not positively affecting the *creative* stage of innovation—may positively affect the *implementation* stage, as described by participants. Those resources may include funding, certain human resources, brand name, and industry "weight", reach, and influence, as described by participants. The importance of brand and industry influence was described earlier by Freeman and Engel (2007). A startup company which experiences resource shortage may still support the creation of novel ideas, but might not have the resources to implement them.

Supervisor, autonomy, and recognition

The role of the supervisor in creating conducive environment is important, but not necessarily through directly encouraging creativity. The supervisor is in a unique position to control several factors that have significant impact on employee creativity, as this study found. First, the supervisor is in a position to provide (or deny) autonomy to employees, as well as their teams. The autonomy to choose direction, technical approach, and how to execute projects has a significant impact on creativity. Burgelman (1983) discussed the structure for corporate entrepreneurship and suggested that top management needs to *acknowledge* middle level strategies rather than *plan* them. Management should not control the low level and specific content of the entrepreneurial activities. There are limitations to the autonomy that mature companies can provide. One of these limitations is that large companies have potential legal exposure and liability due to their "deep pockets", which startup companies lack, as identified by one of the study participants, and therefore large companies must be very restrained in how they behaves in the market. The second impact the supervisor has on creativity is in providing informal recognition (second only to the anticipated financial rewards in a startup company during an exit), which proved to be most meaningful to employees in encouraging their creativity. More important than the supervisor encouraging creativity—the supervisor can acknowledge and celebrate it after it occurred. Finally, the impact that the supervisor has on autonomy and effectiveness of informal recognition is positively linked to the respect that employees have towards this supervisor, and the supervisor must earn this respect.

One factor that the mature company could have hard time replicating is the anticipation of significant financial rewards that, in a startup company, caused the participants to ignore all other rewards and recognition. As one participant described:

> "[During] the period of 1997-2000, you only heard about hundred of million [dollar] IPOs. Our dilemma was whether the founders will make 10 million or 40 million.... I remember conversations we had where we said, well if the worse comes to worst, then maybe we only get $2-3m out of it."

One of the participants, though, described an "extra special" financial reward he received in the *mature* company for a successful project completion. It is therefore not inconceivable that mature companies could develop special financial rewards. However, based on the findings from this study—those rewards have to be anticipated much like the financial reward in startup companies.

Team dynamics

This study and prior research showed several team dynamics factors that affected creativity. Open communications and open debate had positive impact on creativity, while internal competition and personal conflict had negative impact. Those appeared through this study to all be related to *trust* built within the team. This trust is positively affected by the time the team spent together, the friendships created between team members, and the perceived competency of team members by their peers. The trust is negatively affected by continuous churn within team members and by geographical and cultural differences. Increasing this trust could be achieved through keeping team structures intact over long periods of time, promoting off work events to stimulate personal friendships, prevent churn, and collocating the teams. Participants experienced less internal competition in startup companies because there was nothing to compete for. No promotions were available within the small and flat startup organization. Mature companies need to assure that the promotion process does not create internal rivalries within the team, and that the team members are proving themselves to their *peers* rather than to managers outside the team.

Formalization and bureaucracy

Formalization, bureaucracy, internal challenges, and inflexible "one-size-fits-all" processes were some of the most destructive factors to creativity, as the current study revealed, and the conclusion is that those should be minimized. There should be a set of boundary rules that guide the team's work (Eisenhardt & Sull, 2001), but the team should be allowed to operate within those boundaries and create its own processes, based on *voluntary* use of experiences and best practices from the rest of the company. The company should attempt to minimize unnecessary bureaucracy and formalization (one example given by several participants was the bureaucracy involved in purchasing external materials or travel). Pierce and Delbecq (1977) identified 13 variables within the structural, contextual, and individual categories that affected the three stages of innovation (initiation, adoption, and implementation). While most factors had similar (or similar direction) impact on the different phases—two factors appeared to have different impact on the different phases. Formalization had a negative effect on the *initiation* phase (creativity), as was also supported by Amabile (1988) and the current study. However, formalization had a positive impact on the *adoption* and *implementation* stages of innovation. Similarly, decentralization had a strong positive impact on the *initiation* (creativity) stage and a negative impact on the *implementation* phase. Separating the *creative* environment from the *implementation* environment would allow creating a supportive environment for creativity, and a formalized environment required for successful implementation. Andrew et al. (2008) identified Apple as the most innovative company in 2008 in an executive survey. Morrison (2009) described innovation in Apple as separated into the "innovative elite" who works in an environment extremely conducive to creativity, while the rest of the organization is highly formalized, and operates in constant fear and under a veil of secrecy. The implementation phase needs a high degree of formalization, low decentralization, and appropriate processes.

External challenges

This study showed that external challenges existed always. Participants considered external challenges interesting and stimulating. Amabile (1988) considered those conducive to creativity. Most participants described more external challenges in the startup companies simply because of the burden of the internal challenges in the mature companies in comparison. If the company minimizes the internal challenges—it would free up the employees to focus on the intellectual, technical, and market challenges.

Dynamism

Dynamism was found by this study to have significant impact on employee creativity, supporting the same conclusion by Ekvall (1996). The ability to break projects into manageable pieces that could be handled by independent cohesive, collocated teams would have a positive effect on the impact participants feel they have on the success of their company (or their team), and the ability to see the big picture. Beginning with a clean slate and no restrictions is tied to autonomy as well as dynamism, and should be implemented where possible. Unnecessary restrictions and "this is the way it is done around here" should be avoided. Team members should be allowed to assume different roles within the team, and should never be told not to "fall in love" with the product, as one general manager told a participant in this study. The team should perceive an ability to assume risks, within the boundary rules set for it.

Personal context

As stated earlier in the introduction to this study—the company does not have much control over the personal context which could affect creativity. The good news from this study is that no significant differences in personal context factors (job satisfaction, mood, home support, and home pressure) were found between startup companies and mature companies, while employees experienced higher degrees of creativity in the startup companies than in the mature ones. These factors, out of the organization's control— were least impactful on creativity.

Other sources of differences in the factors

This study discovered six additional sources of influence not related to the company itself that could affect the factors explored in this study. Three sources were in the organizational side: the type of technology, the stage in the product cycle, and the stage in the overall business cycle. The other three sources were in the personal side: the employee's financial state, personal maturity, and family stage. As discussed above—the company has no control over the personal sources of impact, but since the factors they impacted showed a lower effect on creativity and insignificant difference between the two types of companies—they could be ignored. The company cannot affect the other sources of impact, either. First, if the company is in the semiconductor industry, with longer product cycle, that would cause employees to see less of an immediate impact they have on the company's success, as participants reported, but the company will not become a software company just to change that. Second, the company will have to go through the entire product life cycle. Even though the early stages in the product life cycle are characterized by higher dynamism which lends itself to creativity more—the company will still have to go through the later stages of productization, even if those are characterized with lower dynamism and lower creativity. Creativity is less required in these stages anyway. Third, the company cannot control the business cycle. When the economy is booming and funding is abundant, companies will tend to give more autonomy to their employees, and when the economy is in a trough and cost cutting measures are taken—funding will be limited, although managers should try to keep the level of autonomy as high as feasible, within a set of boundary rules applicable to that situation.

Limitations

The study is limited first by confining it to the electronics industry, and specifically to electronic hardware and software companies. Different studies showed that different industries behaved differently (Baldridge & Burnham, 1975; Stevens & Burley, 1997), and therefore it is not clear that the findings of this study could be generalized to other industries.

Merriam (1998) acknowledged the limitations of the case study method in general: it is less descriptive of a large population, and less predictive in nature. Due to the limited data collection, a case study is limited in its generalizability, reliability, and validity. Rubin and Rubin (2005) also recognized that both the researcher and participant are people with feelings, personality, interests, and experiences, and that the researcher cannot be expected to be neutral.

The use of t test is based on the following assumptions: the observations are independent of each other, and distribution of values must be normal (Norusis, 2006). The first assumption was met, as the sample was made of 20 independent participants. Moore (1995, as cited by Norusis, 2006) required that for a sample of between 15 and 40 cases, "the data should not have outliers or be very skewed" (p. 131). Given that each variable had only three possible values, none of those values could be an outlier or highly skewed. However, the assumption of normality could still be challenged. Using more than three scale points could have improved reliability (Churchill Jr. & Peter,1984).

Finally, although good case studies were conducted even with a single case (Yin, 2003), and Creswell (2007) stated that using four to five cases in a single study should "provide ample opportunity to identify themes of the cases as well as conduct cross-cases theme analysis" (p. 128)—increasing the sample size could help generalizability, even though the intent of qualitative research is not to generalize the information.

Recommendations for Future Research

The current study was exploratory and based on qualitative interviews and narrative analysis, with coding done by the researcher to provide some statistical support to the conclusions drawn from the narrative analysis. In order to increase the validity, reliability, and generalizability of the conclusions from this study (or to modify or reject some of them), the researcher recommends to conduct a survey study on a larger sample, in the order of the sample size of 120 participants in the Amabile and Gryskiewicz (1987) exploratory interview study that led to the development of KEYS, or the later longitudinal study conducted by Amabile et al. (2005) with 222 participants. A second opportunity is to develop a new survey instrument to measure the factors as described in this study. Another opportunity is to use existing survey instruments such as KEYS CCQ, and KAI to measure most of the factors described in this study.   Previous studies were conducted to correlate factors from different creativity survey instruments (Isaksen & Lauer, 1999; Carne & Kirton, 1982), but not to use the different instruments to compare different environments between the different types of companies. Attributes of the companies should be added to the survey instruments, and the correlation of those attributes to the organizational factors affecting creativity should be tested.

Summary

The purpose of this study was to explore the perceived changes in creativity of individuals who moved between mature companies and startup companies (in both directions), and how they perceived the differences in the organizational climate and in their personal context that may have affected those changes in their creativity. The first research question was: *How do employees who worked in both startup and mature companies experience the differences in their own creativity between the two types of organizations?* The study participants experienced higher creativity in startup companies than in mature companies. The second research question was: *How do employees who worked in both startup and mature companies experience the differences in the organizational climate for creativity between the two types of organizations?*   The research participants experienced the factors positively affecting creativity more in the startup companies, and the factors negatively affecting creativity more in the mature companies.   The third research question was: *How do employees who worked in both startup and mature companies experience the differences in their personal context between the two types of organizations?* The study participants did not experience the personal context factors significantly differently between startup and mature companies.

While this study focused on how the differences between startup and mature companies affected creativity and organizational climate—additional sources of differences were discovered throughout the study, including the technology, product cycle, business cycle, personal maturity, individual financial situation, and family stage.

All hope was not lost for mature companies if they choose to be more innovative and promote creativity: even though not all factors are within the company's control, a list of actions that mature companies can take to improve creativity were proposed here.

Finally, this study generally supported existing creativity climate models, but also proposed a few possible limitations in those models, that create opportunities for further research.

References

Abbey, A., & Dickson, J. W. (1983). R&D work climate and innovation in semiconductors. *Academy of Management Journal, 26*(2), 362-368.

Abedi, J. (2002). A Latent-variable modeling approach to assessing reliability and validity of a creativity instrument. *Creativity Research Journal, 14*(2), 267-276.

Abernathy, W. J., & Utterback, J. M. (1978). Patterns of industrial innovation. *Technology Review, 80*(7), 41-47.

Academy of Management. (2002). Academy of Management code of ethical conduct. *Academy of Management Journal, 45*(1), 291–295.

Acs, Z. J., & Audretsch, D. B. (1988). Innovation in large and small firms: An empirical analysis. *American Economic Review, 78*(4), 678-690.

Ahuja, G., Lampert, C. M., & Tandon, V. (2008). Chapter 1: Moving beyond Schumpeter: Management research on the determinants of technological innovation. *The Academy of Management Annals, 2*, 1 - 98.

Amabile, T. M. (1988). A Model of creativity and innovation in organizations. In B. M. Staw & L. L. Cummings (Eds.), *Research in Organizational Behavior* (Vol. 10, pp. 123-167). Greenwich, CT: JAI Press.

Amabile, T. M. (1995). KEYS: Assessing the climate for creativity. *A Survey from the Center for Creative Leadership.* Colorado Springs, CO: Center for Creative Leadership.

Amabile, T. M. (1996). *Creativity in context.* Boulder, CO: Waterview Press.

Amabile, T. M. (1998). How to kill creativity. *Harvard Business Review, 76*(5), 76-87.

Amabile, T. M., Barsade, S. G., Mueller, J. S., & Staw, B. M. (2005). Affect and creativity at work. *Administrative Science Quarterly, 50*(3), 367-403.

Amabile, T. M., Conti, R., Coon, H., Lazenby, J., & Herron, M. (1996). Assessing the work environment for creativity. *Academy of Management Journal, 39*(5), 1154-1184.

Amabile, T. M., & Gryskiewicz, S. S. (1987). *Creativity in the R&D laboratory.* Colorado Springs, CO: Center for Creative Leadership.

Ancona, D., & Caldwell, D. (1987). Management issues facing new product teams in big technology companies. In D. Lewin, D. Lipsky, & D. Sokel (Eds.), *Advances in industrial and labor relations*, vol. 4: 191-221. Greenwich, CT: JAI Press

Anderson, J. V. (1992). Weirder than fiction: the reality and myths of creativity. *Academy of Management Executive, 6*(4), 40-47.

Anderson, N., de Drew, C. K. W., & Nijstad, B. A. (2004). The routinization of innovation research: a constructively critical review of the state-of-the-science. *Journal of Organizational Behavior, 25*(2), 147-173.

Anderson, N. R., & West, M. A. (1998). Measuring climate for work group innovation: Development and validation of the team climate inventory. *Journal of Organizational Behavior, 19*(3), 235-258.

Andrew, J. P., Haanaes, K., Michael, D. C., Sirkin, H. L., & Taylor, A. (2008). *Innovation 2008: Is the tide turning? A BCG senior management survey*. Boston, MA: The Boston Consulting Group, Inc.

Arbnor, I., & Bjerke, B. (1997). *Methodology for creating business knowledge* (2nd ed.). Thousand Oaks, CA: Sage.

Baldridge, J. V., & Burnham, R. A. (1975). Organizational innovation: Individual, organizational, and environmental impacts. *Administrative Science Quarterly, 20*(2), 165-176.

Barney, J. (1991). Firm resources and sustained competitive advantage. *Journal of Management, 17*(1), 99-120.

Barron, F., & Harrington, D. M. (1981). Creativity, intelligence, and personality. *Annual Review of Psychology, 32*, 439-476.

Bartlett, K. R. (2005). Survey research in organizations. In R. A. Swanson & E. F. H. III (Eds.), *Research in organizations: Foundations and methods of inquiry* (pp. 97-113). San Francisco: Berrett-Koehler Publishers.

Basadur, M., & Gelade, G. A. (2006). The role of knowledge management in the innovation process. *Creativity & Innovation Management, 15*(1), 45-62.

Basadur, M., Graen, G. B., & Green, G. (1982). Training in creative problem solving: Effects on ideation and problem finding and solving in an industrial research organization. *Organizational Behaviour and Human Performance, 30*, 41-70.

Basadur, M., & Hausdorf, P. A. (1996). Measuring divergent thinking attitudes related to creative problem solving and innovation management. *Creativity Research Journal, 9*(1), 21-32.

Bassett-Jones, N. (2005). The paradox of diversity management, creativity and innovation. *Creativity & Innovation Management, 14*(2), 169-175.

Benabou, R., & Tirole, J. (2003). Intrinsic and extrinsic motivation. *Review of economic studies, 70*(244), 489-520.

Bharadwaj, S., & Menon, A. (2000). Making innovation happen in organizations: Individual creativity mechanisms, organizational creativity mechanisms or both? *Journal of Product Innovation Management, 17*(6), 424-434.

Brown, R. T. (1989). Creativity: What are we to measure? In J. A. Glover, R. R. Ronning, & C. R. Reynolds (Eds.), *Handbook of creativity* (pp. 3-32). New York: Plenum.

Brown, S., & Eisenhardt, K. M. (1995). Product development: Past research, present findings, and future directions. *Academy of Management Journal, 20*, 343–378.

Burgelman, R. A. (1983). Corporate entrepreneurship and strategic management: Insights from a process study. *Management Science, 29*(12), 1349-1364.

Burgelman, R. A. (1984). Designs for corporate entrepreneurship in established firms. *California Management Review, 26*(3), 154-166.

Burnside, R. M. (1990). Improving corporate climates for creativity. In M. A. West & I. L. Farr (Eds.), *Innovation and creativity at work* (pp. 265-284). New York: Wiley.

Carne, J. C. & Kirton, M. J. (1982). Styles of creativity: Test score correlations between the Kirton Adaption-Innovation Inventory and the Myers-Briggs Type Indicator. *Psychological Reports, 50*, 31-36.

Capozzi, M. M., & Chakravorti, B. (2006). Innovating at scale. *McKinsey Quarterly, 3*, 26-26

Challenge. (n.d.). *Dictionary.com Unabridged* (v 1.1). Retrieved February 08, 2009, from Dictionary.com website: http://dictionary.reference.com/browse/challenge

Christensen, C. M. (1997). *The innovator's dilemma*. Boston: Harvard Business School Press.

Churchill , G. A. Jr., & Peter, J. P. (1984). Research design effects on the reliability of rating scales: A meta-analysis. *Journal of Marketing Research, 21*(4), 360-375.

Collins, J. C., & Porras, J. I. (1994). *Built to last: Successful habits of visionary companies*. New York: Harper Business.

Cooper, C. R., & Schindler, P. S. (2006). *Business research methods* (9th ed.). Boston: McGraw-Hill Irwin.

Corbin, J., & Strauss, A. C. (2008) Basics of qualitative research: Techniques and procedures for developing grounded theory (3rd ed.). Thousand Oaks, CA: Sage Publications.

Creswell, J. W. (2003). *Research design: Qualitative, quantitative and mixed methods approaches* (2nd ed.). Thousand Oaks, CA: Sage Publishing Inc.

Creswell, J. W. (2007). *Qualitative inquiry & research design: Choosing among five approaches* (2nd ed.). Thousand Oaks, CA: Sage Publishing Inc.

Crotty, M. (1998). The foundations of social research: Meaning and perspective in the research process. Thousand Oaks, CA: Sage Publishing Inc.

Cummings, L. (1965). Organizational climates for creativity. *Academy of Management Journal, 8*(3), 220-227.

Cummings, L. L., Hinton, B. L., & Gobdel, B. C. (1975). Creative behavior as a function of task environment: Impact of objectives, procedures, and controls. *Academy of Management Journal, 18*(3), 489-499.

Cutler, L. S. (2000). Creativity: Essential to technological innovation. *Research Technology Management, 43*(6), 29.

Damanpour, F. (1990). Innovation effectiveness, adoption and organizational performance. In M. A. West & I. L. Farr (Eds.), *Innovation and creativity at work* (pp. 125-141). New York: Wiley.

Damanpour, F. (1991). Organizational innovation: A meta-analysis of effects of determinants and moderators. *Academy of Management Journal, 34*(3), 555-590.

Davis, M. A. (2009). Understanding the relationship between mood and creativity: A meta-analysis. *Organizational Behavior & Human Decision Processes, 108*(1), 25-38.

Devanna, M. A., & Tichy, N. (1990). Creating the competitive organization of the 21st Century: The boundaryless corporation. *Human Resource Management, 29*(4), 455-471.

Dormen, L., & Edidin, P. (1989). Original spin. *Psychology Today, 23*(7-8), 46-51.

Dougherty, D., & Hardy, C. (1996). Sustained product innovation in large, mature organizations: Overcoming innovation-to-organization problems. *Academy of Management Journal, 39*(5), 1120-1153.

Downs Jr, G. W., & Mohr, L. B. (1976). Conceptual issues in the study of innovation. *Administrative Science Quarterly, 21*(4), 700-714.

Drucker, P. F. (1954). *The practice of management.* New York: Harper & Row.

Drucker, P. F. (1985a). *Innovation and entrepreneurship.* New York: Harper Collins.

Drucker, P. F. (1985b). The discipline of innovation. *Harvard Business Review, 63*(3), 67-72.

Eisenhardt, K. M. (1989). Building theories from case study research. *Academy of Management Review, 14*(4), 532-550.

Ekvall, G. (1996). Organizational climate for creativity and innovation. *European Journal of Work and Organizational Psychology, 5*, 105–123.

Ekvall, G. (1997). Organizational conditions and levels of creativity. *Creativity and Innovation Management, 6*(4), 195–205.

Elkington, J., & Hartigan, P. (2008). The power of unreasonable people: How social entrepreneurs create markets that change the world. Boston: Harvard Business School Publishing.

Emerson, R. M. (1962). Power-dependence relations. *American Sociological Review, 27*(1), 31-41.

Engle, D. E., Mah, J. J., & Sadri, G. (1997). An empirical comparison of entrepreneurs and employees: Implications for innovation. *Creativity Research Journal, 10*(1), 45.

Farr, I. L. (1990). Facilitating individual role innovation. In M. A. West & I. L. Farr (Eds.), *Innovation and creativity at work* (pp. 207-230). New York: Wiley.

Farr, I. L. & Ford, C. M. (1990). Individual innovation. In M. A. West & I. L. Farr (Eds.), *Innovation and creativity at work* (pp. 63-80). New York: Wiley.

Feldhusen, J. F., & Goh, B. E. (1995). Assessing and accessing creativity: An integrative review of theory, research, and development. *Creativity Research Journal, 8*(3), 231.

Fong, C. T. (2006). The effects of emotional ambivalence on creativity. *Academy of Management Journal, 49*(5), 1016-1030.

Fortune 1000. (2008, May 5). Retrieved March 14, 2009 from http://money.cnn.com/magazines/fortune/fortune500/2008/full_list/index.html

Fowler, F. J. (2002). *Survey research methods.* Thousand Oaks, CA: Sage Publications.

Freeman, J., & Engel, J. S. (2007). Models of innovation: Startups and mature corporations. *California Management Review, 50*(1), 94-119.

Galbraith, J. R. (1982). Designing the innovating organization. *Organizational Dynamics, 10*(3), 4-25.

Gans, J. S., Hsu, D. H., & Stern, S. (2002). When does start-up innovation spur the gale of creative destruction? *RAND Journal of Economics, 33*(4), 571-586.

George, J. M., & Jing, Z. (2007). Dual tuning in a supportive context: Joint contributions of positive mood, negative mood, and supervisory behaviors to employee creativity. *Academy of Management Journal, 50*(3), 605-622.

George, J. M., & Zhou, J. (2002). Understanding when bad moods foster creativity and good ones don't: The role of context and clarity of feelings. *Journal of Applied Psychology, 87*(4), 687-697.

George, M. L., Works, J., & Watson-Hemphill, K. (2005). Fast innovation: Achieving superior differentiation, speed to market, and increased profitability. New York: McGraw Hill.

Gephart, R. (1999). Paradigms and research methods. *Research Methods Forum, 4.* Retrieved October 20, 2008 from http://division.aomonline.org/rm/1999_RMD_Forum_Paradigms_and_Research_Methods.htm

Gough, H. G. (1979). A creative personality scale for the adjective check list. *Journal of Personality and Social Psychology, 37*(8), 1398-1405.

Gryskiewicz, S., & Taylor, S. (2003). *Making creativity practical: Innovation that gets results.* Colorado Springs: Center for Creative Leadership.

Hamel, G. (Speaker). (1998). *Creating the future.* (Presentation at the Stanford Executive Briefing). Mill Valley, CA: KANTOLA Productions.

Haner, U. E. (2005). Spaces for creativity and innovation in two established organizations. *Creativity & Innovation Management, 14*(3), 288-298.

Hocevar, D., & Bachelor, P. (1989). A taxonomy and critique of measurements used in the study of creativity. In J. A. Glover, R. R. Ronning, & C. R. Reynolds (Eds.), *Handbook of creativity* (pp. 53-75). New York: Plenum.

Howe, K., & Eisenhardt, K. M. (1990). Standards for qualitative (and quantitative) research: A prolegomenon. *Educational Researcher, 19*(4), 2-9.

Ireland, R. D., Kuratko, D. F., & Covin, J. G. (2003). *Antecedents, elements, and consequences of corporate entrepreneurship strategy.* Paper presented at the Academy of Management 2003 Proceedings.

Isaksen, S. G., & Lauer, K. J. (1999). Relationship between cognitive style and individual psychological climate: Reflections on a previous study. *Studia Psychologica 41*(3), 177-191

Isaksen, S. G., & Lauer, K. J. (2002). The climate for creativity and change in teams. *Creativity & Innovation Management, 11*(1), 74-86.

Isaksen, S. G., Lauer, K. J., Ekvall, G., & Britz, A. (2000). Perceptions of the best and worst climates for creativity: Preliminary validation evidence for the Situational Outlook Questionnaire. *Creativity Research Journal, 13*(2), 171-184.

Jennings, D. F., & Lumpkin, J. R. (1989). Functioning modeling corporate entrepreneurship: An empirical integrative analysis. *Journal of Management, 15*(3), 485-502.

Jones, O., Edwards, T., & Beckinsale, M. (2000). Technology management in a mature firm: Structuration theory and the innovation process. *Technology Analysis & Strategic Management, 12*(2), 161-177.

Kanter. R. (1988). When a thousand flowers bloom: Structural, collective, and social conditions for innovation in organizations. In B. M. Staw & L. L. Cummings (Eds,), *Research in organizational behavior*, vol 10: 169-211. Greenwich, CT: JAI Press.

Kanter, R. M. (1989). Swimming in newstreams: Mastering innovation dilemmas. *California Management Review, 31*(4), 45-69.

Katz, R. (2004a). How the team at Digital Equipment design the 'Alpha' chip. In R. Katz (Ed.), *The human side of managing technological innovation.* (2nd ed., pp. 121-133). New York: Oxford University Press.

Katz, R. (2004b). Managing creative performance in R&D teams. In R. Katz (Ed.), *The human side of managing technological innovation.* (2nd ed., pp. 161-170). New York: Oxford University Press.

Khan, A. M., & Manopichetwattana, V. (1989). Innovative and noninnovative small firms: Types and characteristics. *Management Science, 35*(5), 597-606.

King, N. (1990). Innovation at work: The research literature. In M. A. West & I. L. Farr (Eds.), *Innovation and creativity at work* (pp. 15-59). New York: Wiley.

Kirton, M. (1976). Adaptors and innovators: A description and measure. *Journal of Applied Psychology, 61*(5), 622-629.

Kirton, M. (1976, 1976-1998). Kirton adaption-innovation inventory [1998 Edition]. Retrieved August 10, 2008, from Mental Measurements Yearbook database.

Krueger, R. A., & Casey, M. A. (2000). Focus groups: *A practical guide for applied research* (3rd ed.). Thousand Oaks, CA: Sage Publications, Inc.

Lant, T. K., & Mezias, S. J. (1990). Managing discontinuous change: A simulation study of organizational learning and entrepreneurship. *Strategic Management Journal, 11*(4), 147-179.

Lawrence, P. R., & Lorsch, J. W. (1967). Differentiation and integration in complex organizations. *Administrative Science Quarterly, 12*(1), 1-47.

Lee, R. M., & Esterhuizen, L. (2000). Computer software and qualitative analysis: trends, issues and resources. *International Journal of Social Research Methodology, 3*(3), 231-243.

Leifer, R., McDermott, C. M., O'Connor, G. C., Peters, L. S., Rice, M. P., & Veryzer, R. W. (2000). *Radical innovation: How mature companies can outsmart upstarts*. Boston: Harvard Business School Press.

Leifer, R., O'Connor, G. C., & Rice, M. (2001). Implementing radical innovation in mature firms: The role of hubs. *Academy of Management Executive, 15*(3), 102-113.

Lynn, G. S., Morone, J. G., & Paulson, A. S. (1996). Marketing and discontinuous innovation: The probe and learn process. *California Management Review, 38*(3), 8-37.

Madjar, N., Oldham, G. R., & Pratt, M. G. (2002). There's no place like home? The contributions of work and nonwork creativity support to employees' creative performance. *Academy of Management Journal, 45*(4), 757-767.

Malterud, K. (2001). Qualitative research: Standards, challenges, and guidelines. *The Lancet, 358*, 483-488.

March, J. G. (1991). Exploration and exploitation in organizational learning. *Organization Science, 2*(1), 71-87.

Martin, J. A., & Combs, J. G. (2009). Punishing managers for bad acquisitions: does firm size matter? *Academy of Management Perspectives, 23*(3), 92-93.

Martin, R. (2008). Innovation through acquisition. *Business Week*. Retrieved December 5, 2009, from http://www.businessweek.com/print/innovate/content/feb2008/id20080229_5767 34.htm

Mathisen, G. E., & Einarsen, S. l. (2004). A review of instruments assessing creative and innovative environments within organizations. *Creativity Research Journal, 16*(1), 119-140.

Mauzy, J., & Harriman, R. (2003). *Creativity, Inc.: Building an inventive organization*. Boston: Harvard Business School Publishing.

Maxwell, J. A. (1992). Understanding and validity in qualitative research. *Harvard Educational Review, 62*(3), 279-300.

McCoy, J. M., & Evans, G. W. (2002). The potential role of the physical environment in fostering creativity. *Creativity Research Journal, 14*(3/4), 409-426.

Mednick, S. (1962). The associative basis of the creative process. *Psychological Review, 69*(3), 220-232.

Merriam, S. B. (1998). *Qualitative research and case study applications in education* (2nd ed.). San Francisco: Jossey-Bass.

Miles, M. B., & Huberman, A. M. (1994). *Qualitative data analysis* (2nd ed.). Thousand Oaks, CA: Sage Publications.

Miller, D. J., Fern, M. J., & Cardinal, L. B. (2007). The use of knowledge for technological innovation within diversified firms. *Academy of Management Journal, 50*(2), 307-326.

Mone, M. A., McKinley, W., & Barker III, V. L. (1998). Organizational decline and innovation: A contingency framework. *Academy of Management Review, 23*(1), 115-132.

Montuori, A., & Purser, R. (1995). Deconstructing the lone genius myth: Toward a contextual view of creativity. *Journal of Humanistic Psychology, 35*(3), 69-112.

Moore, G. A. (2004). Darwin and the demon: Innovating within established enterprises. *Harvard Business Review, 82*(7/8), 86-92.

Morgan, G., & Smircich, L. (1980). The case for qualitative research, *Academy of Management Review 5*(4), 491-500.

Morrison, C. (2009). *How to innovate like Apple*. Bnet. Retrieved December 6, 2009 from http://www.bnet.com/2403-13501_23-330240.html

Norusis, M. (2006). *SPSS 15.0 statistical procedures companion*. Upper Saddle River, NJ: Prentice Hall.

Oldham, G. R., & Cummings, A. (1996). Employee creativity: Personal and contextual factors at work. *Academy of Management Journal, 39*(3), 607-634.

Paine, F. T., & Anderson, C. R. (1977). Contingencies affecting strategy formulation and effectiveness: An empirical study. *Journal of Management Studies, 14*(2), 147-158.

Peters, T. J. (1984). Strategy follows structure: Developing distinctive skills. *California Management Review, 26*(3), pp. 111-125.

Peters, T. J. (2004). A skunkworks tale. In R. Katz (Ed.), *The human side of managing technological innovation.* (2nd ed., pp. 405-413). New York: Oxford University Press.

Peters, T. J., & Waterman, R. (1982). *In search of excellence.* New York: Harper & Row.

Pierce, J. L., & Delbecq, A. L. (1977). Organization structure, individual attitudes and innovation. *Academy of Management Review, 2*(1), 27-37.

Pinchot, G., III. (1987). Innovation through intrapreneuring. *Research Technology Management, 30*(2), 14-19.

Prahalad, C. K., & Hamel, G. (1990). The core competence of the corporation. *Harvard Business Review, 68*(3), 79-91.

Ray, M. L. (1987). Strategies for stimulating personal creativity. *Human Resource Planning, 10*(4), 185-193.

Rickards, T., & Moger, S. (2006). Creative leaders: A decade of contributions from Creativity and Innovation Management Journal. *Creativity & Innovation Management, 15*(1), 4-18.

Ripple, R. E. (1989). Ordinary creativity. *Contemporary Educational Psychology, 14*(3), 189-202.

Roberts, N. C. (2006). Public entrepreneurship as social creativity. *World Futures: The Journal of General Evolution, 62*(8), 595-609.

Roethlisberger, F. J., & Dickson, W. J. (1939). *Management and the worker.* Cambridge: Harvard University Press.

Ronan, W. W., & Lathan, G. P. (1974). The reliability and validity of the critical incident technique: A closer look. In *Studies in Personnel Psychology.* Vol. 6 Issue 1, p53-64.

Rosenfeld, R., & Servo, J. C. (1990). Facilitating innovation in large organizations. In M. A. West & I. L. Farr (Eds.), *Innovation and creativity at work* (pp. 251-263). New York: Wiley.

Rubin, H. J., & Rubin, I. S. (2005). *Qualitative interviewing: The art of hearing data* (2nd ed.). Thousand Oaks, CA: Sage Publications.

Runco, M. A (1993). Cognitive and psychometric issues in creativity research. In S. G. Isaksen, M. C. Murdock, R. L. Firestien, & D. J. Treffinger (Eds.), *Understanding and recognizing creativity: The emergence of a discipline* (pp. 331-368). Norwood, NJ: Ablex.

Sandberg, W. R. (1992). Strategic management's potential contributions to a theory of entrepreneurship. *Entrepreneurship: Theory & Practice, 16*(3), 73-90.

Schneider, J., & Locke, E. (1971). A critique of Herzberg's incident classification system and a suggested revision. *Organizational Behavior and Human Performance, 6*, 441-457.

Schumpeter, J. A. (1934). *The theory of economic development.* Cambridge, MA: Harvard University Press.

Schumpeter, J. A. (1942). The process of creative destruction, in capitalism, socialism, and democracy. New York, NY: Harper & Brothers Publishers.

Scott, G., Leritz, L. E., & Mumford, M. D. (2004). The effectiveness of creativity training: A quantitative review. *Creativity Research Journal, 16*(4), 361-388.

Scott, S. G., & Bruce, R. A. (1994). Determinants of innovative behavior: A path model of individual innovation in the workplace. *Academy of Management Journal, 37*(3), 580-607.

Scott, W. E. (1965). The creative individual. *Academy of Management Journal, 8*(3), 211-219.

Shalley, C. E. (1995). Effects of coaching, expected evaluation, and goal setting on creativity and productivity. *Academy of Management Journal, 38*(2), 483-503.

Shapero, A. (1985). Managing creative professionals. *Research Technology Management, 28*(2), 23-28.

Siegel, S. M., & Kaemmerer, W. F. (1978). Measuring the perceived support for innovation in organizations. *Journal of Applied Psychology, 63*(5), 553-562.

Skarzynski, P., & Gibson, R. (2008). Innovation to the core: A blueprint for transforming the way your company innovates. Boston: Harvard Business School Publishing.

Smith, G. J. W. (2005). How should creativity be defined? *Creativity Research Journal, 17*(2/3), 293-295.

Solomon, Y. (2007). Bowling with a crystal ball: How to predict technology trends, create disruptive implementations and navigate them through industry. Charleston, SC: BookSurge Publishing.

Souder, W. E. (1988). Managing relations between R&D and marketing in new product development projects. *Journal of Product Innovation Management, 5*(1), 6-19.

Stake, R. E. (1995). *The art of case study research.* Thousand Oaks, CA: Sage Publications.

Staw, B. M. (1990). An evolutionary approach to creativity and innovation. In M. A. West & I. L. Farr (Eds.), *Innovation and creativity at work* (pp. 287-308). New York: Wiley.

Stevens, G. A., & Burley, J. (1997). 3,000 raw ideas = 1 commercial success! *Research Technology Management, 40*(3), 16-27.

Stokols, D., Clitheroe, C., & Zmuidzinas, M. (2002). Qualities of work environments that promote perceived support for creativity. *Creativity Research Journal, 14*(2), 137-147.

Szymanski, D. M., Kroff, M. W., & Troy, L. C. (2007). Innovativeness and new product success: insights from the cumulative evidence. *Journal of the Academy of Marketing Science, 35*(1), 35-52.

Taylor, W. (1990). The business of innovation: An interview with Paul Cook. *Harvard Business Review, 68*(2), 97-106.

Tellis, G. J., & Golder, P. N. (1996). First to market, first to fail? Real causes of enduring market leadership. *MIT Sloan Management Review, 37*(2), 65-75.

Tellis, G. J., Prabhu, J. C., & Chandy, R. K. (2009). Radical innovation across nations: The preeminence of corporate culture. *Journal of Marketing, 73*(1), 3-23.

Thomke, S. (2001). Enlightened experimentation: The new imperative for innovation. *Harvard Business Review, 79*(2), 67-75.

Thompson, V. A. (1965). Bureaucracy and innovation. *Administrative Science Quarterly, 10*(1), 1-20.

Treacy, M. (2004). Innovation as a last resort. *Harvard Business Review, 82*(7/8), 29-30.

Trochim, W. M. K. (2006a). *Qualitative validity.* Retrieved October 20, 2008, from http://www.socialresearchmethods.net/kb/qualval.php

Trochim, W. M. K. (2006b). *The qualitative debate.* Retrieved October 20, 2008, from http://www.socialresearchmethods.net/kb/qualdeb.php

Turnipseed, D. (1994). The relationship between the social environment of organizations and the climate for innovation and creativity. *Creativity and Innovation Management, 3*(3), 184–195.

Tushman, M. L., & Anderson, P. (1986). Technological discontinuities and organizational environments. *Administrative Science Quarterly, 31*(3), 439-465.

Tversky, A. (1977). Features of similarity. *Psychological Review, 84*(4), 327-352.

van de Ven, A. H. (1986). Central problems in the management or innovation. *Management Science, 32*(5), 590-607.

Wanke, M., & Schwarz, N. (1995). Asking comparative questions: The impact of the direction of comparison. *Public Opinion Quarterly, 59*(3), 347-372.

Webster, L., & Mertova, P. (2007). Using narrative inquiry as a research method: An introduction to using critical event narrative analysis in research on learning and teaching. New York: Routledge.

Wengraf, T. (2001). *Qualitative research interviewing.* Thousand Oaks, CA: Sage Publications.

West, M. A., & Farr, J. L. (1990a). Innovation and creativity at work: Psychological and organizational strategies. New York: Wiley.

West, M. A., & Farr, J. L. (1990b). Innovation at work. In M. A. West, & J. L. Farr (Eds.), *Innovation and creativity at work: Psychological and organizational strategies* (pp. 3-13). New York: Wiley.

White, F. M., & Locke, E. A. (1981). Perceived determinants of high and low productivity in three occupational groups: A critical incident study. *Journal of Management Studies, 18*(4), 375-387.

Woodman, R. W., & Schoenfeldt, L. F. (1989). Individual differences in creativity: An interactionist perspective. In J. A. Glover, R. R. Ronning, & C. R. Reynolds (Eds.), *Handbook of creativity* (pp. 77-91). New York: Plenum.

Yin, R. K. (2003). *Case study research: Design and methods* (3rd ed.). Thousand Oaks, CA: Sage Publications.

Zahra, S. A. (1993). New product innovation in established companies: Associations with industry and strategy variables. *Entrepreneurship: Theory & Practice, 18*(2), 47-69.

Zhou, J. (2003). When the presence of creative coworkers is related to creativity: Role of supervisor close monitoring, developmental feedback, and creative personality. *Journal of Applied Psychology, 88*(3), 413-422.

Zhou, J., & George, J. M. (2001). When job dissatisfaction leads to creativity: Encouraging the expression of voice. *Academy of Management Journal, 44*(4), 682-696.

Zien, K. A., & Buckler, S. A. (1997). Dreams to market: Crafting a culture of innovation. *Journal of Product Innovation Management, 14*(4), 274-287.

Appendix A. The Interview Schedule

Introduction

First of all, I would like to thank you for your participation in this study. It means a lot to me, and it will allow you and others understand the differences between startup and mature companies that affect the level of creativity, especially in the context of radical innovation. I would like you to think about one *typical* project you participated in at the startup company, and one *typical* project you participated in at the mature company. Please think about those when you answer the questions I will ask next.

Main Questions

1. I would like to talk about experiencing creativity.
    a. Tell me about the typical project you were involved with in the startup company.
    b. How would you define "being creative" in your own words? Do you feel you were creative there?
    c. Now tell me about the typical project you were involved with in the mature company.
    d. Do you feel you were creative there?
    e. Was it more or less than what you felt in the startup company? How so?
    f. [Possible probes for creativity]
        i. How frequently did you have creative ideas?
        ii. Give me examples of creative ideas you had.
        iii. Would you consider those ideas novel? How so?
        iv. Would you consider them useful? How so?
        v. What did you do with creative ideas you had? Did you share them? Submit them to someone? Did anything prevent you from submitting or sharing?

2. I would like to talk about freedom and autonomy now.
    a. Let's go back to the startup company. How would you describe the freedom (or autonomy) you had in doing your job?
    b. How did it make you feel?
    c. Let's move now to the mature company.
    d. Can you describe the freedom (autonomy) you had there there?
    e. How was it different than the startup company?

3. Let's talk about your immediate supervisor and higher management.
    a. Let's start with the startup company. Tell me about the support or encouragement (or lack thereof) you received from your direct supervisor in the company regarding your ideas?
    b. How would you describe the support and encouragement (direct or indirect) you received from upper management (CEO, executive team) in the startup organization?
    c. Now let's move to the mature company. Tell me about the support or encouragement (or lack thereof) you received from your direct supervisor in the company regarding your ideas?
    d. How would you describe the support and encouragement (direct or indirect) you received from upper management (CEO, executive team) in the mature organization?
    e. Where did you feel you received more support and encouragement from your direct supervisor and higher management? Why do you feel that way? How did it affect your creativity?

4. The next topic is recognition.
    a. Tell me how you were recognized for your creativity in the startup company. What did it make you feel? How did it affect your creativity further?
    b. Now tell me how you were recognized for your creativity in the mature company. What did it make you feel? How did it affect your creativity further?
    c. How did the difference in recognition between the two companies affect your creativity?

5. The next set of questions will be about the challenges you encountered.
    a. Think about the startup company project. How challenging was it? What was it about the project that made it challenging (or not challenging)?
    b. Think about the startup company project now. How challenging was it? What was it about the project that made it challenging (or not challenging)?
    c. How would you compare the challenge level between the two companies? How did it affect your creativity?

6. I would like to talk now about resources.
    a. Think about the startup company. How did the availability (or lack thereof) affect your ability to be creative there?

b. Think about the mature company now. How did the availability (or lack thereof) affect your ability to be creative there?

c. How different was the availability of resources in both companies?

d. [Possible probes:]
i. By resources I mean, in general, to funding, people, and time to try new things.
ii. Enough resources? What was enough and what wasn't?

7. I would like to discuss team dynamics in both companies.
a. Think about the startup company first. Think about a specific team you were part of. Tell me about that team and the other members. Tell me about the relationships between team members (professional and personal, if applicable).

b. How would you describe the team in terms of supporting your creativity?

c. Think about the mature company now, and the team you were part of. Tell me about that team and the other members. Tell me about the relationships between team members (professional and personal, if applicable).

d. How would you describe the team in terms of supporting your creativity?

e. How different was it from the startup company?

f. How did that difference affect your creativity?

g. [Possible probes:]
i. Was it legitimate to have conflict?
ii. Was conflict productive?
iii. Did you debate ideas?
iv. Was there trust? How would you describe trust?
v. Were you open?
vi. Describe the communication flow among team members?
vii. Was there internal competition?

8. Let's talk about formalization, bureaucracy, and processes.
a. Think about the startup company first. How would you describe the formality, bureaucracy, and processes of that company? How did it affect you in general? How did it affect your creativity?

b. Now think about the mature company. How would you describe the formality, bureaucracy, and processes of that

company? How did it affect you in general? How did it
affect your creativity?

    c. How was it different than the startup company? How did
that difference affect your creativity?

    d. [Possible probes:]

        i. Was formality a good thing?

        ii. Was bureaucracy a good thing?

        iii. What processes affected your ability to be creative?

9. I would like to discuss job satisfaction.

    a. Think about the job you held in the mature company. How
satisfied where you with that job?

    b. How did your job satisfaction affect you? How did it affect
your creativity, if at all?

    c. Now think about the job you held in the startup company.
How satisfied where you with that job?

    d. How did your job satisfaction affect you? How did it affect
your creativity, if at all?

    e. In what areas were you more satisfied in one company versus
another? In what areas were you less satisfied? How did it
affect you in general? How did it affect your ability to be
creative?

    f. [Possible probes:]

        i. What did you feel when you went home every day?

        ii. What did you feel when you went to work?

        iii. What did you feel on Friday before the end of the
work week?

        iv. What did you feel on Sunday before the beginning of
the week?

10. We are almost at the end. Now try to think about your mood in both
companies.

    a. When you worked for the startup company, how would you
describe your mood in general? How did work affect your
mood? How did your mood affect work? How did your
mood affect your creativity?

    b. When you worked for the mature company, how would you
describe your mood in general? How did work affect your
mood? How did your mood affect work? How did your
mood affect your creativity?

    c. How was your mood different between the two companies?
Did the companies have an effect on this difference? Did this
difference create a difference in your creativity when you
were in the two different companies?

11. This is my last question. I would like to talk about the pressures and support from home that might have affected you at work.
    a. When you worked for the startup company, where there pressures from home associated with your job? How did your family feel about you working for a startup company? How did it help (or obstruct) your work? How did it help (or obstruct) your creativity?
    b. Did you feel you had support from home (family, friends) for working at the startup company? How would you describe it? How did it help (or obstruct) your work? How did it help (or obstruct) your creativity?
    c. When you worked for the mature company, where there pressures from home associated with your job? How did your family feel about you working for a mature company? How did it help (or obstruct) your work? How did it help (or obstruct) your creativity?
    d. Did you feel you had support from home (family, friends) for working at the mature company? How would you describe it? How did it help (or obstruct) your work? How did it help (or obstruct) your creativity?
    e. Why were the pressures and supports different?

12. Is there anything I missed in this interview? Was there any other difference that you feel was significant to the difference you described in your level of creativity?

Summary

That's it. I want to thank you very much for your help today. Would it be OK if I call you again to clarify something later? As soon as I complete this study and upon its approval by the school, I will be more than happy to send you a copy.

Appendix B. Within Case Analysis

P1

P1 worked in a startup company (S) for five years in a technical role. S was acquired by the mature company (M), and P1 continued to work in M, still filling a technical role for nine more years in two different sites. P1 no longer works in M.

Creativity

P1 felt that creativity was a personal characteristic of him more than influenced by the environment, regardless of being in S or in M. He felt that creativity was in his nature. For him, creativity would occur in the shower, while he was driving, and not necessarily at work. In those locations—the work environment was not as influential on him as in the office. P1 categorized the creativity in S as "survival" creativity, and sometimes even described "cutting corners" as an example of creativity. When comparing his creativity between S and M, he claimed that his creativity at M was more "breakthrough" creativity, more radical, whereas his creativity in S was more basic, although new to the market. P1 claimed that his creativity in M allowed him to publish peer reviewed papers and present in conferences, due to the novel nature of his creative ideas there, whereas his creativity in S would not have allowed him to publish and present. P1 also claimed that much of his innovation in M was patentable, so he filed many patents when he worked in M. P1 believed he had a similar rate of creative ideas in M as in S, but felt that in M some of his creative ideas were suppressed, although he was not discouraged from being creative. P1 felt that his creativity was broad (domain wise) in S, and narrow (linked to very specific domain areas) in M.

Autonomy

P1 was one of the founders of S, and as such felt he had a high degree of autonomy:

> As one of the co-founders and as one of the senior technical position I obviously had a lot of freedom, and if I said that something was a good idea, that was typically automatically generally accepted.

In M, in contrast, he described that when his ideas went against a statement made by his supervisors—they did not want to hear about it, and he felt he lost his freedom. However, P1 felt that his real freedom was an internal thing to him, and that he could carve out his own freedom to think and be creative. He was "slapped" when he tried to go beyond his formal boundaries, but he did not care. P1 described working with another group and testing product concepts without any formal authority, as he felt he did not need formal authority. P1 described that in M he was "taking a beating" and criticized for taking risk, whereas in S he was expected to take risks. At the same time, he described M as an environment that allowed him to make "side trips" and innovate (and file patents) in areas that were not directly related to his official tasks. In S, due to the "survival mode"—he could not deviate from the immediate projects he was working on. In summary, P1 described having less formal autonomy in M compared to S, but that he carved his own autonomy. For the purpose of this study, his experience is interpreted as S providing more autonomy than M.

Supervisor

P1 described his supervisor in S (the CEO) as very driven to success, a business person, willing to "cut corners", but did not think highly of him as a technical contributor. Being a technical contributor himself, P1 thought highly of people who were respected and competent technical contributors. He saw his supervisors in M as such. At the same time, he described them (his supervisors in M) as highly political, who sometimes discounted his ideas if they were not in line with their own. In general, he felt that his supervisors both in S and in M were supportive of his creativity. P1 reported that his supervisors in M were supportive of his academic education, while his supervisor in S was dismissive of it. The supervisor was also dismissive of P1's publications of research, whereas P1 experienced support from the supervisors in M.

Recognition

P1 felt recognized for his contribution and creativity in both companies, but in different ways: formal and informal. He felt both types in M. There was a formal recognition system that recognized and rewarded him for achievements, and there was informal recognition:

> Informal recognition is just the general opinion that people have about you, and you... feel it. They talk about you behind your back,... and you might hear it from somebody, but they also talk about it in front of you.

P1 stated that he cared about receiving informal recognition, and that it was an encouraging factor for him. In S, in contrast, neither formal nor informal recognition existed. P1 felt that in such a small company, in his role, he could only disappoint and not exceed expectations, as the expectations were very high. He did not care about recognition in S, because there was none. However, he expected recognition in the form of company success, when the financial rewards could be very significant through equity ownership that will be material through an exit, an IPO, or an acquisition.

Challenges

P1 only addressed technological and external challenges in both companies. He claimed that S was dealing with "low tech", so the technology there was not very challenging. In contrast, he was dealing with cutting edge technology in M:

> In M, from the very first day, I was in a group whose flag, whose target was to revolutionize [the product]... And people were saying, specifically other people in the field said: you can't build [the technology]... it can't be done. So if experienced people say it, it has to be challenging.... Not only that I felt more challenge. They were officially, "approved by the community" of being greater challenges.

P1 compared S to other startups who were much more radically innovative, and claimed that the innovation in S "was a joke". Throughout the interview P1 describe internal challenges in getting his ideas implemented in M, and how he had to be creative in bypassing those challenges.

Resources

P1 felt that M definitely had more resources for his projects than S. Even when he complained about not having enough resources in M, he could always find ways to get the missing resources. In one example, he asked another team to develop a concept product for his project, and even though he had no authority over them—they still developed the product for him. In S, he described an environment very low on resources, where he had to share tools with others. P1 believed that his creative throughput was similar in both companies, but the availability of resources in M allowed him to implement much more of his creative ideas than in S. P1 also claimed that M allocated more funding than S to file patents, a resource he believed was important to creativity.

Team dynamics

P1 claimed he was a strong team player because he hated to work alone. He enjoyed the interaction with other people, and cross pollination of ideas. He had a stronger relationship with the team at S due to the history they had together prior to working in S. In M, he kept the friendships he had with S employees after the acquisition, but did not make new friends among any of the employees in M that were not part of S before. P1 felt that the environment even within the original S team after the acquisition became a little more political. P1 described more internal competition in M than in S, and gave an example of a fight over who discovered a certain invention and got to file a patent for it. P1 felt that the team in S had more trust and open communications, whereas the team in M had more internal competition and negative conflicts. He felt that a positive debate of ideas existed in both companies equally.

Formalization, bureaucracy, and processes

P1 stated that without a doubt there was more bureaucracy in M than there was in S. He described S as being run by "kids"—young employees with no process experience, whereas M was run by professionals with years of process experience. P1 accepted the fact that formalization is necessary to run a large and complex organization. He admitted that the processes were big and cumbersome, but they did not suppress his creativity. It would have suppressed the implementation of his ideas, and he did feel at times that the organization was "against him", but he found creative ways to bypass the system and get his ideas implemented.

Job satisfaction

P1 felt equally satisfied in both places. He believed he is a happy person by nature, and carried this trait into both S and M. There were days when he felt unhappy going to work, but that happened in both places. As examples, he gave a technical challenge that made him unhappy in S, and an internal-political challenge that made him unhappy in M. However, these two examples were not enough to generalize the source of situational unhappiness in those companies.

Mood

P1 could not describe a significant and consistent difference in his mood between the two companies. He described differences in his family that could have affected his mood, but there were ups and downs during the time he worked for both companies, so he could not describe a significant difference one way or the other.

Home pressure and support

P1 felt more pressure when he worked for M (later) than when he worked for S (earlier). This pressure was attributed to several reasons: (1) the family was smaller when he worked for S, he had no children, and his wife had other things to do while he was working late; and (2) he did not have financial constraints when he worked in the small company, he did not have to pay mortgage, whereas in M he had a much bigger family to support and a mortgage. He added that his wife was more supportive of him working late at S because she understood that it was required for a startup to succeed, and anticipated the financial reward from the company's success. She was less understanding when he worked late at M, where the financial reward was not anticipated as much. She expected him not to care so much in M.

Other insights

P1 described filling multiple roles in S, from a development engineer to a technical support person, marketing person, and beyond. He felt that in S he had a stake in the company's success, while in M he had less feeling of belonging. He felt that such feelings have a direct impact on his creativity (felt more creative in S for that reason). P1 described the interaction between people and projects in M as fertilizing, and provided several examples where interacting with people working on different projects allowed him to help them and create new ideas himself. He also described the environment in M as very dynamic and less monotonous for him. The different projects around him were challenging and stimulating to him.

P2

P2 was the CEO of a small startup company (S) with ten employees for three years, after which he left S and joined a mature company (M) in a marketing role, a role he filled for more than three years, to the date of this study.

Creativity

P2 defined creativity as "being able to find a solution that is differentiated in the market to a particular product, [or] a particular customer problem". He later added novelty and usefulness to the definition. P2 felt he was more creative in S, because the company started with a clean slate, with no prior history, image, conservatism, or business approach, whereas in M he felt that he had to deal with a lot of "baggage". He also felt that the novelty of ideas was critical for the startup company to differentiate itself in the market, whereas in M novelty was not always perceived as positive, and the bigger the departure was from existing products, the more new ideas were rejected.

Autonomy

Being the CEO of S, P2 felt that he had a lot of autonomy, even with the oversight of the board of directors. However, the board of directors was relying on him to know how to run the business, so he enjoyed full autonomy and free reign, once there was agreement on the strategic goals of the company at the high level. In M, he felt that his "sandbox" was defined pretty narrowly, limiting his autonomy.

Supervisor

In S, the board of directors was not made of people who worked full time for the company, so the interaction with the board was more strategic, focused on increasing the value of the company, and raising funds to it. P2 was not often second guessed by the board. He described his supervisor in M as someone who supported his creativity, as long as it matched with his own position.

Recognition

In S, there was no question of who was accountable for everything, and everyone focused on the same goals, which made recognition straight forward. However, in M there were many people who affected every decision, good or bad, and it was hard to link accountability with results and recognition. Both accountability and responsibility were highly distributed. P2 felt recognized at M, mostly for smaller, group wise achievements, as those were the easiest to recognize.

Challenges

P2 described the challenges in S as external: building the business, getting investments, and solving customer and technical problems. However, in M he described the mostly internal challenges: addressing all internal constituencies, reaching compromises, and "feeding the bureaucracy". He claimed he spent used much more energy in addressing the internal challenges than addressing the external ones in M.

Resources

P2 experienced having more resources available to him for his projects in M than in S. Not only that M had a higher absolute number of resources than S, but also more resources were allocated to his specific projects. He also identified another area where M had better resources: the availability of experts on different topics. In S, P2 noted that most people were generalists, while in M he could find an expert on almost every topic, even if outside his immediate business unit. P2 had to work harder in S to compensate for lack of resources than in M, where resources were available. P2 did not associate that with more creativity. P2 claimed that it is easier to fund projects in M compared with seeking investments from VC and shareholders in S.

Team dynamics

P2 described the team in S as very cohesive:

> We spent time to gel the team, really had common vision, common alignment, understood what the objective was. It was very clear what we needed to try to accomplish.

He did not experience the same in M. He also noted that the team in M was distributed across multiple states, countries, time zones, and cultures, whereas the S team was collocated. The collocation in S allowed the team to gel quickly and strongly, whereas the geographic distribution and cultural diversity of the team in M made the relationship more complex. P2 did not notice any internal competition in S, because every individual was going to succeed or fail based on whether the entire company succeeds or fails, and therefore internal competition was meaningless. However, he observed that since it was hard to identify contribution of individuals to the success of the project in M—internal competition and self promotion became more important than moving forward. P2 also noticed that communications in S were more open because everyone could see the big picture, whereas in M communication was withheld by individuals as a way to gain organizational power.

Formalization, bureaucracy, and processes

P2 described the processes in M as time consuming. There were many constituencies in the company that could be affected by any decision he could make, with different objectives. The compromises required diluted the effectiveness of decisions, and a lot of time was consumed in achieving such alignment. P2 noticed the existence of processes in both companies, but observed that the processes in S were optimized to the single project S was working on, whereas the processes in M could not be optimized, and had to be generalized to address multiple projects that existed in M at any moment. P2 claimed that in S they needed to move quickly forward, and would make decisions based on 80% of the knowledge required, whereas extra time was spent in M to gain the additional 20% of the information. P2 attributed this to unwillingness to make decisions in M, causing significant delays.

Job satisfaction

P2's body language and tone of voice unequivocally stated that he was more satisfied in S than in M. His satisfaction in S resulted from the direct impact he had on the company's success, the building of something new, and making a difference. His lower satisfaction in M resulted from having to spend more time on "feeding the internal machine", a lower value activity, than on "real" problems in the outside world.

Mood

P2 could not separate his mood during the two periods from the satisfaction he experienced in the companies, which affected his mood. When he worked for S he experienced significantly more fear and anxiety, more optimism, and happiness, whereas when he worked for M he experienced more comfort, safety, and cynicism.

Home pressure and support

P2 worked longer hours in S than in M, and he experienced pressure from his family, especially since the salary was low to non-existent in the beginning. However, his family did notice that he was happier in S, and had expectation for a potential payoff from a successful exit. At the same time, there was also pressure when he worked long hours at M, as there was no potential for a significant payoff at an exit, and the expectation was that he will not work as hard in M.

Other insights

P2 discussed the differences in risk taking. He observed that people working in M did not want to take risk, as their philosophy was "I can be successful as long as I don't mess it up", thus creating risk aversion. S was the antithesis to that. He took significant risks at S, and adding some small risk to it was not as significant as taking such risk was to M. P2 believed that the risks were objectively the same, but were typically perceived as much higher in a large company, conditioning people to take lower risk and smaller steps forward as a result. P2 himself took less risks at M, to the extent he believed his supervisor's comfort zone was.

P3

P3 worked in M in several different marketing and general management roles for six years. He then left to join S, where he worked as the Vice President of Marketing for two years, and then left S to join another company.

Creativity

P3 felt that his creativity was required and instrumental to both S and M. He defined creativity as "the formulation and process of putting ideas into action that benefits the company, its employees, and shareholders." He felt creative when he first joined M, creating a new business, but less creative when the new business was converted into the formal operations structure of M. This cycle repeated itself through the different roles he filled in M, whereas in S he felt that the opportunity to be creative was more consistent over time. P3 also described his role in S as very broad, thus lending itself to more creativity.

Autonomy

P3 experienced different levels of autonomy at M. When he was part of a smaller organization in the formation phase, he experienced a high degree of autonomy, which diminished as that organization became part of a larger structure. P3 observed that even when the organization was small, there were those who were trying to restrict the autonomy, and do it "the M way". P3 experienced much higher degree of autonomy in S, as there was so much to do, and not enough people to do it, so trust had to be established and autonomy given to individuals. At the same time, there was a strong dependency that cross-functional alignment will be achieved.

Supervisor

P3 attributed troughs in his creativity to lack of leadership in M, and was amazed how quickly someone in a leadership position can dampen or kill creativity. He observed that his supervisors at M were pushing him hard to cut costs and control programs, but mainly because their own supervisors were pushing them. He called this "the gravity effect of leadership". When P3 was hired into S, his supervisor (the CEO) was not sure about him. However, he gained the respect and the trust of the CEO, who was very supportive of his job. There were only few times when he sensed the CEO acting dictatorial. From the interview, P3 seems to have respected the CEO, too.

Recognition

In M, P3 experienced several types of recognition, varying from financial rewards, promotions, and management planning, to informal recognition that included presenting to members of the board, press, and other public venues. That exposure seemed very meaningful to P3. The recognition came not only from his supervisor, but also from other senior executives and technical people at M. P3 participated in promoting other technical people in the organization, and consider that as recognition for himself, especially since he was not a technical person. In S, P3 experienced more informal recognition than in M. That recognition took the form of exposures to VC firms, and the trust he received from the CEO and his peers, especially the technical leaders in the company. The financial recognition at S was mostly in the form of equity and promise of the future, but P3 appreciated the immediate financial recognition he received at M more ("In enjoy the finer things in life. I'm not afraid to work for them").

Challenges

P3 observed that the challenges in general were developing in a cycle. He felt that he needed those challenges so he would thrive, and suffered when there was a trough in the challenge cycle, to the point he felt a need to move to the next challenge. He experienced several of those cycles in M due to his six year tenure there, but only one cycle in S, due to his shorter time there. P3 identified the challenges at S as "do or die". The challenges were directly related to the survival of the company, and were definitely external, whereas the challenges in M were internal, getting management excited about projects, and with overall lower intensity. P3 never felt desperate in M, or that the challenges there were related to the survival of the company.

Resources

P3 lacked resources at S, which was bootstrapping itself to growth. The resource shortage was across people, time, tools, and everything else.

However, P3 felt that the company's success in the face of that lack of resources was all the more meaningful. He also felt more creative due to the finite resources in S. In M, P3 had more resources. At the same time, a temporary shortage in resources could not have affected M as severely as it would have S, causing him to perform some creative actions to compensate for that lack of resources. M was more tolerant to carry and supply resources. P3 also recognized that people at M were working "9 to 5", which would have limited their contribution as resources, and that was tolerated at M.

Team dynamics

P3 characterized the team dynamics at S as strong, with trusting relationships, good communications and good balance, in a consistent manner. The relationships between team members extended beyond working hours, and those relationships improved trust and communications at work. In M, he experienced a constant churn in personnel, as people moved between different businesses, and competed over promotions to higher positions in the organization. P3 formed few personal relationships in M, but not to the same extent as in S, where:

> We laughed together, we cried together, we popped the champagne cork at the end when we sold the company.

Formalization, bureaucracy, and processes

P3 attended many more meetings in M than he did in S. He attributed that to having many more interdependencies among "moving parts" in M. He accepted that as a consequence of a large and complex organization. P3 observed that the leadership team at S came from a heritage of good companies and good practices, and brought processes into S, so S was not completely without processes. There was no bureaucracy in S in implementing and managing those processes. However, at M he observed strong bureaucracy in implementing processes. In both S and M, P3 reported serving "tier 1" customers, complying with ISO quality standards, reporting, and auditing, but he felt that S was more purposeful in implementing processes, whereas in M there was a forced bureaucracy in the implementation. He claimed that the biggest difference in implementing the processes was in the effort it took, how many people were involved, and how long did it take (all of those were more at M).

Job satisfaction

P3 had good times, good memories, and lifelong relationships in both companies. From his description, the peak satisfaction was very similar between both companies. However, in M he experienced more anxiety and "baggage that dragged him down." P3 experienced the challenge cycle several times in M, and having to lay off employees weighed heavy on him.

He enjoyed the successful product launch in S, and was disappointed by the unsuccessful product launch at M, in spite of the team's best effort. A significant contributing factor to his job satisfaction was the financial rewards.

Mood

P3 believed that his non-work related mood was relatively similar during the times he worked in both companies. On the other hand, he felt a significant impact of the level of anxiety he had at work over his mood outside of work. He experienced a constant level of anxiety in S associated with the company's survival, whereas at M he experienced different periods of higher and lower anxiety.

Home pressure and support

P3's wife stopped working, making him the sole provider to the family. She supported him relatively similarly in both companies. She was neither worried nor stressed over his ability to keep their quality of life. She was, however, stressed when she saw him unhappy, entering a time of reflection, and encouraged him to make a change. P3 was respectful of the amount of time he should spend with the family and the attention he needed to give them, and in return he received similar support from his family when he worked in both companies. P3 experienced cycles in his family situation, as his children were growing and had different needs and different times, but it was never to the point of creating more or less pressure on him with respect to a specific company. He mentioned a slightly increased support from his family when he worked for S, due to the survival nature of the startup, which could run out of money any moment.

Other insights

P3 observed an open and supportive environment, providing a lot of autonomy in 1995, "when business was good". However, he described that as business got worse for the specific market M participated in—management got a lot more involved, autonomy was significantly reduced, and he found it harder to stay creative.

P4

P4 was the Vice President of Engineering in a startup company (S) for two years. Then the startup company was acquired by the mature company (M), where he was filling the role of Vice President of Engineering to the date of this study, for over three years. His role was in the engineering discipline, mostly as a manager, rather than an individual contributor.

Creativity

P4 defined creativity as "decisions made in the absence of prior precedents, in pursuit of a defined goal." This definition included the novelty and usefulness elements of the standard definition of creativity. In S, he claimed that everything he did was done for the first time. He found this to be true, in certain activities, even in M. P4 contrasted the consistency of creativity between the companies as:

> The peak feeling of creativity has been the same in S and in M, but I guess I'd say that within the S experience there was a sort of a daily sense of being creative, like the length of the peak was almost the entire time I was there, whereas in M, the feelings of being creative are very spiky, at times prolonged intervals of sort of feeling much less creative.

Autonomy

P4 described experiencing "extreme autonomy" in both companies. However, after further consideration, he defined the autonomy in S as *group* autonomy, developing the strategy for the company, and having a significant impact on achieving company objectives, whereas in M he experienced *individual* autonomy. Working from a home office in a remote site in a different state, he stated, jokingly: "nobody cares where I am". Even considering his VP position, he had no doubt that his work really had no significant impact on the company.

Supervisor

In general, P4 had supervisors he felt respected by, who gave him autonomy, and were available as sounding boards, in a very similar way in both companies. He, though, preferred working alone. He later added that his supervisors in S were supportive of his creativity, claiming this was why they brought him in, whereas in M his supervisor was more reluctant, and *tolerated* his creativity, rather than *encouraged* it. Beyond his immediate supervisor, P4 described a situation in M where he was working on a project with full higher management support, when all of a sudden, arbitrarily to him, upper management decided to stop the project with no explanation. Many decisions were made by upper management in solitude, creating an atmosphere of uncertainty with the team.

Recognition

The most satisfying form of recognition P4 experienced was the informal recognition of his peers in S. The informal recognition of his supervisors was meaningful to him because he respected them. Formal and financial recognition were also noticed at S, but P4 mentioned them only as the third meaningful recognition, mostly in the form of stock options. In M, the formal recognition was the most important to him, and P4 cited a lack of deep and meaningful informal recognition there.   P4 did not appreciate being recognized even by the CEO, as he did not feel the same respect towards the CEO as he felt towards his supervisors at S.   P4 linked his respect towards supervisors or executives as very important to the meaningfulness of their recognition of him.

Challenges

The challenges in S were *extreme*, and exclusively external. Some of the challenges were technical, some were associated with addressing customer needs, and some were in gaining industry support to the company's approach.   In M, none of the external challenges were insurmountable. However, P4 realized that his biggest challenges in his job were *internal*, negotiating inside the company, keeping people aligned and, at times, he counted 30 people inside the company he had to get permission from to speak with a customer, none of which he had in S.

Resources

P4 never felt resource constraints in either company. S was well funded all the time until the acquisition, and M always had enough resources for the projects he was involved in. He did not feel constraints even when S had only 10 employees. He only felt impatient to get moving, and "could not hire people fast enough." However, when it came to having the *right* resources, he claimed that in M, many of the people, at least at the higher positions, where related to other senior executives, and there was a lot of "recycling" of people who have not done well in one position and moved to another.

Team dynamics

P4 described the team dynamics in S as very cohesive and collaborative. The team was truly cross-functional, and he felt connected to every individual in the company, as the company grew from 10 to 150 employees. Being closely bound to the team in S versus working from his home office in a different state had impact on his team interaction. The relationships P4 had with the team at S was very close. He knew the names, wife names, and kids' names of the 150 employees who worked in S, and people worked long hours to support traveling comrades, as a result of that friendship. Furthermore, in S he felt he was really heard. In M, on the other hand, while citing strong work ethic, that type of friendship did not exist, reducing his motivation. He described the atmosphere as "fatalistic", and described going into meetings with top management, not knowing what the outcome will be, often surprised by arbitrary decisions made by top management behind closed doors. P4 did not feel competition within the team at S. He stayed focused on technology and stayed away from internal competition in M, but acknowledged that there was a lot of competition, including over the position he himself got after the acquisition of S by M. One of his ways to disengage from internal competition was to move to a home office in a remote location. P4 associated the internal competition in M with multiple layers of management, and observed such *political action* at the higher levels of management. He was affected by it when one day, without warning, the human resources department informed him of an organizational change, removing him from being a general manager of the business unit that once was S. In S, in contrast, the organizational structure was flat, so things like that could not have happened.

Formalization, bureaucracy, and processes

P4 described the creation of processes from scratch in S an act of creativity. He described that in M he was "fighting factions within the company to make progress". However, in general, he claimed that both companies were light on bureaucracy. There were decision making processes in both companies, but the main difference was that in S, when he needed to make a decision, he only had to involve 4 or 5 people, whereas in M, so many people and so many business units could have been impacted by those decisions, that he literally counted 32 people who needed to be involved in making a certain decision, to the point that there was a tremendous amount of communication that needed to take place. P4 accepted the fact that a large company has multiple "moving parts" and stakeholders, and that such coordination was required, but complained that it slowed decision making significantly.

Job satisfaction

P4 said: "the S experience was the peak experience of my career. Nothing equals that by any stretch of imagination". He later ranked the ratio of his satisfaction in S to that in M as ten to one. In S, what drove his high satisfaction was the teamwork, autonomy, challenging boundaries, rich and meaningful interaction with management, constant learning, filling multiple roles, and ownership of, and impact on the outcome. What made P4 less satisfied in M was mostly the small and narrow role he played in the company, and the lack of significant impact on the outcome.

Mood

P4 described his mood at S as "euphoric", and half jokingly described his mood at M as "bored". Separating the impact of work on his mood, he acknowledged that his personal life was going through significant changes, but those were cyclic, so within the periods of working for S and M his average mood was the same. Cynically he claimed he was in constant denial, and thus happy all the time.

Home pressure and support

P4 felt he had family support both at S and M. The family pressure he felt when working for S was because he worked on weekends and very long hours. At the same time, he felt that the family was more understanding, and also expected the eventual payoff. He claimed that he felt more pressure when he worked in M, since his family expected him to work less in a big company.

Other insights

Six months after the acquisition of S, while working for M, P4 and a colleague realized that they were exchanging e-mails at 1 AM, and tried to understand why they were doing that, after already receiving the financial payoff from the acquisition. They both realized they still feel the impact they have, not only on the company outcome, but on society with a product that increases quality of life. They realized that producing a product that increased quality of life was more important to them than the financial rewards they received.

P5

P5 worked for the mature company (M) for a period of four years, filling roles in a traditional business unit (MBU), as well as creating an internal startup (MS) in that company. She left the company to join a startup company (S), where she worked for two more years. She filled marketing and general management positions in both companies. P5 eventually left S to join another mature company. Throughout these experiences, she went through four periods that showed significant differences in her experience of creativity and the factors affecting it. The first period was when she worked for the MBU in the mature company (M). The second period was during the early days of the creation of the internal startup (MS) within the mature company M. The third period was during the later days of MS, when it became more of a MBU. Finally, the fourth period was when she worked for the real startup company, S, after leaving M altogether. P5 provided insight on two major transitions: the transition from the MBU to MS in M, and the transition from M to S, and in the data analysis, she provided content to two cases.

P5 described her role in general as a marketing and business development in both companies. However, she described filling multiple roles in MS, from marketing to general management, technical marketing, product management, and business development. She was part of the team that created MS, when it only included a dozen people, and stayed there until it grew to a few hundred people.

Creativity

P5 defined being creative as coming up with a new idea and using it. She felt the most creative in MS, mainly because the ideas she came up were the ones that were used, and because of the latitude she had to come up with those ideas. She described her creativity there as spanning across the business and technical sides. She further described being the most creative at MS because the ideas she came up (and were implemented by the company) were novel to the market, representing breakthrough technology. Her creativity in the MBU was limited to the directions that were received from the business unit headquarters, which were in a remote site. Those directions limited her creativity to localization of global ideas generated by the company to the locale of the site she worked in, ideas that she described as incremental rather than radical or novel. P5 described the creativity at S the "survival mode" creativity: "they were dying, thirsty, wanting anything, because they had essentially nothing", but similarly described her own creativity as limited to implementing (in her marketing role) the creative technical ideas that were created by the technical people in the company, rather than generating her own creative ideas. However, she later referred to the innovative product and business model as new to the market. P5 claimed she was the most creative at M, and specifically MS, and found it hard to decide where she was the least creative, but finally identified S as where she was least creative.

Autonomy

P5 claimed she had no autonomy at MBU. Her work was highly directed and structured by the headquarters, which were located at a remote site. At MS she described the charter from management as "while we figure out what the strategy is going to be, just go do something and don't hurt anybody"— very high autonomy. She described the last days in MS as having lower autonomy, as roles became more clearly defined, and so did the focus areas and what needed to be executed. She described the autonomy at the S as being high too, but for different reasons. In S she had free reign because nobody else in the company knew how to do her job. P5 used the phrase "just take care of it" to describe the relationships her supervisors had with her, but in different contexts. In both MS and S she described it as high autonomy, where she was given very wide latitude to define her work, whereas she used the same term to describe very low autonomy in MBU, indicating that she needed to execute a set strategy.

Supervisor

P5 stated decisively that she received absolutely no support from her supervisor at MBU, claiming that this is probably the reason he was fired from the company later. She described him as a very bright individual, but lacking leadership and management skills she expected from a Vice President in a multi-billion dollar company. In contrast, she described her supervisor at MS as a very competent individual, offering great sense of direction, and a great leader. A significant part of why P5 described the later days of MS as lower in creativity and satisfaction were attributed to having a new VP who did not fully understand the business, as well as resided in a different state. She described her supervisor in S as a very bright and technically competent person, but with very little people management skills, lacking structure and organizational mentality, someone who ones told her that he should have been working for her, and not the other way around. However, she described him as very supportive of her.

Recognition

P5 experienced the most recognition in an informal form. In MBU she did not experience any recognition. The only type of recognition was a promotion, but P5 had to define her own objectives and then exceed them in order to earn that promotion, as otherwise she suspected that she would not have received any promotion, as "this guy doesn't have a clue" (referring to her supervisor). She appreciated the Management by Objectives (MBO) program that M had, and was able to use this system to get significantly financially rewarded. At MS, she still enjoyed the MBO program, but seemed to have experienced informal recognition in front of the team, and the exposure to executives. She appreciated the recognition of her contribution by executives in this company much more than the financial recognition she received. Finally, although she received recognition in S, she considered it the least effective. It was not financial as it was in M, and it seemed that she did not respect the supervisors and executives in S as much as she has at MS to value the informal recognition as much.

Challenges

P5 counted three challenges in MBU, two of which were internal: a location challenge, remote from headquarters, and process challenges ("this is the way we do it"). Only the third challenge was technical, facing the market. In general, working in M, she identified the constant reorganizations as a major challenge that disrupted working towards an end. When speaking about the initial period at MS, P5 discussed the external challenges in the market significantly more than any of the internal challenges. In S, P5 described a relative balance between the internal challenges (being a remote employee in a different state, staying connected, internal resistance to move from R&D phase to productization and commercialization) and external challenges in the market, through introducing a new product and a new business model.

Resources

When asked about her creativity, P5 mentioned her ability to generate multiple creative ideas at MS "because it was a startup type environment but with a large company [company name masked] money". She further mentioned the brand name of the large company as opening doors for her, whereas in S there was no such brand or funding available. P5 considered *low resources* as the reason she was least creative in S. The resources P5 had in MS were much less than in MBU in the same company, including people and funding. She cited this as causing her to be more creative: "I had to creatively borrow resources, using other people's people... money,... I had to sell internally". In S, P5 had no resources at all. Even then she had to "bet, borrow, plea" for resources, like MS, but the difference was that in M there were resources to tap onto (including software and other resources beyond people and funding), if she was creative enough, whereas in S there were not enough resources in the company to borrow.

Team dynamics

In MS, P5 described an environment of strong teamwork, all working towards the same goal, with a lot of bonds and lifelong friendships created. She described a team environment where each team member filled multiple roles, and covered for each other on different activities. The team had worked together in the company for a while, and knew each other prior to the formation of MS. P5 had a lot of respect to other team members, describing them as "very bright". She further portrayed an environment of openness, where ideas were debated openly without fear, and where people could enter each other's office, close the door, and vent. P5 described the environment in MBU as "cutthroat", and stated that there was no trust. She attributed the lack of team building to lack of leadership. There was strong competition there for positions, especially due to the continuous cycle of reorganization. P5 also described strong turf wars across groups, where in order to get something done, she needed to get a lot of people with conflicting agendas aligned. In S, P5 described no internal fighting, but rather a very cooperative environment, where a lot of bonding and friendship took place. Her only "complaint" was that the team lacked diversity, being made of mostly engineers, compared to M where the team was much more professionally diverse.

Job satisfaction

P5 decisively indicated she was the happiest in MS. It was a fun place to work in, because she was working on fun things. She attributed that to her experiencing creativity, autonomy, the informal recognition, and the "bleeding edge technology". She did not mind working 12 hours a day, and defined the environment as the best of both worlds, a small organization within a big company. P5 also cited the team bonds as a major source of job satisfaction. She was the least satisfied with her job at MBU, attributing it mostly to the cutthroat environment, and the small impact she had on achieving the business unit objectives. In the first opportunity she had—she moved into MS. P5 was not satisfied in both MBU and S, attributing it mainly to the lack of leadership in both.

Home pressure and support

The support and encouragement P5 received from her family was very similar across all three situations. She had to travel a lot in all three positions, and she described her family as trying hard to support her so that she can travel. P5 described getting her kids involved with trying new products when she worked for MS, something that made them proud and even more supportive. The support was more challenging when she worked for S, given the fact she worked out of her home office, but did not describe this as a significant challenge.

Other insights

P5 described the early time at MS as being highly dynamic, with a new Vice President in charge, a whole new area, new environment, and new structure. She also described the environment in M as being dynamic, but for different reasons: the company was reorganized every 18 months: "you're just getting momentum and it's like [dismissive tone], now they're going to screw the whole thing up."

P6

P6 worked for a startup company S and joined the mature company M through an acquisition, and worked for M for three years. He then left along with a team of people from M to start another startup company, where he worked for five years. P6 filled a technical role in the mature company, and was the founder and CEO of the second startup company. This case describes the transition P6 made from the first startup company to the mature company that acquired it.

Creativity

P6 associated the creativity in S with the success, failure, and survival of the company, and the focus the company had on its objectives. Being a startup company, P6 associated its survival with differentiation against mature companies in the market. He claimed to have been creative in both companies in his technical role. He had unique ideas. However, P6 claimed that his creativity was embraced in S, whereas it was hard to get ideas implemented in M. In fact, he estimated that one in four of his ideas ever got implemented. In S, he claimed, "the project was the company", whereas in

M—each project was just one of many, and had no significant impact on the company's success. He further estimated that he had the same amount of ideas in both companies, and the major difference was the percentage of those that got implemented.

Autonomy

P6 realized that S relied on him to succeed, and that he had the autonomy to do whatever was required for that, autonomy that grew from being an individual contributor to a group manager. He claimed this autonomy was born out of necessity. He realized that some of his decisions needed to be coordinated with others on the team, and could not be made in a vacuum, but he did not feel that was limiting his autonomy. The autonomy in M was limited simply by the position that his research group had within the organization, a step remote from products and customers. When asked to compare the autonomy between S and M, P6 was surprised to realize that he enjoyed more autonomy in M, being able to research adjacent areas to the one he was "officially" working on, whereas in S, the focus of the company on its survival and its main (and only) project limited his autonomy.

Supervisor

P6 descried that his supervisor in S, the CEO, could make decisions immediately and implement ideas. In M, in contrast, his supervisor had to convince another level (or several levels) of management before a decision could be made. P6 respected his supervisor at S, the CEO, as a technical person, much more than he respected his supervisor at M, who was a business person.

Recognition

P6 felt more recognized in S, and associated that to the respect he had for his supervisor, which made any recognition coming from him more meaningful, and to the unanticipated nature of rewards, whereas the anticipated rewards in M desensitized him to those. P6 also appreciated that he could be more recognized (formally and informally) and rewarded regardless of his age in S, whereas in M his recognition and rewards were linked to his tenure. Even though recognition in M could have come from a very senior executive, the respect that P6 had toward his supervisor in S made his recognition more meaningful to him. P6 felt that his supervisor in M was struggling for survival of his group, which was driving his behaviors, and did not respect that trait much. Although P6 enjoyed financial rewards in M, he felt they were not as linked to his performance as they were in S, and thus he appreciated the latter more.

Challenges

One of the reasons P6 claimed that a smaller percentage of his ideas got implemented in M was the number of people who needed to be convinced with the value of his ideas. In S, he needed to speak with a small number of people who were immediately available to make decisions, whereas in M he needed to convince a much larger group of people, who was not easily accessible. P6 described technical challenges equally between the companies. However, P6 described a kind of challenge in M that did not exist in S—internal challenge. He compared M to a huge ship, that could not make quick course corrections, and is not as nimble as S was. P6 emphasized the severity of the internal challenge in preventing progress. In contrast, he described the challenges in S as productive: overcoming them will increase shareholder value and achieve the company goals, whereas the internal challenges at M were not productive.

Resources

P6 described the resources in M as abundant, and at the highest quality. He respected the market clout that M had and its global sales force that allowed him to get support from current and potential customers of M in standardization activities. M had the best equipment, and spared no expenses when it needed to acquire it. In S, he had to settle for used equipment that could get the job done. However, P6 claimed that whenever a resource was absolutely needed for the success of a project at S—they would find this resource and make it available.

Team dynamics

In general, P6 described good team dynamics at both companies. He attributed very positive dynamics in S to the team being focused on the same clear objectives. P6 described the geographical separation of the different groups in M as a source of delay in making decisions, as well as a source of internal competition between groups, which was fueled by fear of certain groups getting closed. This fear caused teams and individuals to withhold information from one another. The team in S was collocated, thus eliminating decision making delays and intra-group competition. P6 described very open debate of ideas in S, resulting from trust and lack of fear and competition. He said:

> ...we have to remember that the competition is outside, not inside... and I think that at S we realized that. Our competition was other companies, but inside M sometimes competition became the other sites.

P6 described friendships in S between team members, and with the CEO. They met outside work, and participated in many social activities together.

In M, in contrast, it was hard to establish such relationships, or get management to support or participate. He distinctly remembered his supervisor telling a team member not to bother him over the weekend.

Formalization, bureaucracy, and processes.

P6 stated that M was much more bureaucratic. He provided two examples where rigid processes prevented employee satisfaction and promotions, to the point of reducing his own motivation. He appreciated the fact that as companies grow, they need more rules and processes due to the complexity of the large company, but claimed that those were too rigid and inconsiderate of real life situations. He described a situation in which a senior manager in M intervened to bypass processes, and liked that, but this was the exception rather than the rule.

Job satisfaction

P6 was more satisfied in S than in M. He attributed that mainly to his ability to focus on external challenges that increase shareholder value in S, versus the energy he had to waste on internal challenges that were unproductive.

Mood

P6 could not identify non-work related factors that might have affected his mood differently in the two companies. He saw a strong effect of his work on his mood, but not the other way around.

Home pressure and support

P6 worked longer hours in S, but did not have any children at that time, so it was easier for his wife to support him. While he was working in S, she got involved with other activities. In general, he claimed that her support was constant and equal between the companies, but also that it was a function of his happiness and satisfaction more than other factors such as working hours and financial reward or stability.

Other insights

P6 emphasized the survival of the organization (S) and the focus on the company objectives, as well as the impact of his contribution on the success of the company. He finally compared the two companies in the relationship with the product:

> ...at S, I think some of us really loved our product and loved what we were doing. At M, the last GM I worked under would actually say: don't fall in love with your product. It's a difference in mentality. We loved what we were doing. We wanted to make a difference, and so I think the comment "don't fall in love with your product" is a distancing comment.

P7

P7 joined M through an acquisition, and filled a marketing role in M for four years following the acquisition. He then left M along with a team that started S, a startup company. He filled the position of Vice President of Marketing in S for more than two years, a role he was still filling at the date of this study.

Creativity

P7 defined creativity as "coming up with unique ideas". He thought he was as creative in S as he was in M, and that creativity was an individual thing. However, he did state that his creativity in S translated to actions more often than in M. He also claimed that creativity in S had to be more unique and radical, whereas in M creativity could result in "me too" products. In M, radical ideas were shot down often, as they meant turning a huge ship around. At some point, he stopped coming up with radical ideas. In S, he felt more responsible for coming up with creative ideas than in M, given the impact they have on company success. He eventually realized he was more creative in S.

Autonomy

P7 felt complete freedom and autonomy in S. Part of it was attributed to the company being so small, and him being in charge of the marketing function. Another part of it he attributed to being in a remote site with significant time zone difference. He felt the freedom to create the marketing strategy and execute it the best way he could. In M, there was a lot of overlap between his job and others', and the need to coordinate his actions with people who might be affected by them limited his autonomy.

Recognition

P7 felt significantly more recognized in M than in S, but at the same time claimed that in S he cared much less about being recognized in order to be motivated. The recognition in M was more important because of the small impact that he had on the company. He appreciated the recognition he received in M, especially when it was associated with higher levels of management, by a general manager he respected a lot. At the same time, P7 identified situations where he and his team in M were recognized for project success, but consequently their project got cancelled, making that recognition meaningless.

Challenges

P7 stated that the biggest challenge in M was internal politics, and figuring out who the decision makes were who needed to be convinced in order to get an idea through the decision process. The biggest challenge in S was execution, mainly due to limited resources. The challenges in S were mostly technical. P7 claimed that the technical challenges in existing products in the market gave rise to S, which could not have competed with large companies with incremental challenges. Those significant challenges were the only barrier that the large companies face.

Resources

When it came to human resources, P7 experienced that M had much more than S. While specific programs in M might have been understaffed, it was really a matter of priorities, and if programs were prioritized higher—the required resources were found and reallocated. However, in S the resources simply did not exist, and there was a dilemma of whether to hire new resources and train them, or simply work longer hours with the resources at hand. Non human resources were available in S as much as they were available in M—enough to get the job done. Maybe M had excess resources overall, but he had what he needed in both. P7 linked resources to creativity:

...you have to be more creative when you have less resources, because you have to do more with less and it kind of spurs the creativity process.

Team dynamics

P7 described internal competition in M as "a bunch of people trying to pull themselves out of the pack and get recognition so they can move up the organization". Some of the challenges in both S and M were the geographical distance, time zone, and cultural differences between the teams. When P7 joined the team in M, he had to earn the team's trust. The team was experienced and cohesive when he joined them from an unproven startup company. The dynamics were characterized with tremendous internal competition, focused on the technical approaches, and on gaining access to resources. However, once he earned their trust, he became "one of the guys". When the entire team left to start S, he joined them, enjoying the trusting relationship they had in M. When they worked in M, he felt the classical tension between marketing and technical people, but once the team left and created S—he felt they were on the same side for the first time, and that their cooperation is critical for S to be successful.

Formalization, bureaucracy, and processes

P7 acknowledged that the politics in M served a purpose, given the size and complexity of the company. S lacked the decades of experience that M accumulated, and needed to figure out processes as it went along. P7 experienced a "love-hate" relationship with the processes in M. On one hand, they slowed progress and decision making, but on the other hand—they allowed the team to handle unexpected negative consequences better, and catch possible problems early on.

Job satisfaction

P7 was the most satisfied when he was doing real interesting work. He had times in M when his work was interesting, in a dynamic environment, but when those times were over, making room for a more operational and routine role, he became less satisfied, and left with the team to start S. He looked for a new challenge in S, and described being more satisfied in S than in M.

Mood

P7 described the changes in his life throughout the last 10 years, since he finished business school, moved to a new state, met his wife, got married, and had his first child. However, he could not attribute sustainable differences in his mood to changes in his personal life, whereas work had significant impact on his mood through his job satisfaction.

Home pressure and support

P7 felt a significant increase in his travel in S compared with M, associated with his role and the impact he had. Before taking on that role, he discussed it with his wife, who said:

> When you're happier, you're more pleasant when you're home [laughing], and when you're busy, you're happy, and so, I'd rather have you happier less time than unhappy but here every day.

By showing consideration to his wife's feelings and concerns, P7 believed that in return she was as supportive no matter what he was doing, whether at S or M.

P8

P8 worked in M for eight years, filling technical and operational roles until he left M to join S, filling a very similar role for almost three years, until he left S to be the founder of yet another startup company.

Creativity

P8 defined creativity as "doing something different to get better results. Not doing the same thing." He believed he was creative both in S and M, but considered himself "overhead", being a manager and not an individual contributor. P8 felt more creative in S than in M, as he felt that S was willing to try new things, whereas in M, certain things had to be done in a certain way. He also described the environment in S as a clean slate, allowing him to try those new things. He quantified his (and his team's) increased creativity as the number of people and the amount of time it took to solve a certain problem. As an example he described a project that was conducted in M, using six to seven senior engineers for a year and a half, whereas a more complex project was completed in S with three engineers in less than one year. Some of those creative ideas that P8 created in S were worthy of being patented, although the company chose not to, as those were process improvement ideas, not directly related to the company's main product. P8 also associated creativity with the product design cycle, where there was a much higher opportunity for creativity in the early stages than in the later stages.

Autonomy

P8 experienced much higher autonomy in S, since he was given a clean slate, an objective, and resource constraints, and the freedom to operate within those. He had to make a business case in S to get the funding he needed, but he felt that as long as he made a sound business case—he had the autonomy he needed. In M, in contrast, he felt that his ideas would have required a significant deviation from the company's current modus operandi and M was not ready for that. He believed that his ideas did not even go beyond his manager, and were stopped there. P8 associated his autonomy with the product life cycle. At the early stages, even in M, he felt some autonomy. However, in the later stages, where in S he was still experiencing autonomy—the autonomy in M diminished.

Supervisor

P8 enjoyed working for his supervisor in M. He described his supervisor as a good promoter, who let him speak publicly in meetings, but P8 did not respect his supervisor's technical abilities. His supervisor in S was less knowledgeable in P8's specific technical area of expertise, but P8 was surprised how quickly his supervisor mastered that area, and described him as having an overall technical knowledge of everything. The supervisor in S knew how to provide guidance, and combined it with autonomy. P8 respected his supervisor in S more than he respected the one in M, and seemed to have been supported by his supervisor in S slightly more than the one in M.

Recognition

P8 felt fortunate that he was formally recognized in M, but at the same time claimed that the "buddy system" was prevailing in the company, formally recognizing and promoting people based on internal politics. This system did not exist in S. However, P8 felt formal recognition in the form of promotion to a Vice President position. P8 described both formal recognition and financial rewards very similarly in both S and M. He felt that he was slightly more informally recognized in S, mainly through the exposure that he received in the company.

Challenges

The challenges P8 experienced in M were almost exclusively internal—changing people's minds, proving to them that a new and creative approach was viable, time and time again, to the point he became annoyed. In S, he described challenges mostly with resources shortage, and external challenges of delivering products to customers. P8 described those external challenges in S as much more interesting than those in M.

Resources

P8 identified cash shortage, cash preservation, and equipment shortage as stimuli to creativity. He felt that he had more resources in M, and had to outsource many activities in S where he did not have resources in house. However, he felt that the availability of resources in M became a bottleneck, as they did not allow utilizing them in a novel way. In general, P8 did not suffer from resource shortage in M, but he did not think those resources were used efficiently, due to having to do things the same way they were done before. In S, on the other hand, he suffered from resource shortage, but he also felt that the resources he was given (people, equipment, etc.) were used more effectively, and at a higher efficiency. P8 described the human resources at his disposal in S as having the right mindset and the right synergy.

Team dynamics

P8 described very open communications between team in S. This open communication allowed teams to see the "big picture", and address future issues before they occur. He described the team in M as having productive debates, mentoring, learning, but had limited trust, which restricted open communications. He identified in M internal competition of a positive nature, trying to excel and get promoted, but also of a negative nature, based on jealousy. He blamed part of it on managers who gave new and interesting assignments to employees who excelled before, without trying to mentor those who failed, causing this competition and jealousy. Teamwork in S was enjoyable, characterized with open communications. Disagreements could be strong, but task related and respectful, not leading to competition between people, competition that P8 did not experience in S.

Formalization, bureaucracy, and processes

Initially there were no processes in S for P8's area of expertise, and he had to develop his own processes, which were thus optimized for S's only project. The processes developed in S came from people's experiences from companies they worked for before. They brought best practices from those companies, and avoided poor practices. Later, as S grew, the processes became aligned and mandated under a big "umbrella" of process and structure, but P8 did not complain that those processes were restrictive. In M, all processes already existed, and P8 felt they were restrictive, unnecessarily. The processes were unified and applied to all products in the company, not addressing the differences between the products that might have warranted different processes.

Job satisfaction

P8 enjoyed getting up in the morning and going to work in S. In M, he described his work as sometimes mechanical, and sometimes boring. He was happier in S due to the experience, the exposure, and the people he referred to as talented. He enjoyed having everyone working towards the same goal— the success of the company. He compared that to his work in M, when his business unit was declining, and people left it without looking back.

Home pressure and support

P8 stated that in general his wife supported him the same way when he worked in both companies. She knew everyone in S, and felt more like a part of a family there. P8 was surprised during the interview to realize that he spent more time at home when he worked in S than when he worked in M. He attributed that to the flexibility and trust he had in S, versus the lack of trust and increase formalization in M. His wife would probably have liked it more when he worked in S, as he was happier there, and spent more time at home. P8 recognized a change in his family situation with the arrival of his children, but he and his wife found ways to compensate for the growing family to the point it did not create different pressure.

Other insights

P8 described learning a lot in M, through filling multiple roles over the years, and trying different things. In S, in contrast, he felt that he (and others) was filling multiple roles at the same time, with a clear picture of the entire project. P8 described that he learned a lot in the nine years he spent in M, but that he learned more in the two years he spent in S, which eventually led him to start his own startup company later.

P9

P9 worked in M for three years in various marketing and business development roles. He left M and joined an unrelated startup company (S), where he worked until the date of this study, for more than three years.

Creativity

P9 initially felt he was as creative in M as he was in S. He felt more creative when he worked for a new business unit in M than when he worked in a more generic role in M prior to that. P9 felt his creativity was associated with the empowerment he had in M, which was similar to the empowerment he experienced in S. When creativity was broken down to different elements of the standard definition (novelty and usefulness), P9 started feeling that he was more creative in S than in M. He felt that his ideas in S were much more "out of the ether", as there were a lot of unknowns and he started with a clean slate. In M, in contrast, there were a lot of assumptions and constraints that were made that limited the novelty of his ideas. P9 felt that his ideas were more useful in S because S was a software company, which allowed him to see the fruits of his ideas much faster than the ideas he had in M, a semiconductor company, where the product life cycle is much longer, and idea usefulness is seen years after they are conceived. Finally, he felt that he had more creative ideas in S:

> I would say that you're really starting with a blank board, or a white sheet of paper here at S, and that allows for creativity on a daily basis. I'm not sure that I was creative on a daily basis at M.

Autonomy

P9 felt that his autonomy in M was limited mostly by the need to align with multiple stakeholders within the company, as M was much more complex than S, and any decision made in one business unit could affect other business units. This had put constraints on his autonomy to make decisions and the time he could spent productively. In S, he did not feel the need to coordinate with multiple constituencies, and spent most of his time outside of the company, promoting the products.

Supervisor

P9 experienced several different supervisors in M, and reported directly to the CEO in S. He seemed to have respected his last supervisor in M more than previous ones, mainly because he experienced a lot of flexibility and autonomy from his last supervisor. He felt slightly more flexibility from the CEO in S, but relatively comparable to the flexibility he had from his last supervisor in M. He felt that this flexibility was more a function of the individual supervisor than the size of the company.

Recognition

P9 felt the lack of formal recognition in M and in S, but felt some form of informal recognition in both companies. In S, he felt he was recognizing people more than being recognized himself, as he was a member of the executive team, and felt recognized in getting exposure to the board of directors. He definitely felt more recognized in S than in M, as it was a lot easier and tangible to associate his efforts with company success. It was hard for him to get noticed for his efforts outside of the small business unit in M, and he acknowledged the fact that his efforts were small compared to the overall business in M.

Challenges

P9 divided the challenges at the different companies into several categories. He felt that the *technical* challenges were relatively equal at both companies, although in general he stated that semiconductor technology challenges (M) were greater than software challenges (S). He also felt that the *external* challenges in S were far greater than the external challenges in M. In S, there was the constant challenge of survival of the company, and engaging with customer carrying a business card of a small company, compared with the large company business card he used to carry in M. Finally, P9 compared the *internal* challenges at the two companies. He claimed that the internal challenges in M were greater. He had to align efforts with multiple constituencies, and cited long time to get decisions made.

Resources

P9 decisively stated that he had more resources in M: people, equipment, funding, and more. Everything was easy to get in M, except offices. There was also flexibility with the ability to move resources between projects. However, while he had fewer resources in S, those resources were sufficient and very focused on achieving the goals of the company. The resource availability in M allowed the company to start new initiatives that were unrelated to current projects, something that would have been hard to do in S. P9 observed the negative relationship between resource availability and creativity:

> The more resource constrained you are—the more creative you end up being, and I think, when you have more resources, you come up with maybe less efficient ideas, or maybe more resource intensive ideas, whereas when you know you have a lot more finite resources, you typically tend to be more creative.

Team dynamics

The team in S was very collaborative. While the structure of the teams that P9 was part of in S and M were very similar—he described much "stronger" relationships within the team. He described strong relationships as characterized by open communications, without fear of discussing contentious issues. P9 described personality conflicts in M, and the lack of constant exposure due to the multinational distribution of the team in M. P9 had a lot of respect for one of the team members in M, but he only saw him once a quarter, which prevented him from developing the type of strong relationships he later experienced with his team members in S. P9 developed more personal relationships with team members in M than he did in S. He felt internal competition in M, because individuals were thinking about the next career move in M, and used politics to rise inside the large organization. In S he did not feel any internal competition, as the company was too small for such politics. The only competition was external to the company. P9 described a higher level of productive debate in S, in order to resolve issues quickly and move forward. However, he felt a higher level of personal conflicts in M, due to the desire to climb in the organization, due to misunderstandings, and low exposure to team members. He also felt that his own part in personal conflicts in M was higher than in S due to his own maturity level.

Formalization, bureaucracy, and processes

While P9 appreciated the fact that a large company like M required complex processes that are strictly enforced, or chaos will reign—he also stated that those processes stifled creativity there. He claimed he wasted a lot of energy on meeting the process to the letter, energy that could have been spent more productively on the real objectives of the business unit. In S, in contrast, the team developed its own processes. Since everyone in S had a "big picture" view, as S was smaller than M—there was no need for complex processes. Those processes needed to be developed as the company grew beyond 50 employees, but even then—those processes were limited to the absolute necessary.

Job satisfaction

P9 felt definitely more satisfied in S than in M. When breaking it down, he claimed that satisfaction is a function of the excitement he had, as well as the monetary rewards linked to his efforts. He felt that his efforts were more rewarded in S than in M. He associated his excitement level lasted longer in S due to the dynamic nature of the business, and the greater challenges he felt compared to M.

Mood

In general, P9 felt better in S than in M. He definitely felt the impact of his work on his mood, and less the other way around. In S, he felt that his work had a stronger effect on his mood than it did in M. He described difficult circumstances in S that had more severe impact emotionally on him, whereas he felt isolation in M. During the first year in S, he felt a higher level of personal stress, due to the move to a new state with a higher cost of living.

However, after the first year, once he settled in with his family—he was experiencing the same personal mood as he did in M.

Home pressure and support

P9 felt the same level of support from his wife in S, as he did in M. He felt that her support was driven by his own happiness and demeanor at home, and when she felt he was unhappy—she encouraged him to move and confirmed what he already decided. He was traveling much more when he worked in M, but he was consumed with the business more when he worked in S. He did not feel any pressure from his family during the time he worked in S that was a result of the future unpredictability inherent to a startup company. By the time his first child was born, he felt that S was stable enough not to worry financially. P9 felt pressure to spend more time at home, both in S and in M. He felt more pressure when he got married, and even more when he had his first and second child. However, that pressure came from him, and not from his family. He claimed that his wife was more stressed during the first year in S, due to the transition to the new location, and his own stress level associated with the new position. However, later he felt that her pressure level was lower than when he worked in M.

Other insights

P9 emphasized the importance of the impact he had on S compared with the impact he had on M:

> At a small company like S, if you can increase revenue by a $1m, that's a big deal. If you increase revenue by a $1m in M, it's meaningless. No one even really cares.

P10

P10 joined S and filled a marketing role for four years. He then left S and joined M, still filling a marketing and business development role. P10 was still working in M at the date of the interview for this study, for more than two years.

Creativity

P10 defined creativity as being given the opportunity to think outside the box, identify what he wanted to do, who he wanted to do it with, and having the flexibility to implement it. He felt he had "full artistic creativity" in both S and M. P10 believed that in M he had more novel and radical ideas, because of the breadth of technologies and applications he was involved with, compared to a very limited and focused application he was involved with in S. The breadth of applications gave him more opportunity to be creative. P10 described M as giving a lot of decision making power to the business units, with very visionary management that treats the small business units like a VC does. He filed patents with both companies, and felt that the rate and number of ideas he had were relatively similar.

Autonomy

P10 described S as a pretty flat organization, very quick to respond and to implement ideas. He described M as relatively similar, but with several formal challenges that would limit flexibility. Some of them were associated with the size of the company and its potential legal exposure as such, and some with rigidity within the company. When asked to compare the autonomy, he decisively stated he had more in S, due to his ability to work directly with investors and press (in his marketing role), in contrast to having to work through legal, public relations, investor relations, and venture groups within M. M had many more people and structured processes involved, whereas he described the environment in S as much more dynamic, where he was wearing many different hats.

Recognition

P10 attributed recognition to the amount of self-marketing he conducted for himself in both companies. He felt that the informal recognition in both companies was relatively similar. He added that when everybody delivered high performance in S, the expectation for recognition was lower, as it was hard to single out an individual contributor. Formal recognition in S was almost absent, whereas in M—there was a clear formal recognition mechanism in place. Overall, P10 felt recognized at the same level in both companies.

Challenges

The biggest challenge for P10 in M was that, as a large company, he felt there was a big target mark on his back, causing him to be very pragmatic in how he represented the company, due to the potential exposure that a large, public company has. His legal department assured he was careful. A second challenge in M was the numerous competing priorities that affected the support and availability of resources for his projects. S, in contrast, was focused on a single product, which always had the highest priority. He did not feel he had to convince many people that he was doing the right thing. Working for a small company (S), P10 did not feel the big target mark on his back, and was therefore making statements, stirring up controversy, and issuing press releases that he would be restricted from issuing in M. In M, when a project reached commercialization stage, there was an infrastructure in place for a swift product launch and production. In S, on the other hand, there was much higher risk and little infrastructure to support it. There was a challenge in implementing ideas associated with customer validation. The requirement in M was higher for customer need validation before an idea would be implemented, compared with a lower requirement in S.

Resources

P10 faced resource challenges in both companies. S was a small company with a finite amount of resources, but could attract top talent due to the payoff potential, whereas M had many more resources, but such that were allocated and not readily available for his projects due to being allocated to other prioritized projects. P10 observed that the CEO in S was concerned with growing too fast, and as a result the company was never fully staffed. However, when there was a clear need for resources—the company hired them quickly. In M there were many more resources, but P10 described this as sometimes working against the project. On one hand, the resources might not have been at high enough quality, even if abundant, and on the other hand—sometimes there were great resources available for projects, but they were engaged in unproductive philosophical debates. An advantage in S was that it allowed management to be dictatorial at times, directing resources towards the real problem.

Team dynamics

The team dynamics in S was much more open and trusting, lacking the need for political correctness. On the other hand, P10 described the team environment as having a high degree of political correctness, to the point of not being able to move forward at time, and being caught up in rhetoric. He did acknowledge that the never ending planning process in M could have slowed projects down, but at the same time acknowledged that S was more prone to make bad decisions due to the lack of sufficient debate. Overall, P10 preferred not to be dealing with the internal politics he experienced in M. He described having earned the trust of all people in S and that he trusted them, in turn, whereas in M, due to the size of the company, while earning the trust of the people close to him—he could not earn the trust of everybody he had to interact with. At the same time, he did not trust anybody, due to knowing they have competing priorities and individual agendas, and sometime due to what he described as incompetency. P10 associated trust with informal relationships between team members, much higher in S than in M, where the engagements were more formal, and included a lot of posturing. P10 did not feel internal competition in S. There was not a lot of room to be promoted in a small company, so there was nothing to fight over. In M, in contrast, he felt some internal competition for promotions, although he stated that seniority and tenure were not always a deciding factor in promotion, thus reducing such internal competition somewhat.

Formalization, bureaucracy, and processes

P10 described M as more formalized than S. However, he was familiar with larger and more rigid companies in their formalization than M, and described the formalization in M between those companies and S. He claimed that M was not overly bureaucratic, and that even with the processes in place, everyone was moving pretty quickly, like in a startup. There were few hurdles, but not too many. In S, bureaucracy was not a term that ever came up. P10 felt more accountable in S, and more in control of his career, compared with M, where he felt less accountability and less in control of his career.

Job satisfaction

P10 felt satisfied in both companies and attributed that to the dynamic environment in both companies, and to his job being meaningful to both companies. He felt empowered in both companies.

Home pressure and support

P10 was not married when he worked in S or in M. He did have girlfriends (different ones) then. He did not feel pressure from them when he worked in S or in M, but he also acknowledged that he didn't care, as he was in a selfish mode, due to lack of maturity. He claimed that later he became less selfish, as he matured, and started balancing work and life.

Other insights

P10 was surprised to realize how satisfied he was working for a large company after working for a small company. He attributed it mostly to the dynamic environment in M. He felt that working in S before he moved to M gave him an appreciation for things that people who might have only worked for large companies take for granted: resource availability, secretaries, administrators, budget and overhead.

P11

P11 worked in M for five years, filling various marketing and business development roles in different business units, until a reduction in force in the company. Less than a year later, he joined S as the Vice President of Marketing, a role that he filled until his interview for this study, for almost two years.

Creativity

P11 looked at creativity as a discipline that involves passion and emotion. He sensed that M defined him as being creative when he took initiative without waiting for instructions. He felt creative in M when he felt strongly about certain ideas to push forward. He felt that being creative in S meant more than having an idea—it mean implementing it. P11 believed that his ideas were more novel in S, because he started with a clean slate, with no need to conform to rules, policies, procedures, or "anti-innovation" culture. He also believed that the product developed by S was very disruptive to the market. He felt that in M he was less creative because nothing was really new, and he was limited by those rules, policies, procedures, and culture. P11 claimed that his ideas were more useful in S simply because it was easier to measure them there, whereas it was hard to measure his ideas in M, as they were not directly related to revenue, specific new customers, or bottom line financial contribution.

Autonomy

P11 felt he had a reasonable amount of autonomy in M. It seemed that his group was new and unknown, and could have created its own mandate of what the job should be. In S, he needed to keep himself within the budget, but did not have many restrictions beyond that. Later he described that there was a mandate the team was working for that limited his autonomy. However, he felt he had a much higher level of autonomy in S, where he needed to build a marketing team from scratch. In S, he really needed to develop the mandate. It seemed that the dependence of the organization on him in S, versus the small impact he had on the organization in M, made him feel that the autonomy in S was much higher, and that even if he gets a free reign, but with no significant impact—it limited his autonomy.

Supervisor

In S, his supervisor did more than support his creativity—he *relied* on P11 to do his job, as nobody else in the company could do it. The CEO also relied on P11 to mentor the other executives based on his experience as an executive before S. He also felt the support in that the CEO gave him full access to advise the board of directors. He felt a very high level of trust from the CEO and the board, and they called him often to get his advice. He never received such a call from the CEO or a senior executive in M, and when he received such call, it was when the caller already knew the answer, and wanted only to verify. He did not feel trusted in M. P11 had a good relationship with his immediate supervisor in M, as they shared an entrepreneurial background. P11 respected him, and they had a relationship that resembled a partnership. However, he felt that even his own supervisor's "sandbox" was limited, and those limitations trickled through to him. While his respect to his current CEO in S and his direct supervisor in M were relatively on par—he lacked respect to upper management in M, due to their directive interactions, and the perception of them not caring or listening to his opinions:

> Because some of those guys think, well, they made it there
> and they've got into that position... they don't need to explain

themselves.... Because they think their time is so precious, "I don't have time to waste with you."

Recognition

In M, most of the recognition that P11 received was from his direct supervisor, and he did not feel recognized by higher levels of management. He felt informal recognition for a job well done, and some formal monetary rewards in the form of stock options and cash bonuses. He felt that the financial recognition was very good in M, but he also added that he felt that his contribution was much higher than the recognition he received there. In S, in contrast, P11 did not enjoy formal cash bonuses, since those did not exist. He received stock options instead, and claimed that the CEO, who had financial background, was very aware of the value of stock options, to the point that P11 claimed he received a sizeable percentage of ownership in S. The CEO in S recognized P11 informally, but he did it so often that P11 became desensitized to it. He felt that the exposure to the board of directors, the autonomy he has, and the ability to influence is a form of informal recognition he enjoyed in S.

Challenges

P11 did not feel challenged in M because he wasn't able to use his full capacity. He felt that the company and the executives in it were rejecting new ideas that did not fit the company's mold. The biggest challenge for him in M was trying to convince the VP to move forward with new initiatives. When asked about technological or external challenges, P11 described another internal challenge: M was driven by engineers, and as such exercised technology push more than market pull. The engineering teams were the company's "elite", and he described their products as "solutions looking for problems." There seemed to have been a disconnect between market demand and company technology supply. In S, on the other hand, the main challenge was operational: the limited resources and capacity to execute the plan. P11 did not feel any internal challenges in S. There, decisions could be made within 24 hours, as the entire company was focused on a single product. A large company (M), he admitted, had to deal with many different ideas, and could not be as focused as S, and thus it was over-thinking new ideas, slowing down innovation. P11 did not feel an external challenge in carrying the S business card. He claimed that the technology was so novel and disruptive, that it did not matter where it came from and, in fact, it might have even helped.

Resources

P11 claimed that M had a lot more resources, but the availability of specific resources to specific projects was challenging. The company had multiple projects, and a complex prioritization system. His project could have been de-prioritized almost arbitrarily, to the point he would not have enough resources to complete it. In S, on the other hand, the overall number of resources was much smaller, but since the company was focused on one project—the resources were sufficient, and could never be de-prioritized to other projects.

Team dynamics

P11 described the team dynamics in M as one of constant conflict. He separated the engineers who he described as typically introverted and happy doing what they do, from the marketing and business people (the group he was part of), who always wants to get ahead. On one hand he described this competition as positive, when they challenged each other, but on the other hand he described:

> We're always pushing each other, and that dynamic environment sometimes makes people step on other people's feet. And sometimes people will stab you in the back to get ahead of the pack.

P11 described the team dynamics in S as much more collaborative, with everyone pushing in the same direction, everybody clearly knowing their roles and responsibilities, and everybody understanding that only collaborations will yield success. He described being "continuously in dialogue and building opinions and making decisions quickly to get to our target". He did not feel any internal competition in S whatsoever. He only felt they were debating ideas regarding the way to move forward. He described open communications, sharing of ideas, listening to different perspectives, and benefiting from the diversity of experience that the different members bring to the team. P11 added that open communication through sharing of ideas and open and respectful criticism helped the organization (S) to learn. He stated that senior managers in M restricted such open debate, and rejected ideas that were not consistent with their own. He claimed that M redefined the team "teamwork" as follows:

> ... like to throw around the word team, be part of the team, play with the team, you got to be part of the team, you got to be a team player, be a member, you know? And I don't think they know what it means.... In most cases they think that being a team player, team member means you follow as I tell you to do and you will execute to my plan and if you follow all my instructions and you execute—you're a team player, and you've done a good job. Be it good or bad. And the difference is they don't know when it's good and when it's bad because they don't listen well.

In S, P11 felt he was part of a family. He never felt like that was in M, and attributed that to the distance he felt from the leadership, and the fact they did not listen well.

Formalization, bureaucracy, and processes

P11 described that M had procedures and policies already in place when he worked there, and those defined the roles and responsibilities, as well as the interaction between the different departments in the company. In S he created processes from scratch. The fact that there were no processes before in S caused people to do above and beyond what their titles suggest their roles and responsibilities are. They had to create procedures that would fit the company. The needed to be compliant with quality standards such as ISO, but they were creating the compliance processes from scratch. P11 accepted the fact that a large and complex company such as M needed to have that amount of processes and procedures to prevent chaos. Those processes were difficult, and slowed progress, but he felt he needed to live by them. They were "the nature of the beast".

Job satisfaction

For P11 the choice was clear—he was more satisfied in S than in M. He attributed that mainly to the fact that he had management and board interaction, and that he was involved in the decision making. In M, in contrast, decisions were made for him. He could make recommendations, and nothing more. He felt that he spent a lot of energy in M on developing use cases, scenarios, plans, and recommendations to present to management, all as part of internal selling. He enjoyed the external selling that was part of S. The impact he had on S made him feel definitely more satisfied there.

Mood

P11, like many other participants, could not notice a difference in his mood that could have affected his work in S or in M. He felt the opposite— the effect of job satisfaction on his mood, but even then he felt there were good moments and bad moments in both companies, and saw no significant mood differences.

Home pressure and support

P11 claimed he received no pressure from his family associated with his work in either S or M. His family was very supportive of him as long as he was happy and feeling he was reaching his potential. To assure that support—P11 made sure he balanced his work and family life. It was more difficult for him to balance life and work in S, as his office was in another state, and he has to commute and stay there five days a week, away from his family, whereas in M he worked close to home. Part of balancing work and life when he was in S was to assure that he attended important family functions, take vacation, and spend the holiday seasons with his family. He never felt any pressure regarding finances, or a concern that the startup company offered less financial security than the mature company. P11 attributed that to a solid financial situation of his family that allowed him to assume risks. He stated that his wife would probably have preferred the time he worked in M, because he was not traveling as much, and that is possibly the only difference in her support.

Other insights

P11 felt there was a higher degree of diversity in S than in M. In S, he was exposed much more to people from different teams and different disciplines, whereas in M his exposure to people outside his business development team was minimal, and he was exposed only to representatives of those teams. The team in S came from many different other companies, backgrounds, and experiences, thus increasing the level of diversity, whereas in M people worked for the company for a long period of time, thus fitting the company mold.

P12

P12 joined M as a technical researcher, and worked there for eight years. He left M to start a startup company (S) as one of the founders, and continued to fill a technical role in S until the date of this study, for five years.

Creativity

P12 described founding S on the basis of his creative idea, something that did not exist in the market prior to the formation of S. He described that creative ideas in M may not have had an immediate impact (unlike the ideas in S), and potentially never made an impact on M's products. However, he also stated that in M he had room to try things that were not directly related to the projects he was working on, allowing for creativity. He described the pressures in S to develop ideas that had immediate impact, and could not allow himself to pursue ideas without immediate impact. He felt less of this pressure in M. He could not state that his ideas were more radical or novel in one of the companies than the other, but felt that the ideas in S were more useful than those in M. P12 filed more patents in M than he did in S, but claimed that only few of his innovations saw the light of day in M, or were useful in the marketplace.

Autonomy

In S, P12 had all the autonomy he could want (supervisor wise), since he was one of the founders, and the company was founded on the basis of his idea. However, external forces in the market and the financial situation restricted his autonomy to areas that are most related to immediate impact. He felt that he had a lot of autonomy in M to do the work, which was combined with the ability to deviate and research new avenues.

Recognition

P12 felt formal recognition that was associated with technical expertise in M. He felt that his contribution was recognized by his technical supervisor, as well as his business counterparts. In S, he felt he could not be recognized internally. Being at the top of the company—he could not get promoted. However, the recognition in S came from external sources: the customers that granted his company business. When asked to compare the two types of recognition—he claimed that M did not have a good way of recognizing people, specifically innovators. He felt the recognition in M was significantly inferior to the external recognition in S.

Challenges

The biggest challenge P12 identified in M was getting the support of the business unit to novel creative ideas which, as a result, caused many of those ideas to never see the light of day. Additional challenges were his small team that was limited in resources, and the limitation on the scope of innovation. All of those were internal challenges. The biggest challenges he saw in S were to get funding, people, and resources to innovate. The biggest challenge of all in S was to align the product timeline with market adoption. When comparing the different types of challenges, P12 felt that internal challenges were high in M, external/market challenges were high in S, and he did not list any major technological challenges in either S or M.

Resources

P12 stated decisively he had more resources in S than in M. True that M has an overall larger number of resources, but a smaller amount of those was available for his projects than in S. Once funding was secured in S—he had all the people he needed. He had a bigger team than in M. The projects developed in S were capital efficient, and did not require significant investment in capital equipment as projects in M did. Whatever tools he needed for his projects in S—he had. On a relative basis, once investment was secured—he had more funding in S for his projects than in M.

Team dynamics

P12 described positive team dynamics in both companies, but for different reasons. In S, there was not a lot of conflict or competition as there is nothing to compete for. He claimed that nobody in the team planed to be working there for 10 years, and thus nobody was trying to get promoted. People worked there because of their interest in work, and the potential financial reward resulting from the success of the company. In M, the team members were pretty autonomous, and working on individual projects, so team interactions were minimal. Still, P12 felt that the team in M missed the feeling of everybody being on board together, as in S.

Job satisfaction

P12 definitely experienced higher job satisfaction in S than in M, due to one factor: he was a founder, he created the company, he had the idea, and he could do whatever he wanted to do. In M, in contrast, he was an employee, with minimal impact on the company or ability to make decisions.

Home pressure and support

P12 was traveling a lot in S. He could be away from home for three weeks at a time. Initially, this has put pressure on his family. His wife would prefer to see him more at home. When he worked in M, he traveled very little. However, his family got used to his travel in S. P12 felt support from his family equally in S and in M. While his wife preferred him to be home more, she preferred to see him happy even more, realizing his potential, and potentially getting financially rewarded with the success of the startup.

P13

P13 worked for startup companies as well as mature companies before he joined M. When he joined M, it was into an internal startup (MS), where he worked in a technical role for six years. After MS became a mature business unit, he moved into a more traditional business unit in the same company (M), and filled several roles there for four more years. P13 then left M to join a different mature company. Using P13 for this study was inspired by P5, who worked for an internal startup in her own company, and could compare the internal startup to a traditional business unit in the mature company, as well as to a real startup. P13 helped add more insight into the differences between internal startups and traditional business units in mature companies. For the following analysis, MS represents the internal startup in the mature company, and M represents the time after the internal startup became a traditional business unit, and P13 began working for a larger, more traditional business unit within the mature company.

Creativity

P13 believed he was as creative in MS as he was in M. However, in MS he claimed that a larger number of his ideas reached fruition, whereas in M many of his ideas never reached the market. He also felt that in MS he (and the team) really created something new. He did not feel creating new things later in M.

Autonomy

P13 described that his group was very autonomous in MS. With the exception of monthly meetings with an oversight committee, the team had the autonomy to do what they thought was necessary. Their project seemed to have been experimental, and the management above them did not interfere. P13 described that he did not fear that the plug will be pulled on his project. Every now and then they needed to conduct a study to address an oversight committee member's concern, but that was the only exception to their complete freedom. P13 described autonomy to modify the roadmap, and decide on the product features. That autonomy disappeared when customers started buying the products, and MS became a traditional business unit. At that point, the team became exposed to more executive scrutiny. Later, in M, the size of P13's "sandbox" became much smaller. He still felt he had autonomy, but in a much narrower domain. He also felt that he was being held to a much higher "burden of proof" to convince stakeholders to do something for the business unit.

Supervisor

P13 reported to two people when he was in MS. He described his supervisors as "enablers". They did not ask him to do things arbitrarily, and offered advice without enforcing its implementation. He did not feel that his supervisors micro-managed him then. In contrast, when MS grew to become a traditional business unit, and later in M, P13 felt that the communication with his supervisors became more distant and he received less encouragement. He described his later supervisor in M as generally supportive, but P13 was not really sure if he cared about what he did.

Recognition

P13 felt recognized in MS. He recalled receiving a cash bonus at some point, which surprised even him with its magnitude. To date, P13 claimed that this was a very significant bonus, and that his supervisor emphasized that he had received an "extra special" bonus for an "extra special" achievement. P13 also felt the respect, "all the way up and down": from his team mates to senior VPs. He was asked for opinion on other things, and he felt that as a form of informal recognition. P13 felt recognized later in M, too, but he never felt as special as he did when he was recognized in MS. He was part of a much bigger group in M, and it was hard to identify individual contribution and recognize it then.

Challenges

P13 stated that the biggest challenge in MS was the external competition. The company entered a market it had not been considered a player in, and went against giant players in that market. Later, in M, P13 claimed that the biggest challenges were internal: showing the value of what he was doing, convincing people to spend resources, and getting support from different groups were all very hard. In MS he felt he had all the support that he needed to implement his ideas, as radical as they might be. He could implement them internally in the company, with the help of other groups, or externally, cooperating with other companies. However, later in M, he felt that it was much harder to get ideas through to implementation, whether due to unclear roles and responsibilities, or due to people not disposed to help him. Another challenge in M was the disposition that everything had to be done inside the company, and there was no willingness to go outside and partner with other companies to expedite time to market. That disposition, according to P13, slowed things down significantly.

Resources

P13 described having significantly less resources in MS than in M, with a lower quality variability, and a substantial overall higher quality of the resources. At the same time, they had the ability to get more resources when he needed:

> It was a very small team, everybody was super high quality, and when we needed more, and we made the case for it, at that point we had the support and we were able to get it. Not a blank check, but we were clearly not held back.

Later, in M, P13 described a much larger team, but with higher variability of quality, and overall lower average quality of the resources. P13 described that the efficiency of the resources at MS was significantly higher too. Later in M, it took 10 times the amount of people and time to execute a similar task that earlier in MS it took a tenth of the time and people. P13 also described working in a frantic way during his time in MS, and having a lot of "down time" in M when things were less efficient. P13 described having access to general M facilities when he was in MS, which an ordinary startup will not have.

Team dynamics

Very early on in MS, some of the team members were new to each other, there was geographical distribution across two countries, and there was some overlap of work done by different members of the team. All of those contributed to lack of trust there. Later on in MS, though, as the team started gelling, members built trust and strong communications. Nothing was formal, but the roles and responsibilities became much clearer, and that was the normal state in MS. Later, in M, when the team grew bigger, P13 felt he could go back to be an individual contributor, which he enjoyed a lot. However, there was a down side to it: people were asserting political power and prevented progress. Internal competition became the norm. P13 also felt that a big part of the team involvement in MS was attributed to seeing the big picture, and understanding the customer and the design-in process. However, when the team grew bigger, in M, people became disconnected from the customer, and he described people actually amazed that their product ended up in customer hands. P13 felt he developed strong relationships with everyone in the team in MS. He knew everyone in the team, and they knew him. But as he moved into M, he described:

> I distinctly remember, at a certain point, I think, we got so many people, and somebody said "hi" to me in the hallway, and I had no idea who that was. And I felt terrible. I honestly felt really, really bad. I felt like I've let somebody down.

Later, P13 described the camaraderie in MS in similar terms to the brotherhood in arms that soldiers have in the battlefield. He described a team that hated to lose, and worked really hard to win. He did not experience those feelings later in M.

Formalization, bureaucracy, and processes

P13 described two processes and how they affected his work in MS and in M. As both were in the same company—the processes were similar. One process was the phase-gate product development process, and the other was the handover to manufacturing process. Both processes applied to MS and M equally. However, P13 claimed than in MS, the process was used typically to *guide* progress. It was a good process, and following it helped the team develop the product with no mistakes. However, the focus was on the results, not letting the process be too overbearing:

> Everybody in the team knew that whatever was the goal, the process wasn't a barrier to get to the goal, but it was one of the milestones we had to get through. And so, I'm sure that we did things, that we didn't strictly meet whatever the criteria were, meet some process goals, but we had to get through that goal.

However, later P13 described that in M the same process was very strictly enforced and followed, which slowed progress almost arbitrarily. It seemed that people used the process to assert power:

> I remember people trying to schedule [a process phase gate], and it would take an act of God to get everybody in the room that you needed to have, I don't know what they needed. It takes a lot logistically just to get everybody in the room.

P13 also described another process, the one that was required to move a product into manufacturing. This process involved the manufacturing group, external to both business units P13 worked for, and was thus enforced equally. While admitting that it did take time and energy to follow that process and fill the required paperwork—P13 was more understanding of why it was needed.

Job satisfaction

P13 described the early days in MS as the time he had the highest job satisfaction when working for the company:

[Those were] the best days. It was frantic, it was fun, and it was challenging, whatever, but everybody was sort of on the same page, everybody was fighting the same cause, and it goes a long way.

He added to that the impact that he had on the results in MS as another major source of satisfaction. Later, in M, he claimed that he felt that there was strong internal competition for power, and people's agendas were not aligned. He did not feel he had as strong an impact on the results in M as he had in MS.

Mood

P13 emphasized the cyclical relationship between his mood at home and his satisfaction at work. He described that when he is more satisfied at work—he would be happier at home, and as a result—he would get more support from home, and would be more effective and happier at work. The only difference he could feel between his time at MS and his time at M that was not related to work was that it was more challenging at home once his first, and then second child were born. He had sleepless nights, and had to do more at home. This happened during his time in M, and not in MS. In general—he was happier in MS than he was in M, but he associated that with the cyclical relationship between mood and job satisfaction, and he had higher job satisfaction at MS.

Home pressure and support

P13 traveled a lot for his job during his time in MS, as well as his time in M later. He felt a difference in the level of support he received from home. When he worked in MS, initially he had no children. His wife could be more understanding of his travel and, in fact, joined him on certain trips. However, as his family grew, she became less supportive of his travel, as it was more difficult for her to raise the family alone when he was traveling. On the other hand—once his family started growing, P13 started restricting his travel more, to be more supportive of his family. It was to the point that he heard that his supervisor was not happy about the fact that P13 was limiting his travel.

Other insights

P13 described that the entire team in MS could get their hands around the entire business, and saw the big picture of it, and he claimed that it gave team members a sense of ownership. This has changed later, with people becoming more focused on small pieces of the puzzle, as the picture became more complex.

P13 described a link between how important was a specific customer to M as a whole, and the level of interference he had. When in MS he had a small customer, that was not strategic to M, he had enough autonomy to work.

However, the autonomy declined significantly when a larger customer, more strategic to M, was interested in the product that MS developed. That was probably the reason for a much higher level of management interference, and eventually turning MS into a traditional business unit within M.

P14

P14 was the founder of a startup company, which was acquired by a mature company (M). He filled a technical role in M for three years. He then left M to join a second startup company (S), where he worked as a Vice President of Engineering for six years. The focus of the interview with P14 is in the more recent transition from M to S.

Creativity

P14 did not feel very creative in M. However, he did not associate this to the company, but rather to the stage of the product life cycle. When he was involved with the development of the product before his previous startup company was acquired by M, he was creative. However, after the acquisition, the product was in its commercialization stage, which did not allow him to be very creative. The type of work associated with this product stage did not lend itself to creativity:

> I figured our creative ways to work around their accounting and inventory report systems. That was probably the most creative thing I did. Which is kind of ironic.... I don't know, I'm trying to think of creative stuff I did there. There wasn't a lot of creative time there.

In S, on the other hand, P14 felt creative, because the product was in its definition stage, and defining it lent itself to creative approaches. The undefined nature of the product attracted him to the company. "There were so many opportunities to be creative there," he said, and added a description of that creativity: "Figuring out completely new ways to do those things nobody actually knew how to do before." P14 insisted that the differences in his creativity in the two companies were attributed first and foremost to the stage in the product life cycle:

> I think that the design cycle had the most impact on creativity. The early stage of the design cycle is so much, everything you do, you have to do from absolutely scratch, and you had to figure out how to do it from scratch and do it with absolutely no baseline, and it just lent itself to creativity, and lent itself to great solutions, and to be honest, some God awful solutions for other things. Once you get to the later side of the design cycle, productization and operations and applications, there's some creativity, in the debug cycle, but it's much less

profound. It's more of a routine level of good debug practice than true creativity.

P14 eventually defined the creativity differences as radical in S, and incremental in M.

Autonomy

P14 felt he had "almost complete autonomy" in M. When his previous startup company was acquired by M, he came with a lot of credibility, so "they let us run our own show". He had the autonomy to step outside the established processes in M, and he had no interference in his decision making, and had the autonomy to do what he thought needed to be done, and what he thought was right. P14 had complete autonomy over technical issues, in defining the product development process. Oddly enough, P14 felt that his input to marketing activities were much more accepted and appreciated in M than in S. He complained that S was driven by marketing, which sometimes dictated performing engineering tasks only to achieve marketing milestones, and not to create real value.

Supervisor

P14 did not have any problems with any of his supervisors in S or in M. He believed his relationships with both were pretty good. However, he felt more respected and listened to in M than he did in S. He did not feel appreciated in S, and associated that to a company driven by sales and marketing, where engineers were "second class citizens".

Recognition

When asked about recognition in M, P14 started by describing the informal recognition: exposure at trade shows, exposure to executive management, and the acknowledgement of the marketing group of his engineering contribution. Formal recognition and financial rewards existed, but were very limited in M. P14 felt very recognized in S based on the fact he was entrusted with a group of 60-70 people reporting to him. He did not feel that the engineering group was appreciated, or recognized by the executive suite in S, which was driven by marketing. In general, P14 felt that recognition lacked in both companies.

Challenges

P14 described the first challenge in M as learning how this particular large company worked. It was a learning curve for him. He had to understand how the existing development process worked. P14 did not feel he had significant technical challenges in M, but associated this fact mostly with the product life cycle, which was in productization in M, rather than initial design, which would have been much more challenging technically. P14 described the challenges in S as much more significant: there were industry challenges in designing a standards-based product while the standard is still evolving, getting funding for the company, and technical challenges in the design process itself. The latter was the most fun for him, whereas the "industry politics" challenge was the most frustrating. In general, P14 felt much more challenged (in a positive way) in S than in M.

Resources

P14 admitted that he had an abundance of resources in M, and minimal resources in S. Those resources included people, equipment, and software that he needed. He gave several examples of how easy it was to get access to existing resources in M compared to S. He had to struggle to make do with the resources that were available in S. However, the story was different when he talked about resources that did not exist in the companies. In S, he could simply go out and buy them immediately, whereas in M he described a logistical purchasing nightmare, where it took a very long time to get something purchased, even if it was a $500 item. The purchasing process slowed progress significantly in M. P14 preferred the resources availability in S over M, mostly because of the ability to go and get existing resources immediately when he needed them. He stated that even the risk of losing a customer was not enough to have M move faster in purchasing what was needed. P14 described a relatively similar situation when he discussed human resources. The pool of engineers in M was much bigger than that in S. However, the amount of high quality, talented engineers, to his surprise, was much smaller in M. Given that M dealt with many projects—access to the limited core of high-quality engineers was restricted, and they were over allocated to other projects. In S, he described a smaller overall engineering team, but of much higher quality, that was completely allocated to his project—the only project in S.

Team dynamics

P14 described a "massive political conflict" at the management level in M, especially between different businesses, competing for resources and mindshare. At lower levels, the level of internal conflict or competition was minimal. P14 illustrated an open environment, where the team was focused on the same goals. He specifically described the openness between the engineering and marketing people, and attributed a lot of the harmony between people to a strong project manager, who also separated the team from the upper level conflicts. P14 also attributed the harmony to the fact that most of the team was acquired as one company, and therefore had a history of working together. There was no competition from any of the other corporate functions that worked with this team. P14 described instances of task related debate, but no conflict. In contrast, in S he described a strong case of the typical marketing-engineering conflict. Those conflicts were regarding allocating finite resources and time to product development, public relation activities, developing the next generation technologies, etc. Trust, however, was stronger in S, mainly because everybody knew everybody there. P14 thought it was ironic that there was more trust there even though they disagreed far more. There was less trust in M since people did not know each other as well as the team in S did.

Formalization, bureaucracy, and processes

P14 described that in S there were no processes, and as the founding VP of Engineering he was responsible to create the processes, whereas in M he had existing process he had to comply with, although he felt he had enough autonomy to step outside the process and come back later. However, he still needed to go through all the stages of a phase-gate development process. P14 compared this with larger companies he worked for before, and that level of flexibility did not exist in those companies. He felt better that he could, for a while, step outside the process to achieve something without the fear if incompliance consequences. At the same time, P14 complained about some of the processes that slowed progress in M. One of them was the procurement process described above, that limited his autonomy to go outside and purchase something that was required immediately. Another was the return on investment (ROI) process that slowed the sales process down until sufficient ROI was calculated for a specific customer inquiry, also leading to rejecting customers that might have eventually turned into large customers. This process was the final productization phase that took a product from design to manufacturing that slowed the product release timing significantly. P14 also claimed that some of the design flow processes seemed to have been designed for inexperienced designers, thus overly burdening experienced ones.

Job satisfaction

Overall, P14 definitely experienced higher job satisfaction in S than in M. He associated that to having the opportunity to be creative, creating something new that did not exist before, and starting from scratch. He associated lower job satisfaction in M mainly to the mature stage in the product life cycle that he was involved with in M, where most of the creative work was already done, and the rest was very procedural and logistical.

Home pressure and support

P14 was single when he worked in M, and dedicated almost all of his time to work. He got married while he was working in S, and then had his first child. He described:

> ...it was always sort of a split thing between the time at home, time with my wife, my son... and the time at work. And there was always a tug of war between the two, which certainly

affected the amount of time I could spend at work, and the amount of time I could travel for work, and to be honest, probably hurt my stay at S.

He felt he was only 60-70% dedicated to work in S, compared to 100% before (in M). He claimed his wife did apply pressure for him to spend no more than 40 hours at work, and spend more time at home. P14 did not feel any financial pressure from home to work for a large and safe company, as he had a strong enough financial situation resulting from the sale of his first startup company to M.

P15

P15 worked in M for five years, filling a marketing and business development role, until leaving the company to join S, filling a very similar marketing and business development role for three more years, and then left S.

Creativity

P15 did not feel that his work or creativity were much appreciated in M. He was left to do whatever would be compatible with the overall direction of the company, but did not feel support or specific direction. It was compatible with his work style, as it allowed him to be creative with no supervision. He could not feel the direct impact of his creativity and company success. In S, P15 felt relatively similar, with the exception of a tighter link between his work and the survival of the company. He felt the freedom to pursue a creative agenda, but he felt more involvement and guidance from the company. P15 worked from home, remotely from the office, both in M and in S, and felt that being accountable and creative are prerequisites for remote workers. P15 did not feel that his ideas were more novel in one company versus the other. However, he did feel that his ideas were more useful in S than in M, simply because they were implemented more often by the company.

Autonomy

P15 felt that he had more autonomy in M than he did in S. He attributed that to feeling less connected to the business in M, which as a remote employee gave him very broad autonomy. In S, in contrast, even though he was still a remote employee, he was more connected to the business, and received more guidance from the company headquarters, and thus felt a lower degree of freedom, although not dramatically lower.

Supervisor

P15 respected both supervisors, in S and in M, in the same way. They both understood the importance of what he did. While his supervisor in M gave him more autonomy, it was harder to push his ideas through in the business unit. On the other hand, while his supervisor in S was more directional and authoritative—P15 could see the impact of his work and creative ideas on the company. In fact, P15 described the S leader almost as dictatorial:

> It became a very polarized situation where you had M thinking about the world the way he always thought about it, and everybody else worrying for their jobs if they think differently.

P15 described the supervisor in M as very erratic, who "would promise you something and then take in back in the next breadth".

Recognition

P15 did not feel a significant difference in the formal or informal recognition between the two companies. At the same time, he claimed that recognition is not a strong motivator for him. He felt that both organizations recognized him. The connectedness of what he did to the organization, and the impact of his work and ideas on company success were the recognition he needed. Since the definition of recognition in this study ties to other people in the company recognizing a participant's work—in P15's case that recognition was considered similar.

Challenges

The challenge that P15 enjoyed the most, and was motivated by the most, which existed equally in both S and M was the intellectual challenge, external to the company:

> I like it because it's a game. I enjoy the intellectual challenge, looking at big complex problems and kind of postulating how they may be solved, and then trying to influence the solution that seems the most advantageous for what I know needs to be done. And for me, it's playing the game.

P15 found that in M it was hard to get people to move in the same direction and to collaborate. One of the reasons was the geographical distribution of people, which made coordination harder. Every now and then he found that individuals were unilaterally not delivering on their promises, without having any consequences to that. He did not feel this issue in S. In S, P15 felt that his task was very important, and as a result saw the company rallying around helping him achieve his goals. There, however, he felt that his supervisor was very authoritative, and did not tolerate opinions that conflicted with his. That was the biggest internal challenge that P15 felt in S. P15 felt external challenges in both companies with market adoption of new and changing technologies. However, he felt those challenges were higher in S than at M:

> I think it was much bigger challenge in the case of S, because it was a new company, in a new market, unproven people,

unproven product, unproven technology, unproven market viability, and so overcoming all those barriers was an extremely difficult proposition. M had a reputation, and the brand of M, and what it may stand for, for whoever is looking at it, it is a big company, so there is an authority that comes with being a big company, the kind of maybe gives you, in the work that you do for a company like that, more authority or leverage.

At the same time, P15 also described the possibility that M was viewed as a company that might have lost its technological edge, whereas S would be viewed as an up-and-comer.

Resources

P15 felt that he had more resources available to him in S than in M. While M had a higher absolute number of resources in the company, availability to a single project was higher in S, since S had a single mission focus. P15 felt that in M:

> ...the bigger the organization got, the more dispersed it became, the more political it became, the less I saw the ability for the team and our business to find the resources necessary to achieve its objectives.

The most important resource to P15 was people's bandwidth, and specifically management mindshare, both of which he enjoyed both more in S than in M. While describing that at times he was held back in S as resources were allocated for other parts of the project, he was more understanding of that, versus not having access to resources at all in M.

Team dynamics

P15 worked from a remote location while in both companies. He travelled often to both companies' headquarters, but he felt much more connected to the team in S than he did to the team in M. In M, he felt he was cut adrift. After leaving a meeting in M, P15 felt he would have to work especially hard to stay synchronized with the team, and had to be the initiator of that. In S, he felt that the team was entirely on board with his activities. He did not have to be the one who keeps everyone synchronized with his activities. P15 also described very tight professional relationships with his counterparts at the team in S. He felt they were complementing each other very well, more so than in M. P15 experienced a high degree of communication and openness in S. He described the communications in M as "communication without action", and discounted the value of that communication. P15 trusted his colleagues in S much more than the team in M. He claimed that he never established trust with the team in M, which was an interesting statement considering that P15 worked longer with the team in M than with the team in S. Finally, P15 felt internal competition within the team in M, and had the feeling that if he did not "play the game" internally in M—he would not be considered a team player, whereas in S he did not feel any internal competition, mainly because there was no redundancy in responsibilities or duties that will give rise to members competing over positions. Both teams in S and M were globally distributed, but P15 described a much stronger alignment between the teams in S than between the teams in M. From his description, it seemed that the teams in S, although globally distributed, shared the same objectives, communicated effectively, and collaborated, whereas the teams in M each "lived on their own island" and did not reach out to bridge the gaps. Finally, P15 described M as having a much higher level of organizational politics. People in the organization were working to make themselves look better:

> It's friction, it wastes time, and it causes unnecessary energy spent on things that are unproductive.... I thought it was just way too many games. I thought it was just—you guys are here to play that game when we're here to actually do work.

In S, he felt no such politics. There was no time for politics in S.

Formalization, bureaucracy, and processes

P15 felt there were many processes, and lot of bureaucracy in M. Being part of a startup that got acquired by M, he felt that once they got acquired—everything stopped as they all had to learn "the M way" of doing things, even at the expense of carrying the business. S, on the other hand, had much less bureaucracy, and few processes, and people often skipped steps in the process, sacrificing a "perfect" product in favor of a "working" product that could be delivered faster. When S was about to start manufacturing the products in volume—following process became more important, as mistakes could be costly at that phase. In general, P15 claimed that M was much more formalized than S, and that this formalization always slowed him down in his job.

Job satisfaction

P15 was surprised to realize that he experienced higher job satisfaction in M than in S. He attributed this to none of the previously discussed factors, and exclusively to the impact that he had on the outcome, and the pervasiveness of the technology he evangelized in the market while he was working in M. The technology that he evangelized in S was not very successful in the market, leading him to lower job satisfaction. P15 described traveling in M much more than in S, and he enjoyed the lesser amount of travel in S. However, even less travel and all the other factors where he preferred the S environment still left him more satisfied in M, due to the impact he had.

Home pressure and support

P15 felt the support of his family in a similar way in S and in M. He felt a little more pressure when he worked in M due to the amount of travel he had there, and at the same time a little less pressure in M due to the fact that M had a brand name, and offered higher job security than S. Overall, he felt the same support in both companies, and a little more pressure when he worked in M due to travel.

P16

P16 worked in M for six years in two different sites, filling various technical roles. He then left with a team to start a startup company (S), where he worked for nine more years, until S was acquired by another company.

Creativity

P16 thought very highly of the team he was part of in M. The selection criteria were very high, and when he was hired, he was one of two new hires out of four hundred candidates, so the quality of people was very high. He experienced working on eight to ten different projects, which exposed him to diversity of technologies. However, when compared to a startup, he felt that in M he was working on a very narrow niche, which limited his creativity to a specific area. In S, as a founder, he felt that he was responsible to more aspects of the product development, thus giving him more freedom to be creative. In S he felt stronger relationship to customer needs, whereas in M he said he almost did not care. He only wanted to improve existing products. P16 felt his ideas were more radical in S, because for a startup company—incremental development was not enough: the product needed to have radical improvements for market success. In M, innovation was incremental in comparison, and P16 claimed that the focus of creativity was on how to work more efficiently. Finally, P16 stated that in S he was *required* to be more creative. It was not only a result of the circumstances. He filed about the same number of patents in both S and M.

Autonomy

P16 described a higher level of autonomy in S due to several reasons. First, he was a founder in S, and thus at the highest level of decision making. Unless something was completely outrageous and he needed to get the CEO's permission to do something (typically large purchases)—he had the authority to make decisions. In M, on the other hand, he was limited with the decisions he could make, even with respect to radical ideas. He had to get up to four levels of management to approve radical ideas. In M, though, once he did get the appropriate approvals—he could purchase significantly more equipment than in S.

Supervisor

P16 had several supervisors in M. He had high respect for them as professionals. He characterized his relationships with them as based on mutual appreciation. They were supportive of his creativity. They gave him time to develop his ideas, and to file patents if appropriate. In M, intellectual property (and specifically patents) was very important, hence the support from his supervisors. In S, there was a similar support for patents, but when the product needed to be complete, or a customer served—the emphasis on patents declined. P16 knew the CEO in S since they worked together in M. He had a great relationship with the CEO. That relationship was smoother, simpler, and more pleasant after they stopped working together. Overall, he felt more support for his creativity in M, even though the area was narrower. In S, he felt the emphasis on survival that drove efforts in the company, rather than a specific drive for innovation.

Recognition

P16 described the importance of the financial rewards and informal recognition to him as similar. In M there was an organized and formal recognition system engrained in the company. He received many small recognition gifts for successful task completion. While not having a high financial value, those small rewards created pride and satisfaction for him. In S, he did not expect recognition, but rather the success of the company which would lead to financial rewards. S was also less structured than M with respect to formal recognition and rewards, and there was less emphasis on those. P16 described some informal, ad-hoc recognition provided by team leaders, but with no structure.

Challenges

P16 felt the bigger challenges were technical, by his own choice, as he was seeking out those challenges. In M, he felt challenges in leading a team that felt job security in a mature company and that there are many opportunities outside the company, if needed. Keeping such a team cohesive and motivated was a hard challenge for him in M. The challenges in S were mainly technical. P16 worked very long hours, but did not feel problems motivating the people. He could not compare the technological challenges, because they were different:

> The challenge in M was to take the product you have and add special features, and find a way to make the design more efficient. In S, 90% of the challenge was to produce a clean product, on time. Not necessarily the best product, it has to meet all the requirements, but in M, if I had an idea for a new feature,

I would not hesitate to raise it, even if it would have delayed the schedule. In S I wouldn't even think about it.

P16 also described the internal challenges in convincing people in M to adopt new ideas, and challenges in the purchasing process, that did not exist in S. Finally, P16 described an external challenge for S in facing large customers:

> I came [to a customer] as M, the customers were much more open, it's a known, large, public company, but when you come as a startup—you had the burden of proof, big time. And we know how this is [laugh]. Skepticism is high. Many companies don't even speak with you. [A large public customer], I almost couldn't meet with them at all when I was with M. They were very careful.

Resources

Budget in M was virtually unlimited, whereas in S, with limited budget and resources—P16 had to be creative in how he develops products with such limited resources. He claimed the limited budget increased his creativity. However, when it came to human resources, it was much easier to hire people in S in the mid 1990s than it was in M. He felt that this trend turned around after the "dot com bust" in the early 2000s, when it became harder to hire in S, the company had a lower budget, and the board of directors was more restrictive. In general P16 felt he had more access to equipment and budget in M throughout the entire period, but it was easier to hire new employees for the most part in S than in M.

Team dynamics

In M, the formal reward system was very clear, and P16 felt that members were doing exactly what it took to achieve those rewards, and nothing more. In S, on the other hand, he felt that team members were fully committed to the company's success, and did not need a lot of motivation. P16 did not feel a lot of internal politics and conflicts within his small team of four members in M. There was one conflict that P16 described in S, but it was the exception, and he claimed that it was due to specific personalities, and probably regardless of the company. P16 felt a lot more internal competition in M than in S. People in M had aspirations of advancement, and improving their salaries and compensation. In S, in contrast, everyone had the same objective: the company's success. The desire to advance was less obvious, and there were not many places to advance to in S. P16 did not feel a difference in the level of communication across the teams in the different companies, and did not feel that anyone was withholding information to gain power. He experienced stronger relationship with team members outside work in S than in M:

I think it resulted from the joined effort and joint objectives and the successes or failures, I think we had more of a "brothers in arms" friendship.

Formalization, bureaucracy, and processes

P16 felt higher levels of formalization in M than in S. He experienced that in the number of levels he needed to convince in order to get budget for a new activity or project. It was much simpler for him in S: all he needed to do is speak with the CEO and CFO and get their approval. It was much quicker than in M. He felt that the lack of bureaucracy allowed him to do much more than his formal job definition required in S. P16 claimed that the formalization in M slowed creativity on one hand, but also had structured systems to encourage it, on the other. He accepted bureaucracy and formalization as required for large and complex organizations.

Job satisfaction

When P16 was asked to compare his job satisfaction in both companies, he described them as 10 to 1 (in favor of S). He had job satisfaction in M, but it was not comparable to the satisfaction in S. His satisfaction in S was driven by the potential for an IPO worth hundreds of millions of dollars (which, in that period of 1997-2000, was not uncommon), and the potential payout for himself. Beyond that—he felt the satisfaction of building something from scratch, growing quickly, hiring employees, and a high level of Adrenaline.

Home pressure and support

P16 worked relatively long hours in M. He was married then, but did not have children, so his wife used the time to get a degree. However, when he was in S, he had children, and his hours were dramatically longer. He felt more pressure when he was in S due to the long hours, but in general his wife was supportive in both cases.

P17

P17 worked in M for seven years, and then moved to another site of that company for four more years. He filled technical roles in both sites. P17 then left M and joined a mid-size company, which he then left after working there for ten years, and joined the startup company (S), again filling a technical role. The interview focused on P17's work in the first mature company (M) at the second site, and at the recent startup company (S), where P17 was still working at the date of the interview for this study.

Creativity

P17 felt creative in both companies. He defined creativity mainly by coming up with new ideas for new products, but also as solving problems in creative ways, and even in convincing the company to move in a certain direction. That required creativity too. He also felt that he was creative when he was not doing the same things every day. In S, he defined the creativity as coming up with new product ideas. He did not have any of the other types of creativity he defined in M. P17 felt that his ideas in M were incremental, and that it was hard to push radical ideas due to the organizational inertia. It was easier to push radical ideas in S, as long as eventually they result with a new product that could be sold:

> When we are going to define the next product, everything is fair game. Really, everything is open. You can do anything. You can start producing Coca Cola if we thought that's the right thing to do.

Autonomy

P17 felt he had reasonable autonomy in both companies. He behaved as if he did not have a boss, doing what he wanted to do. However, the difference was the size of the "sandbox" he had. In M, his role and domain area were more narrowly defined than in S, but not in a dramatic way.

Supervisor

P17's supervisor in M managed a $500 million division, and was a very busy, operations person. It was hard for P17 to approach him, and he never met him without an appointment. While smart and nice, P17 felt he was never on top of his supervisor's priority list. P17 respected the CEO, his supervisor in S, very much. Not only did he consider him a friend, but he also described him as "an amazing marketing person, good sales person, a strategist, and even a decent engineer". With all the pressure that the CEO was under—P17 felt he could always talk to him, and be very open with him. In fact—he claimed that the CEO would be unhappy if P17 was not completely open with him. P17 also felt that the CEO in S expected him to be creative much more than his supervisor at M.

Recognition

P17 contrasted two recognition systems: formal and informal. The formal recognition system was very strong and established in M. There were rules for recognition. There were bonuses and predefined celebrations for writing patents, for example. S lacked such formal recognition system. However, both companies were relatively similar in their informal, ad-hoc recognition. A pat on the back for a job well done, flowers to en employee's wife to thank her for understanding that he had to spend the last two nights at work—those were critical, and implemented in both companies informally. P17 was not overly excited over any type of recognition, but also claimed that the informal recognition was much more important to him. He described informal recognition as recognition between people, and not company mandated. He felt he had less of that in M, and that it was more local to specific divisions. In S, when the CEO sent an email congratulating the team for success, everyone to the last engineer felt part of it.

Challenges

Like others, P17 separated the challenges into technical (external) and organizational (internal). The technical challenges were relatively similar, with the challenges in S slightly higher than those in M, because the product was more complex in S, it started from scratch, and there was a lot more room for success or failure. In M, in contrast, the projects we built incrementally from previous generation products. New projects, completely from scratch, would occur once in 10 years. P17 experienced a completely new project from scratch only once in M, but many times in S, in comparison. He faced external challenges in both S and M. When he presented himself as an employee of M to potential customers, it brought the brand equity that M had, but it also brought the perception that any innovation would be incremental, and that the project might get cancelled almost arbitrarily. When he presented himself as an employee of S, there was no brand equity, but there was the perception that the startup company may have more radical innovation, although the company might run out of funds and out of business. The biggest challenge P17 experienced in M was an internal challenge, in the last few months he was a team leader in the company, in keeping his team intact, as different groups in the company were vying for his group's budget and resources.

Resources

P17 described fierce competition for resources in M. As a whole, M had many more resources than S, but there was a constant struggle to get access to them, the resources were associated with functional silos, and it was very hard to move them around. In S, in contrast, P17 felt that whenever he needed resources in the company he could get them. The resource allocation process was much less formal in S. Funding issues in S came in waves, associated with external fund raising. In M, resource allocation was linked to a specific group's budget, whereas in S there was no specific group budget. The only budget that existed was the company budget. The same applied to equipment in both companies. The absolute existence of those resources in M was higher, but the local availability was higher in S.

Team dynamics

P17 started by describing internal politics. It was very strong in M, but the competition was for budgets between teams. Teams were questioning the existence of other teams, and were trying to take budgets away. These conflicts included the general managers' level, one level under the CEO. In S the politics did not exist, simply because there was no time for it:

> ...in a startup you don't have time to deal with politics. You have a single objective, and everybody shares this objective. There is only one product line, there is one product, there is one date, so what are you going to do? Are you going to start playing with politics?

P17 did not claim there were no conflicts in S, but he stated that the conflicts were driven by different views of the company's success, and what was needed to be done for it. Everyone had the company's single objective and best interest in mind.

Formalization, bureaucracy, and processes

P17 stated that bureaucracy existed much more in M than in S. In M, "everything had a form, everything had a division that handled it". He gave an example of air travel. There was a long procedure that involved multiple people and approvals just to get travel booked. In S, in contrast, people were booking their own travel. P17 attributed that to a higher level of trust, and high visibility. P17 described a very strict process that defined the product life cycle, from requirement definitions to product obsolescence. He described the process as a good one, but also as a restrictive one, that at times caused delays in product development, as different gates had to be reached. P17 described the ability of S to work without such level of formalization as a great advantage that allowed S to move faster. Some elements of the process, such as the marketing requirements document were mandatory, and used in S, too. P17 accepted that the process in M had to be generic enough to address all possible products in the company, but claimed that this generalization created a process that was not optimized for individual products, and that is where the inefficiencies happened.

Job satisfaction

P17 enjoyed his time in M with the exception of the last few months, when he had to fight to keep his team intact against internal competition over budget and resources. However, he enjoyed his time in S much more, and attributed it to having a significant impact on the success of the entire company: "You are not a small screw. In M, whatever you do will not move the needle".

Home pressure and support

In M, P17 worked at the office. In S, in contrast, he was working from home, in a remote location from the S headquarters, although in the same state. He did not feel a significant difference in the pressure he had from home between the two companies. He was traveling a lot, and could not help the family often, but that was similar in both companies. P17 did not feel any pressure from home associated with the fact that S is a startup company with a more financially questionable future. He claimed that he never had to worry about job security in any place, which helped his career, as he was never afraid that the company might fail. He did feel more support when he worked in S than in M, because his wife felt that he was more relaxed, less stressed, traveled a little less, and stayed home more. He could manage his time more flexibly and support his family more. He did not believe he could have worked from home in M.

P18

P18 worked for several mature companies. He left one of the mature companies to join a startup (S), filling a business development role for two years. In 2002 he left S and began working for a mature company (M), filling very similar business development roles for different business units. P18 was still working for M at the time of this study.

Creativity

P18 felt creative in both companies. His ideas were more novel in S than in M. He associated that to the fact that in S he started with a clean slate, and therefore coming up with novel ideas was easy. However, in M there was an existing framework, and coming up with new ideas was hard, but more important. As a result, he felt that his ideas in M were more incremental:

> When I worked at a startup, it was almost like a campaign level creativity. But when you work for a large company, you are more like a cog in the wheel... you're more granular. Creativity is being applied to certain details.

P18 felt that he had more impact with his ideas on S than he had on M. However, he did not feel that his ideas were more useful in one company versus the other. In summary, P18 stated that he had more creative ideas in S than he did in M.

Autonomy

P18 described himself as a generalist in S, dealing with a lot of topics over a narrow domain area, whereas in M he was a specialist, over a wide area of domains. As a result, he felt less autonomy in S due to the narrow domain. However, when he considered autonomy as a result of how far was the company framework developed, then he felt more autonomy in S, where he had a clean slate, versus M, where the framework was already developed. Finally, he associated the autonomy with specific supervisors, and felt that he had more autonomy to make decisions in S.

Supervisor

P18 described both his supervisors in S and in M as very supportive.

Recognition

P18 felt informal recognition in M in the form of longevity of employment, being trusted to continue to do the same job, being listened to, and that he had influence over decision making in M. He did not feel any formal recognition in M, and at the same time described a formal recognition program in a previous large company he worked for, but he claimed that such a program had an impact on younger employees, whereas he saw it as simply a program, and was not affected by it. The best recognition to him was financial. P18 felt informal recognition in S in the form of team celebrating successes. He described it as a good feeling. When asked to compare the recognition between the companies, P18 felt he received more recognition in S than in M, and attributed it to the ability to see the impact of his work on the end result, and celebrating it.

Challenges

P18 described the biggest challenge in S as external: raising awareness to a new technology in the market. In M he felt that the biggest challenges were internal: some people in the company had an arrogant attitude towards customers, being a large company—they behaved as if the "knew it all"; the second challenge in M was to get internal buy in to ideas he had. He also felt that in M people were not entrepreneurial, and were worried about their next paid holiday more than they were worried about the success of the company.

Resources

P18 felt that he had all the resources he needed in S to get his job done: money, people, and work tools. In M, he felt that some of his creativity was actually in how he overcame resource shortage. While he felt that M had more resources on an absolute level—the company had resources constraints for specific projects. P18 gave an example of a travel freeze in M, and how he creatively found ways around it. On the other hand, he appreciated the resources that M had in influencing government and market makers, resource he never had in S, where he needed to prove himself on a daily basis.

Team dynamics

P18 believed that the team dynamics varied with specific companies more than with the size of the companies, startup or mature. He described people who were hard to work with in both companies, and in both companies they got managed out of the company. In both companies he saw people get promoted based on their performance and not seniority. He did not feel internal politics or competition differently in either company. P18 described different teams he worked with at M. He described one of the teams as cheerful, more collaborative, laughed a little bit more. Then he described another team in M as "dark" and hard to work with. P18 himself described being a little more detached from the team in M, but attributed that to his own maturity, going to lunch less with team members, and hanging around the water cooler less with them. He began to work smarter, and dedicate more time to his family.

Formalization, bureaucracy, and processes

P18 felt that this is an area where the two types of companies differ significantly. He felt much more bureaucracy in M than in S, in the areas of:

> Travel, raises, appropriations of funds, or projects. Getting people to help you. Deciding to go to someplace to see a customer. Especially during a tight fiscal year. In a startup, sure, maybe it's approved by a VP, but it's because you walked by his office and said: "you know? I think I should go visit [a large customer]." In M you would have to go and get 3 pages of company signed by somebody electronically that says I'm going to go over to [the large customer]. So some of it is access. In a large company you don't have access. They can't scale that way.

Job satisfaction

P18 was satisfied in his job in both companies, but for different reasons. He was satisfied in S mainly due to the impact he felt he had on the company and its success, the autonomy he had, and his ability to walk into a Fortune 500 client and talk to them in a way they were never talked to before. He felt empowered. He was satisfied in M, on the other hand, because M was a Fortune 500 company itself, and had a lot of weight they could put in an industry to support his activities, and could really move the industry. That was very rewarding to him too. P18 insisted he was as satisfied in one as he was in the other.

Mood

Although not directly related to affect, P18 described two changes in his own attitude: he felt he matured significantly after he transitioned from S to M, and he felt that he also became more stubborn, as well as more confident. He described:

> As I got older, I've gotten a lot more stubborn, so if somebody asks me to do something I didn't like to do, I would be a lot more likely to stand up to the point that would be like: ok, fire me, fine. Back then, I was more probably trying to impress. I'd look at it as my own maturity though. I'm more confident. You're confident that it's not going to ruin your career, confident that you're going to be able to find another job.

Another aspect was that he felt losing his personal freedom to go out with his wife on a "regular" date, stay up late, since he got his children when he worked in M. He described his time in S, from a family perspective, as more "liberated" and fun. At the same time, he described the reward of having children when he was in M.

Home pressure and support

When P18 worked in S, his wife worked for a large mature company, and they did not have kids. As a result, P18 did not feel pressure from his wife. She had a career so it was fine for him to look for a startup opportunity, and at the same time, her income could have compensated for any risks he was taking with the startup company. However, when P18 started working in M, his wife left her job as his first children were born, and he started feeling more pressure from the family to work less and be home with them more. His confidence in his ability to replace the employment in M with another company prevented financial pressure from the family.

Other insights

P18 felt that he filled many more roles in S than he did in M. In S, he even took out the trash, when needed, and worked cross functionally a lot more than in M, where his role was more narrowly defined. P18 added that he took a lot of experience and formal training from the first mature company he worked for into the startup, training and experience he could not have gained in S. However, in the transition from S to M he took the realization that he can make a difference, and that ideas do matter. P18 concluded stating that he believed that all the factors he described were related to specific companies rather than the size of them, being startup or mature. However, for the purpose of this study, his experiences were catalogued into the appropriate company size, S or M, which he actually worked for.

P19

P19 filled a marketing position in a startup company (S) for four years, until it was acquired by a mature company (M), where P19 continued to fill various marketing roles for more than seven years until the date of the interview for this study.

Creativity

P19 felt a little creative in S. His creativity was expressed by creating new business models for customer engagements. He did not define new products. He felt somewhat creative in M, but felt that the environment in M limited his creativity. M has promised customers several things, which restricted how he can deliver products to those customers. P19 felt that creating new business in M was limited by the availability of engineering resources to work on them. Those resources were deployed to execution of projects with very tight schedules. This high level of resource utilization did not give them breathing room required to be creative. There was another burden of proving that the market for a product existed, and that limited new development. Those burdens were lower in S and decisions were made quicker, and the stakes were smaller. P19 overall felt he was a little more creative in M than in S, since decisions are pushed down to him. The problem he saw was in taking the creative ideas to the next step and implementing them. P19 did not feel than any of his ideas were novel or radical in any of the companies. In general he did not feel very creative in either company because he felt busy with daily tactics, and because he did not feel that creativity was recognized in either company.

Autonomy

P19 felt he had more autonomy in S than in M. As an example, he shared that at S he could create any part number he wanted for a product, whereas in M there was a system for generating part numbers. When a customer asked for a product in S, P19 could immediately develop a project estimate and put together a customer contract very quickly. However, in M he described having to convince two committees and three decision makers, and provide market justification before anything could be done.

Supervisor

P19 described high variability in the relationships he had with his supervisors in S, as he had several different supervisors throughout the years. The relationships varied from "very good" to "horrific". He claimed that one of his supervisors was not inspirational, but he also attributed it to his own level of maturity that changed over time. He had the best relationship with his managers in M (he had two). One of them advocated for him whenever he needed, and the other would let him advocate for himself and thus give him autonomy to propose new ideas. P19 respected the supervisor in M more than he did the supervisor in S. His respect was a combination of competency and capabilities. In a retrospect, P19 respected the supervisor at S more than he did when he worked there, as he later understood the pressures that supervisor was under, and attributed respecting him more to P19's own level of maturity. Since this study focuses on how participants experienced the different factors *at the time* they were at the respective company—P19 is considered to have respected his supervisor in M more than he did his supervisor in S.

Recognition

P19 felt recognized in S through a couple of awards that he received through a formal recognition system in the company, and a few people who told him that the company depended on him, and the products he was working on was going to make or break the company in terms of on-time delivery. From P19's description of those events, it felt that the latter was more important to him. However, P19 felt more recognized in M. He won an excellence award there, again—a part of a formal recognition system. However, it was not the award that made him feel that he was recognized more at M, but rather the efforts of his supervisor, a VP in the group, to assure that P19 received the award that made him feel recognized:

> It was actually the advocating for me to win the award that actually was more important to me than the award itself. So that was a huge deal. It was a sort of public recognition for me.

He felt recognized by that VP both in a private way, during performance reviews, and in a public way, being recognized in front of the whole company.

Challenges

P19 described the challenges in S as task related. He struggled with the tactical activities, being on the phone with customers in Europe in the morning and Asia at night, for example. The challenge was that due to these day to day activities with specific customers, there was no time left to be creative and come up with new product concepts. In M, he did not feel the same challenge. There was a sales force and a technical force that could handle the tactical activities. However, P19 has experienced new challenges in M: while he had time to be creative and come up with new ideas, he had to get buy in from many people in the company, hold many meetings, and decisions took two weeks, at times. The challenge in M was internal, and not task related. Externally, being part of M helped P19, as his customers typically already have a deep relationship with M, and selling new products to them was easier than if he would be part of S.

Resources

The resources available for P19 in his projects in M were mostly the same people that were available to him in S before it was acquired by M. In M, he felt he has many more resources. As long as his projects got high priority (his recent project was of high priority for M)—he had an abundance of resources. In S, he was limited in resources, as S was limited in funding as a startup. Furthermore, P19 claimed that even the human resources available to him in S have matured and gained much more experience over the years. If in S they were young and inexperienced engineers—a few years after the acquisition by M, those same engineers became much more experienced. This fact, combined with access to experienced engineers who worked for M all this time—caused not only the quantity of resources to improve in M, but also their quality. In the business that S and M both operated, human resources were the main resources, as those companies operated in a low capital intensity industry.

Team dynamics

For the most part, P19 was part of the same team he was in S that was acquired by M. He described a much more cordial and formal relationships in S than now in M. When in S, he described avoiding conflicts, and either letting them resolve over time, or simply disappear. P19 described a much more open communication after the team became part of M. He attributed this mainly to the time that the team had spent together over the years, getting to know each other, and developing a trust for each other. In M, P19 stated they still had conflicts, but that they addressed them head on. P19 attributed the buildup in the level of trust to the time this team spent together rather than the companies or the acquisition. P19 also added the formal processes in M as contributing to increased trust, as they defined roles and responsibilities. P19 observed more internal competition in M than in S, due to the increase in levels of management, and aspirations of team members to advance in the company. He also described a stronger inter-team competition than intra-team. Where in S there was only one product line, M had many product lines, and teams were competing for resources for their projects.

Formalization, bureaucracy, and processes

P19 described a higher level of formalization in M than in S. This formalization took the shape of having to convince many people in order to move an idea from creation to execution, and other areas such as the standardized part number scheme that was described before. He described the higher formalization as one of the main internal challenges in M.

Job satisfaction

P19 felt definitely more satisfied in M than he was in S. He gave several reasons for his higher satisfaction level: First, he felt that M was more professional, and had adequate resources to work on tactical issues, allowing him to think more strategically and be creative, which he liked. Second, he felt better compensated than his peers, which he believed reflected his contribution. Third, he enjoyed the success associated with his current product line, especially compared with previous product lines that were not as successful. Finally, he enjoyed the exposure that his recent product line gave him in the company, and externally with the media.

Mood

While P19 did not discuss specific mood changes, he talked about changes in his personal life. When he was in S, due to the workload, he worked long hours and neglected to take care of himself, physically and mentally. As his workload reduced in M, he decided to work less, and start taking better care of himself. He began working out, and spending more time with his family. Personally, this made him feel better in M than he did in S. He also discussed several times how he matured over the years, and felt more mature in M than he did in S. At the same time, he started describing an anxiety regarding his professional future, and moving to the next phase of his career.

Home pressure and support

P19 felt more pressure from his wife when he worked in S, compared to when he worked in M, mainly because when he worked in S he was not taking better care of himself, and in M he did. His wife was very supportive of him in both companies, and motivated him to advance his career, but motivated him more when he worked in M. P19 feels that she was more supportive in M because he managed to successfully negotiate a pay hike (with some help from her), and because he was happier in M, and was taking better care of himself there. P19 was traveling recently in M more than ever, but did not feel any pressure from his wife due to travel.

P20

P20 worked for several small and large companies. In M he filled a marketing role, until his departure four years later to join a startup company (S). P20 continued to fill a marketing role in S for almost two years, when the company was acquired by another company and he left shortly after the acquisition. In M, P20 described two chapters: one under his first supervisor, and the second after his first supervisor left. In S, he described two similar chapters: when his first supervisor was there, and after he left. In both cases, the second chapter (after the original supervisor left) was described as a temporary stage, and was therefore not considered for this analysis.

Creativity

P20 felt creative in M at times. He gave several examples of creative ideas he had that became products, and he filed patents for those. He received management support for those ideas, resources, and took them all the way to the market. P20 felt a very nurturing environment in M for his ideas. He felt less creative in S, as he found less room for creativity. He described the management as dogmatic and authoritative, and although he felt "pockets" of where he could exercise his creativity—those were the exceptions and not the rule. P20 felt that his ideas were more radical, disruptive, and novel in M, and that the management in M embraced them. He also felt his ideas were more useful at M. P20 is a very enthusiastic person, and he felt embraced in M, making him more creative, and less embraced in S, making him less creative there.

Autonomy

P20 described M as having an entrepreneurial spirit, and experienced very broad autonomy:

> Ultimately there are certain deliverables, of course, that you are responsible for, and you're held accountable to, but how you get there, and your work style, your methods, how you prioritize sub tasks within that, as long as we were crossing major milestones people were given a tremendous amount of autonomy.

The autonomy in M was not restricted to how people did their jobs, but also where they did their jobs: "lots of times you didn't even know where people were. People worked from home or remote, or from coffee shops or on the road, when they're traveling." P20 described an environment in M where the goals were much more important than what people had to do to get there. P20 brought the element of the product life cycle, where even his autonomy in the scope of his role changed later, but he still felt a relatively high level of autonomy in getting his job done. P20 described the autonomy in S as more limited than in M. Part of it was associated with his job function which, by definition, had less autonomy associated with it, but part of it he associated with the management team.

Supervisor

P20 knew his supervisor in M from the previous company they worked in, and considered them friends to the date of this study. He described this supervisor as giving him a lot of autonomy and support, and respected his capabilities, vision, and wisdom. P20 worked for the VP of Marketing in S, who he described as "flamboyant" and a stereotypical VP of Marketing. P20 respected his branding capabilities, and felt they complemented each other well, but could not have reached a friendship with him. He did not believe that his supervisor in S had enough technical depth for the job. P20 described a much more formal and professional relationship with his supervisor in S than the one in M. He respected his supervisor in M much more.

Recognition

P20 described a formal recognition-reward mechanism in M as the primary method of recognition, with stock related rewards as the primary reward tool. He claimed there was not a lot of informal recognition in M, probably to a fault. The company lacked team celebrations of successes. It was one of the company's cultural corks. P20 stated that S did not have any mechanisms for recognition, formal or informal. Stock options were granted, in the hope that the company will become public, which never happened. He claimed never even to have had a performance review in S. He observed a lot of disappointed people there for lack of recognition. P20 felt much more recognized in M, and eventually described informal, implicit and explicit recognition. A big part of the recognition was the market success of products based on ideas that he conceived. P20 felt some informal recognition from his supervisor in S, but nowhere near the level he felt in M.

Challenges

P20 described the biggest challenges in M as external and technical. There were challenges in developing the products, in building them fast enough, in delivering them to the market, in winning business: "you know, all those headaches, and challenges, but they were kind of the fun challenges that a company, in growth and success." P20 described the challenges in S as tremendous. While a big part of the challenges in S were external, in the market, he attributed a lot to poor and disorganized management—internal challenges.

Resources

P20 never felt a resource shortage in M. In some instances, some of the teams were stretched ("maybe they had three engineers instead of four"), but that was in the fringes. As long as the projects were prioritized appropriately—he did not feel resource shortages. P20 had fewer resources in S, but he claimed he had enough to get the job done.

Team dynamics

P20 described great relationships within the team in M:

> It was definitely, you know, one of those rare times in your career that you are working with a group of people that, you're thinking: wow, these are all virtually, across the board, really great people, really bright, really motivated, kind of like the all-star team, and you wonder: how did I get so lucky to have such a great group of work colleagues.

He described many personal friendships, a lot of trust, and fun that he had with the team. He described the caliber of people as high, in a consistent manner. In S, P20 described the team dynamics as "good". They were not as good as in M, but were not bad either. He described positive, friendly competition in M, where peer pressure was applied to achieve better results and grow the business. There was no individual, political competition in M during the first chapter, under his original supervisor there.

Formalization, bureaucracy, and processes

The formalization in M was relatively loose. P20 claimed that typically companies could not operate with such loose formalization, but the caliber of people, who knew what they were doing and were committed to the results, compensated for the loose processes and yet delivered the desired results. P20 claimed that S was a little bit more formalized than M, but the reason was that the people in S were more junior and less experienced, and needed the processes to achieve the results. Those processes, P20 claimed, would have slowed experienced, senior people, but were needed for the people in S.

Job satisfaction

When asked which company P20 felt more satisfied in, he laughed and said: "You need to hear it from me... So, just for the record, and you are recording, the answer is obviously M." He attributed his satisfaction in M to working with "some of the best and the brightest". He felt constantly challenged (in a positive way) by his peers. He did not feel bureaucracy, and the team was committed to winning in the marketplace. Another element contributing to his satisfaction was that the company was really winning in the marketplace, which made him feel good. He enjoyed the support of his supervisor, and the camaraderie he felt from his peers who were supportive of his efforts and cheered him as he was successful. In S, on the other hand, P20 did not feel that he worked with a high caliber of people, there was a lack of trust, smart people, and friendships. The company was not successful. P20 did not enjoy his interaction with the management team in S, as he felt they did not understand the technology, and what would it take to make it successful in the market. The executive team was not supportive of his efforts, and he needed to constantly convince them with his direction.

Mood

P20 did not feel any difference in his external environment and family that would make his mood different when he worked for the two companies, other than reasons related to the companies that were described in the previous paragraphs. He enjoyed a good life during both periods.

Home pressure and support

P20 felt that his wife was more supportive of him when he worked in M than when he worked in S. This was driven mainly because she felt he was more satisfied in M. She knew what he was working on there, "at a 50,000 foot level." In S, on the other hand, she realized that the company was not successful, and she noticed that he was not as happy there as he was in M. P20 tried to make sure he was spending as much time at home in both companies. Since his commute was significantly longer in S—he compensated by working significantly less in S. As a result, there was no family pressure on him to work less in one of the companies. P20's wife did not pressure him as a result of financial concerns associated with the startup company, although she was surprised that he wanted to leave M, after all the success and satisfaction he experienced there.

Other insights

P20 felt he had significant impact on both S and M. M was a big company, and its stock price did not increase significantly as a result of his projects. However—he did feel significant impact on company revenue and market success of the products he was involved with. With S being a small company—it was easier to feel his contribution to deliverables, so he felt he made a significant difference in both cases. Since P20 was significantly more satisfied in M than in S, it was interesting to know why did he leave M to join S. As he described it, after his original supervisor in M left, there was some chaos, the company became more hierarchical, and he experienced more internal competition for positions. His role was changing to a less interesting one, and he felt that he needed to challenge himself and join a startup company. The period after his first supervisor in M left was considered atypical, and therefore was not analyzed here.

www.ingramcontent.com/pod-product-compliance
Lightning Source LLC
Chambersburg PA
CBHW051900170526
45168CB00001B/176